SNAKEMASTER

SNAKEMASTER

WILDLIFE ADVENTURES WITH THE
WORLD'S MOST DANGEROUS REPTILES

AUSTIN STEVENS

Skyhorse Publishing

Skyhorse Publishing books may be purchased in bulk at special discounts for sales promotion, corporate gifts, fund-raising, or educational purposes. Special editions can also be created to specifications. For details, contact the Special Sales Department, Skyhorse Publishing, 307 West 36th Street, 11th Floor, New York, NY 10018 or info@ skyhorsepublishing.com.

Skyhorse® and Skyhorse Publishing® are registered trademarks of Skyhorse Publishing, Inc.®, a Delaware corporation.

Visit our website at www.skyhorsepublishing.com.

10 9 8 7 6 5 4 3 2 1

Library of Congress Cataloging-in-Publication Data

Stevens, Austin James, author.
  Snakemaster : wildlife adventures with the world's most dangerous reptiles / Austin Stevens.
     pages cm
  ISBN 978-1-62873-710-3 (hardback)
1. Stevens, Austin James. 2. Herpetologists--South Africa--Biography. 3. Poisonous snakes--Anecdotes. I. Title.
  QL31.S748A3 2014
  597.9092--dc23
  [B]
                        2014002140

Cover design by Qualcom
Cover photo courtesy of the author

Paperback ISBN: 978-1-5107-4239-0
Ebook ISBN: 978-1-5107-4240-6

Printed in the United States of America

For Amy

MEASUREMENT CONVERSIONS:

1 kilometer = .609344 miles
1 meter = 3.28084 feet
1 kilogram = 2.20462 pounds

CONTENTS

Author's Note

This book discloses a part of my life story, lived somewhat randomly and wild, originating from a time before general and scientific information became available to everyone at the click of a mouse. This book is not intended to be an in-depth exploration into the many-faceted science that is herpetology today, but rather a trip across time, offering you, the reader, the opportunity to re-live with me a bygone era of adventures and experiences.

INTRODUCTION

It is generally accepted that one must make allowances for the inexperience of youth. One can of course only appreciate this when one is older, and try as you may to influence those younger or less experienced than yourself, inevitably they, too, must experience life as their youthful minds and enthusiasm dictate. (I, myself, am a typical example.) Thus, considering what knowledge one has gained over—let's say forty or fifty years of life—and knowing with some certainty that we cannot wholly transfer this knowledge to our children (or other youthful acquaintances) but that they must indeed experience life for themselves before attaining full gratification, however disastrous or otherwise the results might be, one might once more be compelled to contemplate the time honored question: *What is life?*

While the whole answer to this question is certainly not a simple one, it is certain that one cannot be what one is not, and one must forge along the path of life as best as possible and, with luck, live to be old and wise, for whatever it may be worth. Unfortunately, society as we know it today, amongst other factors, influences the path of life; sometimes even forcing it in one particular direction . . . good or bad. But here precisely is where what one is truly made of will surface, where the genetic makeup of the person will emerge in that form we simply consider as "character." And though over the years one's surface character may mold, adapt, or even change, that which lies deep inside is forever.

I have always believed that no matter how one attempts to improve his- or herself, one can never be what one is not. The outside influences inflicted on a person by everyday life are to a large extent superficial and will serve only as an option. However, the genetic makeup of each individual is installed at the very beginning of life, never to be changed. This is, after all, what makes each one of us forever unique. However much one would like to emulate the enviable traits of another, one can never truly be what one is not!

Though I do not consider myself particularly endowed with an overabundance of enviable traits, there has always been one favorable aspect to my character, a factor that has served me well through the numerous traumatic events of my life. I am possessed by the most powerful will to live . . . forever, if it were possible. And not for one second have I ever considered the possibility of my own demise, not even in the face of sometimes overwhelming odds. This, I must stress, is not courage. This is simply how I am constructed.

When I was a young boy, I was convinced that physical pain should be endured as far as possible without artificial relief. My theory behind this being that, by so doing, the body and mind would be toughened, and therefore each time be better trained to cope. However, after experiencing a number of broken bones, sprains, and other schoolboy injuries, it became apparent to me that there were limits, though I still tried to maintain a "tough" standard. Later it was explained to me by a doctor that I had, in fact, the "wrong end of the stick." By introducing artificial relief (painkillers), the body and mind are better able to tackle the healing process, without the added disruption incurred by the presence of pain.

Delirium is described as a disordered state of mind, with incoherent speech, hallucinations, and occasional mad ravings. At one point in my young life, I found myself to have all of this, and more. And though I was not at all in full comprehension of my state, my brain registered with some clarity that this was a time to endure . . . *or die.*

For the eight days that it took for the cytotoxic properties of the venom of a puff adder to fully distribute its devastating effects along the length of my arm, I surfaced consciously only between morphine doses, when the terrible pain forced me from the delirious blackness to the living hell of reality. Cytotoxins destroy tissue and blood cell walls, promoting hemorrhaging and necrosis, which if untreated will eventually lead to gangrene poisoning and death. To place one's arm into a fire, without the option of removing it, would roughly describe the painful effects of this tissue-destroying venom, while the resultant swelling, blistering, and exuding of plasmalike fluid from the bitten limb is frightening to witness. The serum created for snake bites is mostly unable to neutralize the cytotoxic properties of puff adder venom, though it is effective against other life-threatening agents.

In my painful state of delirium, I did of course have little comprehension of time and little recollection of actual happenings, other than those briefly taking place between six hourly morphine medications. Usually the burning pain would be returning to its full intensity long before the final hour, rendering me suddenly awake and crying for my arm to be removed from the fire. I remember once desperately searching—if not physically, then in my tormented mind—for my rifle, almost panic-stricken by its absence. I had been trained never to be without my rifle. *Where was my rifle?!* I must have screamed, for the next moment there was someone at my side, and a prick in my arm sent me back to a restless yet pain-free oblivion.

On another such occasion, as the pain once more seemed to be enveloping my whole being, my very fiber of existence, I was aware of people about me, probing me, examining me. A voice pierced my delirium, as though from the mouth of a megaphone, loud and concentrated in my head: "Amputate the hand, or he will die."

And, as though jabbed with a dose of adrenaline (which may very well have been the case by natural reaction of the body), I sat straight up in the bed and screamed "No! Please no!" before a prick in my arm once more rendered me quivering back to the darkness that is chemically induced sleep.

However, my brain now fought the sleep, desperately, pathetically, with the little control it still had. For whatever the developing scenario in my subconscious, I knew I could not accept amputation any more than I was prepared to accept death. Not under any circumstances. *It simply could not be!* And I believed this totally, as such is my design. And in spite of my heavily drugged condition, I continued to mutter my objections, deliriously adamant of my nonacceptance of the diagnosis made and the treatment prescribed.

Fear of losing my hand now rendered my pain irrelevant by comparison, and I fought desperately with the nurses as they attempted to administer my regular dose of morphine. Now I did not want to sleep! In my sick delirium I even welcomed the pain. It meant that my hand was still a part of me. No matter the circumstances, I was *not* going to lose my hand. And I had no intention of dying either. *So there!* And it took many people—nurses, sisters, and doctors alike—to hold me down before the needle was once more inserted into a vein and I was delivered furiously into the world of the unconscious.

Days passed, but for the most part I was oblivious to them. Then suddenly my eyes opened wide and staring . . . and there was no pain. *No pain!* The joy of it soared through my still fuzzy brain. *The pain was g. . . .* Sudden fear cut short my thoughts, constricting my breath, as though my chest were in a vice. *Dear God, no!* I almost screamed as I turned my head to focus on my heavily bandaged arm strapped to a splint along the side of the bed. *Please God no!* I almost tore the splint loose in an attempt to focus on the extremity of my arm. At this point a nurse rushed in, alerted by my screams of distress. Quick to understand, she grabbed me firmly by the shoulders, not so much to restrict my panic but to get my attention—to look into her eyes. And when I did, she said. "It's okay, your arm is whole. It's all there." And the dark blue eyes looking into mine told me that she was not lying. "Rest now," she continued, "The worst is over. But there is still a long road ahead for you." With that she settled me comfortably back in the bed, with my head raised slightly on the pillow, and left the room. And for the first time in ten days I slept a true, uninduced and painless sleep. Christmas had passed, and I didn't even know it.

I was just nineteen years of age.

Another day later I saw my arm unbandaged for the first time, and the shock of it took my breath away. Swollen to twice its normal size, the upper regions were tinged purple, whilst below the elbow the flesh was black and hard, with a number of large, swollen, blood-filled blisters scattered across the top of my hand. One such blister, larger than the others, surrounded the bitten finger at the sight of the fang puncture, from where a greenish brown fluid oozed repulsively. It was a terrible sight, and in my drastically weakened state, dizziness overwhelmed me. I had to lie back on the bed, as it seemed that I would faint.

My entire arm was painful to the touch, as were other areas of my body, especially in the armpits and groin, where my lymph glands were considerably swollen. However, except for the actual bitten finger, the doctors now seemed reasonably confident that, with the help of specific antibiotics, the arm would eventually slough the dead tissue and regenerate itself anew. The finger itself, however, having been exposed to the worst of the cytotoxic effects of the venom, remained another matter. Solemnly I was warned not to get my hopes up, as full recovery of the finger was not likely, with amputation highly probable. It would still be a few more days before the medical staff knew for certain.

Grateful as I was in knowing that my hand and arm would be spared from amputation, deep depression set in as I considered the possibility of life without my right index finger. How would I point? How would I hold my rifle and pull the trigger? For that matter, how would I scratch my buttocks or pick my nose? *Good grief!* Endless combinations of things I would not ever be able to do again loomed menacingly out of proportion in my traumatized mind. *Life as I had known it would never be the same again.* Plunging my face into the pillow, I howled my frustration and fear into its comforting softness.

ৎ ৎ ৎ

So how did I end up contemplating losing my finger to a puff adder's bite? When South Africans leave school, they normally were obligated to take military training in conventional warfare and antiterrorism. Getting oneself bitten by a highly venomous puff adder was not part of the usual military training program, as described by the South African Defense Force manual of operations at the time. This was entirely my own doing, brought about by my somewhat overzealous enthusiasm for reptiles. We came upon this species often while on bush patrol along the border dividing South West Africa from Angola, where at the time the South African Defense Force saw fit to deploy its youthful recruits in defense against hostile insurgence from the north. Snakes were often spotted, both venomous and nonvenomous species, and I had taken it upon myself to somewhat improve my platoon's knowledge of the subject by catching and displaying these interesting reptiles on every possible occasion. Thus I soon became known as the "Snakeman," and when one night a highly venomous puff adder was found to have positioned itself amongst the sandbags of a guard post, it was natural that the "Snakeman" be called to remove it.

And indeed this I did, with somewhat unexpected results, as the snake, angered by my handling, managed to slip one long fang down past its bottom lip, just piercing my index finger deeply enough to inject a few drops of the terrible cytotoxic venom. The drama and trauma that followed became a nightmare blur of pain, distress, and near mayhem as the insufficiently experienced military medics on base strived to administer treatment as best they could, unfortunately much of it incorrectly. (At the time, the matter of snake bite poisoning and the treatment thereof remained somewhat ambiguous.)

This was followed by a two-hundred-kilometer, high-speed dash through enemy bush territory in an open-top army Land Rover and on into the Caprivi Strip panhandle section of northeastern Namibia (then South West Africa). There a military aircraft was on standby to file an emergency flight plan for Windhoek, hundreds of kilometers to the south. After twenty-four hours of mental and physical trauma, discomfort, and agony, they finally delivered me in a state of semiconsciousness to the Windhoek Hospital, with a progressively deteriorating right arm that felt like it was on fire.

It was now some two weeks later. Two weeks of my life lost to delirium, pain, and shock as my entire physical and mental prowess was dedicated to the fight to keep me alive. The remaining question now: Would I lose my finger?

It is amazing how easily one takes so many things for granted until threatened with the loss of them. First came the battle just to survive the episode. The thought that if only my life could be saved, all else thereafter would be a bonus . . . *just to get through it and be alive!* This somehow miraculously achieved, the next desperate fight suddenly materializes: the fight to save the hand. *Oh, if only my hand would be saved, nothing else would ever matter.* And you struggle and fight and demand and even beg to the God you are not sure exists that, should your hand be saved, then all else in your life, for evermore, would be fine. And the doctors fret and strive and apply all their skills and medicinal knowledge until finally, it is done, and your hand is out of danger. *Oh, thank you Lord, doctors, nurses . . . thank you all.*

But now, suddenly, there is a new priority, an all-encompassing and overpowering priority: the original bitten and now mutilated finger, the original source of all the dilemma. And you know you should be thankful for your life, and for your hand, which is now out of danger, but suddenly all that has gone before is overruled. *Oh, if just this one little, now all-important, finger could be saved, there would never again be anything to fear from life.* This index finger . . . this all-important finger, seemed now somehow to overrule even that which was so important before. *If only my finger could be saved, then all else in my life would be gravy. Nothing but gravy!* The entire battle was now reduced to just that one little digit—that one little digit that now seemed as important as the whole hand did before, as saving the *whole* of my life did in the first place.

Human nature is indeed fickle . . . and we so soon forget.

It took another three weeks of further treatment and waiting before the doctors finally concluded that my finger, though looking somewhat disfigured and emaciated from the tissue damage, would remain as part of my hand. I received the good news with a tremendous sigh of relief, thanking the doctors and all medical staff involved for all their efforts on my behalf, and lay back into my cushions, both mentally and physically exhausted. It had been a long, hard, and frantic haul. I had lost weight and seemed to be weak all over from the effects of my ordeal and from being bedridden. Carefully I examined my finger and compared it to that of the opposite hand. It still looked terrible, with a hard, dry scab firmly attached around the original fang puncture. This, I had been assured, would drop off in time. I tried to flex the finger, which was painful, but the very fact that it was painful meant life was returning and all would be healed in time. I took another great sigh of relief, remembering the words so often repeated by my mother, who in her lifetime suffered much pain: "This too shall pass."

In fact, a further month passed in the military hospital before I was finally discharged, and also officially discharged from further military service for that particular period. I was grateful to be well and healed, and in one piece. My finger looked remarkably better, considering what it had been through, but it was thin and tender to the touch and still slightly stiff. This was a situation that would always persist, but barely a discomfort in comparison with amputation. I left the hospital with a bounce in my step, with optimism for the future.

The ongoing border war being fought against Russian and Cuban-backed communist insurgents in the far north of South West Africa afforded the South African government power to recruit all able-bodied graduates into compulsory military service. I had no grounds for exemption and was immediately recruited after leaving school, endured nine grueling months of being trained in the art of conventional and guerrilla warfare and survived a further three months being targeted by the enemy in the operational area in Angola, followed somewhat unceremoniously by two months in a military hospital recovering from snake bite. Not surprisingly, I had not yet experienced much personal time to consider what I wanted to do with my life, or even where to start. It was 1970, and I was just nineteen years old, with my whole life lying ahead of me.

CHAPTER 1
EARLY DAYS IN THE SNAKE AND ANIMAL PARK

Of the roughly three thousand species of snakes recorded on the planet today, approximately 10 percent are venomous and are potentially dangerous to humans. This is a small percentage, making the chances of meeting up with a highly venomous snake much less than those of colliding with a fast-moving car while crossing the road. In most countries, more people are struck by lightning than bitten by snakes.

Venomous snakes can be divided into groups according to their dentition. The back-fanged species, of which only two African species are considered dangerous to humans are the *boomslang* (tree snake) and the *twig snake*, while a further two back-fanged species, one located in South America and the other in Asia, might be considered potentially dangerous because of their size. These are the more primitive of the fanged species, with the usual solid teeth in both upper and lower jaws, together with one or more enlarged grooved fangs on the upper jaw, roughly situated below the eye.

Among front-fanged snakes, those with fixed front fangs are considered one step up the evolutionary ladder. Almost all of these snakes—which include the mambas and cobras of Africa, the coral snakes of North and South America, and the sea snakes of the world—are considered potentially dangerous to humans. The fangs of these species, with some exceptions, are usually fairly short and hollow, injecting the venom in a similar fashion to a hypodermic needle.

Front-fanged snakes whose fangs are hinged possess the most advanced injecting system. These are adders and pit vipers, most of which, again, are considered potentially dangerous to humans. Situated in the front of the upper jaw, their fangs are much enlarged, tubular, and can be folded back into a protective sheath when not in use. When attacking prey, the snake swivels the fangs forward at a great speed. Their extra length makes it possible to secure the prey more accurately and enables deep penetration for a sure kill.

A few snakes amongst the cobra species have evolved hollow fangs that direct the flow of venom forward rather than downward. By contracting the muscles surrounding the venom glands, these snakes are able to direct a spray of venom forcibly towards the eyes of an attacker, purely as a means of self-defense. The venom is harmless on the skin but will cause an extremely painful reaction if it enters the eyes and, if not washed out, could cause blindness.

All these and many more herpetological facts concerning venomous snakes flitted randomly through my thoughts as the hooded snake rose up before me, its dorsal scales gleaming black in the mid-morning sun. Taller and taller, the creature stretched itself upward, a meter or more off the ground, to bring its dark, beady little eyes level with my own, as I crouched motionless in its path. Nervously, the reptile concentrated its unbreakable gaze in my direction, its mouth slightly ajar, the silver-white fangs startlingly contrasted against the surrounding blackness of its scales.

Reaching its full height now, with only a third of its body remaining on the ground for support, the snake swayed somewhat unsteadily, as defensively it employed the muscles surrounding the upper vertebrae and ribs—forcing them back—to magnificently display the famous "hood" of the cobra. And with a slow but forceful exhalation of air from the single expanded lung, the snake hissed its defiance at my intrusion. Stubbornly I stood my ground, still motionless, my face not a meter from that of the angered serpent. I knew the slightest movement would provoke a forward lunge, releasing a fine spray of venom towards my face.

To the novice, the raised body and expanded hood of the snake in question perfectly depicted those characteristics so typically advertised by the "infamous" cobra. However, though the behavior now flaunted in such close proximity before my very eyes was typical of the cobra, I knew that technically speaking, *this* snake was in fact not a *true* cobra. It was a snake known by its common Afrikaans name, *rinkhals*, meaning ring-necked, sometimes incorrectly referred to as the ring-necked spitting cobra. And to all intents and purposes, the snake is indeed much like any cobra, but differs slightly by having keeled scales (a ridge running along the center of each scale) and a difference in dentition. A more substantial distinguishing feature, however, is that, whereas all true cobras are egg layers, the rinkhals retains its eggs within its body until incubation is complete, thus delivering live young incased only in a thin membranous sack, from which they immediately break free once deposited.

Though a number of cobra species have evolved the capability to discharge a spray of venom at an enemy's eyes, here the rinkhals differs again, as it is more correctly a venom thrower than spitter, and must hurl its raised body forward to forcefully discharge the spray. A true spitting cobra need only contract the muscles surrounding the venom glands to exert pressure enough, from any position, to spray venom up to a distance of some three meters or more.

And this now was what the public had come to see at reptile parks . . . what they had paid their money for. Never mind the rows of cages scattered throughout the Hartebeespoort Dam Snake and Animal Park, filled with colorful and interesting species of reptiles, painstakingly collected and imported from the four corners of the earth for these very visitors to view. Never mind the realistically recreated background displays of the natural environment and the miles of informative and creatively stenciled natural-history information supplied. Never mind even the well-stocked African curio shop and restaurant complex so creatively designed to blend in with the rest of the park's construction in a further effort to entice the tourists that flocked through the gates every day, and especially on weekends. Never mind any of this . . . but note the simple wooden makeshift clock fastened outside the entrance gate, the one that advertises the times for the "Live Venomous Snake Handling and Milking Shows." Therein lay the answer to the success of the business! In fact, it is not unlikely that in those early days of the parks during the 1970s, some three quarters of the annual gate revenue was accumulated solely through the advent of this advertisement.

And none were more aware of this than I, as dramatically I crouched down on my haunches before the angered snake, well within its striking range.

Dramatics!

That was what the public wanted. Dramatics and *death*-defying feats! Everybody's seen a snake in a cage at some time or another. And, "once you've seen one . . . you've seen 'em all." Most people are petrified of snakes, considering them evil, dangerous creatures, spawned from the very depths of hell itself. So who wants to go stare at one of those in a cage? Leave that to the interested enthusiasts, few that they are. And indeed these few, patriotic as they might be, certainly number far fewer than is necessary to render the creation of a reptile park a viable business proposition.

However, the slightest indication, however subtle, that human life might be at risk in a public display, be it high-speed vehicles, bull fighting, or venomous serpents, ensures full attendance, irrespective of the attendees' specific like or dislike for the particular subject advertised. The simple fact that danger is involved is all that is needed in an invitation . . . and the house is full. And kneeling then as I was, staring death in the face (as most would see it), the grandstands surrounding the arena filled to capacity with an eager, expectant audience, I knew I was giving them what they had paid for . . . *dramatics!*

With a purposeful sudden jerk of my head, I startle the swaying snake, provoking it to lunge at me, at the same moment strategically maneuvering myself backward out of reach of the deadly head, leaving myself vulnerable only to the twin sprays of clear fluid venom. And the crowd releases a gasp of excited anxiety as again and again the defending reptile hurls itself forward to saturate my face with venom.

But I am not unprepared, and those who had been before know that it is all part of the show; but still they came to see it again and again. After all, one never knows what can happen, and one day the handler might misjudge his distance, allowing the snake a taste of revenge. What a spectacle that would be! The thrill of danger (at someone else's risk) is ever pleasing to the crowd.

But that day, as with many before, I am right on form. I move closer to the arena wall and casually remove my sunglasses from my face and hold them up to clearly display the splattering of sticky venom attached to their outer surface. This pair of sunglasses is my only defense to protect me from the deadly attack of a spitting cobra; one of the most celebrated and feared of all African snakes. The crowd leans forward as I stroll past their seats, uttering *oohs* and *aahs* as they crane their necks for a closer look. And they are astounded—not just by the venom on the glasses but as much by the fact that I am still alive and well and talking to them. Unable to control their amazement any longer, those less informed on the subject bubble over with questions.

"Why has the venom on your face not killed you?"

"Are you immunized against snake venom?"

"Why is the snake not chasing after you?"

"What guarantee is there that the snake won't climb over the wall and spit at us?

I would follow these questions with a speech filled with explanations that I was well familiar with, as every show produced the same reaction from the public, with generally similar questions. Having thus incited their curiosity by the incorporation of dramatic display, the people in the audience, who before had little or no interest in the subject, are now keen to be lectured and informed; and at the end of the day, this is what reptile parks (amongst other things) should be all about: educating the public. And education is so much more easily accepted when a desire to ask questions has been created. Thus, a would-be-boring lecture of facts and figures that are soon to be forgotten have now, by dramatic display, been transformed into a situation of genuine interest. And I play my small part to promote the plight of the dreaded serpent in the hope that eventually the knowledge shared would somehow contribute to the understanding of the much bigger picture—conservation of the planet and all its diverse species of living creatures.

With bated breath the audience now expectantly awaits my return on their assortment of questions. I knew it mattered not how intelligent or ludicrous some of these questions might be, but only that I had generated enough interest for questions to be asked. And this was only the first of an assortment of snakes that I would be displaying within the next half hour of the show. Returning to my original position in the center of the arena where the wary rinkhals still lingered, swaying its hooded neck from side to side, its eyes rigidly fixed on my every movement, I correlate my answers to flow somewhat across the spectrum:

> Firstly, ladies and gentlemen, one must understand that the snake is a creature of nature, designed to play its part in the balance thereof. The fact that some snakes are venomous, and therefore of potential danger to humans, has led to the condemnation of all the species, no matter the purpose they serve or the good they might do. Folklore would have it that all snakes are dangerous to man, but this simply is not true. In fact, no more than 10 percent of the species of snakes recorded on the planet today possess venom that might be considered potentially dangerous to humans. Furthermore, with only one or two exceptions, snakes are too small in size to consider humans as prey and therefore have no reason to attack a human, other than in self-defense. Irrespective of the reptile in question being venomous or not, its only means of defense is its mouth, therefore it will bite in retaliation to attack, just as any wild creature will. So it is not surprising that most snakebite cases reported turn out to be harmless.

There is a hush now across the audience, their interest is palpable. I continue:

> However, should one step on a snake or in some way anger it, it will certainly strike out, and in the case of a venomous species, possibly inject a dangerous dose of venom. In such a case, naturally, it is important to get the victim as

6

calmly and speedily as possible to medical attention. The good news here is that there exists today an antivenom for most species, and in most countries more people die each year from lightning strikes than from snakebite.

There is a murmur of surprised exchanges. I take a breath before continuing.

Venomous snakes are so solely for the purpose of feeding. The more potent venoms are designed to kill the prey as quickly as possible, while milder venoms contribute to slowing the victim down as well as aiding in the digestion of the prey. Here too, proportions of size must be considered, because, for example, a venom that kills a mouse in minutes may take several hours to kill a much-larger adult human. Thus, with the usual one or two exceptions, most snakebite accidents leave the human victim with considerable time to reach medical help. Certain first-aid treatment applied correctly, like the application of an elastic bandage along the length of the bitten limb, can extend this time still further. Thus the odds generally are well in the favor of the human, while the luckless serpent, which was just defending itself from the monster-sized human creature, often ends up with its head bashed in.

At this point I have the audience's full attention, leaning forward to catch my every word. The hush interrupted only by the occasional whispered repeat of a fact, or a giggle at my sometimes subtle, if sarcastic, humor. And for a second or two I allow them time to digest these basic facts before once more proceeding.

All the while, not two meters from where I stand, the rinkhals remains upright and on the defensive but does not attack. Thus, at the same time as I am delivering the facts verbally, I am testing and proving some of them on the spot. And it's true . . . the snake does not attack me, as long as I keep still

7

and keep a fair distance. *Astounding!* Who would have thought it possible, after all the propaganda to the contrary? And with a bit of luck, the next time one of those in the audience that day encounters a snake in the wild, they may just remember my demonstration and allow the snake space to escape rather than make an all-out effort to crush its head in.

And I press on:

> As for the matter of spitting venom, this is purely a self-defense mechanism designed to create time for the snake to escape. Only a few of the cobra species are capable of this feat, and the venom, though deadly in the blood stream, is harmless on the skin. However the design is to spray venom into the eyes of the enemy, where it will cause pain and smarting, allowing enough time for escape. Where humans are concerned, the solution to the problem is no more complex than washing the eyes with water, and it is only in extreme cases where this treatment has been neglected or the eyes rubbed and inflamed that blindness may result.

Moving on now, I gently entice the rinkhals towards a nearby bush, where it quickly forgets about me and darts away to hide safely from view, no doubt greatly relieved to be dismissed.

It was time now for the next display, which takes the form of a meter-long, heavy-bodied puff adder; the African species best known for the fact that it is responsible for the most venomous snakebite cases on the continent.

Here the demonstration takes on a whole new turn, as I have to firmly pin down the snake in question behind the head with a specially designed rod while, with my free hand, I close in to take the now-furious and puffing reptile safely into grip. And there is always that one nerve-wracking moment during transfer from rod to hand when an angry puff adder might jerk violently in an attempt to free itself, and the huge hinging fangs appear suddenly, miraculously, just millimeters from my thumb.

The audience watches in expectant silence. Some are fearful for my safety, while others are hoping for blood. However one becomes accustomed to the technique—as one does to any repetitive move—and I dare say that I probably could eventually have performed the technique blindfolded, though there is no way in hell I would ever attempt to prove this. The painful memories of my first-ever snakebite while in the military remain forever impressed upon my mind, while the fact that, in spite of it all, I still chose to do this work is proof enough of the confidence I have in my ability.

Venom extraction from certain species of snakes is essential for the manu-facture of the antivenom, and in Africa the puff adder supplies one of the numerous venom types necessary to complete the process. The venoms used in the process are sterilized and diluted into nonlethal doses that are then injected into the bloodstream of a horse. This promotes the formation of antibodies designed to fight the venoms. Within a period of months, the horse is capable of accepting, without any ill effect, a cocktail dose consisting of various venoms which, under normal circumstances, would have been fatal to the animal. At this time regulated amounts of blood can be drained from the horse and the antibodies separated and purified into a crystal clear life-saving antivenom.

Thus it came about that reptile parks the world over took to the milking of snake venom (the process of safely extracting venom from a snake to be used for antivenom), which, after being desiccated, was stored for later sale to laboratories as demand prescribed. The Hartebeespoort Dam Snake and Animal Park, situated some forty kilometers outside the capital city of Pretoria, South Africa, where I now found myself employed as curator of reptiles, was no exception, with tourists and the general public alike arriving in their droves to witness these exciting and potentially dangerous "snake milking" exhibitions.

Once I had safely secured the puff adder behind its head, basically minimizing any further existing danger to me, I now only need to coax the reptile's mouth over the edge of the prepared milking flask. The design of the flask is not relevant, but across the open top a thin plastic membrane is stretched through which the snake's fangs must penetrate. Thus simulating a bite, the snake will usually eject a quantity of venom from each fang. After a number of extractions, the flask is cleared and the venom desiccated. In its dried form, snake venom retains its concentrated toxicity indefinitely.

With the demand for certain snake venoms at its peak in the mid- to late 1970s, the reptile parks realized the crowd-attracting potential such displays would render if advertised and performed on a regular basis. Thus a new era was born, with park attendance figures increasing steadily as the word spread that "life-threatening" feats with venomous snakes were being performed on a daily basis . . . in the presence of live audiences. And though to us professional snake handlers the entire matter was considered to be no more than part of the job, I imagine that to the general public, with their ingrained natural (or unnatural) fear of snakes, it was unusual and exciting to witness. And of course, the possibility always existed that someone might get bitten. What a show that would make!

But with the advent of these venom-extraction shows, a shortage of the particular snakes in demand quickly developed. Generally, the parks were forced to rely on the public to supply, or at least report the whereabouts of, snakes, and those in close proximity to the park would be collected by one of the staff. But as the venom extraction process was detrimental to the general health of the snake, the mortality rate was high, while the demand was ever increasing.

Snake venom is in fact a complex protein. Regular draining of this protein forces the snake's body to continuously replenish the loss. Add this to the trauma suffered each time it is handled, and soon the reptile's condition deteriorates. This will often be followed by a reluctance to eat, and inevitably, death.

To prevent the loss of reptilian life, construction of a much larger park was called for that was capable of housing hundreds of hygienic, single-quarter snake enclosures, specifically designed for the needs of the milking stock. In other words, if a very large collection of the desired species could be housed, individuals could be rotated, with longer periods of rest afforded between venom extractions. This would minimize trauma, while allowing plenty of time for correct feeding and replenishing of the lost protein. However, the costs involved in the creation and staffing of such laboratories was substantial, and not within the grasp of any but the larger reptile institutions at the time.

In South Africa, cash rewards were offered for any snakes delivered uninjured to the park, a move that precipitated a craze of catching, especially amongst the farmers living in the hot, dry northern areas of South Africa, where a variety of snake species—especially puff adders—were prolific. And soon, instead of the occasional drum or box container of captured snakes arriving by train at the railway station for collection by the park, the farmers themselves began to arrive, their vehicles fully packed with the luckless reptiles. I recall numerous occasions when more than five hundred puff adders would be delivered at one time, not to mention an assortment of other specimens, both harmless as well as venomous. With such an astonishing abundance of snakes available in these areas, one could at least reason that, were the reptiles not caught for sale to the parks, they would in all likelihood otherwise have been killed on sight, as was the case most anywhere else in the world.

However, as time passed the matter was eventually investigated by the Department of Conservation and, thankfully, by the early 1980s a law had been passed prohibiting the capture or killing of *any* reptile species found in South Africa, venomous or otherwise. For what it's worth, this at least somewhat deterred the further blatant rape of the *herpetofauna* (local reptile and amphibious species), though it is a certainty that many snakes continued to be killed simply because they were snakes.

Entering the next phase of my demonstration now, I grip the neatly captured puff adder firmly behind the head with my right hand while supporting the heavy body with my left (at the same time clasping the plastic covered flask). I then bring the snake and flask together, allowing the snake's mouth to feel the edge of the flask being pressed between its lips.

Instinctively the snake is prompted to bite. With hinging fangs instantly erect, it lunges forward, with the crowd gasping as venom gushes to the bottom of the flask. This is what they had come to see! Dramatic demonstration of snakebite in action! And as I stroll around the arena with snake and flask both raised high for a better view, and with the reptiles huge needle-like fangs now plainly visible through the plastic membrane, the crowd excitedly cranes forward for a better look. And as always, they are amazed, with a hundred new questions bubbling over in their minds. These questions I address on the move, thereby keeping up a constant repertoire of Q&A so as not to lose the interest of those in the crowd I have already passed by. Having completed my rounds, I finally return the puff adder to its holding container. The audience breathes a sigh of relief . . . as I secretly do as well. Gripping a large, venomous adder behind the head as its long hinged fangs relentlessly chew in an attempt to prick a finger is not a matter to be handled brazenly.

Introducing the next reptile for discussion, I produce an African tree snake from the bushy branches of a shrub-like tree growing in the middle of the display arena. A number of these snakes lived in the tree, coming to ground only when food was presented below. This is a back-fanged species, unusual in that, unlike most other back-fanged species, the African tree snake, or boomslang, manufactures a hemotoxic venom of particularly virulent proportions. However these snakes are docile serpents, seldom attempting to bite but rather choosing to disappear with lightning agility into any available overhead vegetation. Securing the snake's tail in one hand while draping the rest of the slender body over the front end of a grab-stick, the audience is now treated to a few jittery moments as the serpent is suspended over the arena wall to dangle ominously in their midst as I pass. The calm disposition of the snake astonishes the crowd. A flood of questions erupts from those more curious, while those more nervous cringe at the close proximity of the reptile. A close encounter with a potentially deadly serpent in the hands of a competent handler—one way or another—is always a crowd pleaser.

The boomslang is eventually returned to its tree, which now leaves only the grand finale of the show. Locating a harmless species in the arena, usually a one-meter-long common mole snake or juvenile African rock python, I offer this to be either held or simply touched by members of the audience, thereby at first hand disproving the popular fallacy that the serpentine skin is slimy and hopefully somewhat dispelling their fear of being in close proximity with the creature. This personal encounter with a snake was always well received, with many of the public volunteering to have the snake draped around their necks for a photograph—a personal prized memento of their exciting visit to the snake and animal park. All in all a practical lesson in nature, in this case concerning a drastically misunderstood creature of some undeserved negative repute.

Throughout my years spent as curator of reptiles at three major parks during the 1970s through the early 90s (two in South Africa, one in Germany), I must have physically handled over a hundred thousand snakes—extracting venom from many of these—as well as performing countless public shows, demonstrations, and lectures. Over that period of time, though experiencing a number of close calls, never was I ever seriously bitten by a venomous snake while performing and lecturing to the public; that all happened behind the scenes!

CHAPTER 2

A BIT OF BACKGROUND AND THE HARTEBEESPOORT DAM SNAKE AND ANIMAL PARK

I was just twelve years old when I brought home my first reptile, a juvenile red-lipped herald snake. Though this species is not considered dangerous to humans, my parents were unimpressed and forced me to dispose of the luckless reptile. I was very upset, having now seen the forbidden fruit but not allowed to eat of it. Thus began my love/hate relationship with my parents as I battled relentlessly to coax them over to my way of thinking, while they in turn threatened to send me off to boarding school if I did not behave as was expected of me.

It is not easy to explain why snakes and other reptiles affect a young child so. It might be the unusual way in which they move, or their incredible color patterns displayed on shiny scales, or it might be because these creatures are so secretive and mysterious, some even reputed to be deadly. It may be one or all of these things. All I know, and what I have witnessed with many people I have introduced to snakes, is that once they have touched a snake, felt its smooth, cool body move effortlessly through their hands, they are never quite the same again. Everything changes, and there seems suddenly to be a new awareness of the beauty of this wondrous natural thing.

Needless to say, my parents did eventually succumb, and by my late teens I had procured an extensive collection of snakes that I housed in a variety of glass enclosures in my bedroom. By this point my parents now proudly discussed my "pets" with all friends and visitors, showing pride and genuine respect for my accumulated knowledge and enthusiasm of the subject. Little did they suspect how these creatures would affect the rest of my life.

I had never touched a camera until some years later, when I first became professionally employed at the then-named Transvaal Snake Park. Suddenly I had access to all these wondrous reptiles from around the world, reptiles of every color and shape. So I purchased a little fixed-lens instamatic camera and began to take pictures. However, within a short while, realizing that I was not doing these magnificent creatures the justice they deserved, I progressed to a more advanced camera, one that incorporated interchangeable lenses that allowed me access, especially, to a variety of close-up macro lenses.

Now I could get down to fine detail, showing all aspects of the wonderful color patterns and scale formations of these reptiles, amongst other features. Soon I was photo crazy, shooting up roll after roll of slide film. Eventually I began writing articles about these exotic creatures, supporting each article with my own photography. (Over the period of my writing, I have had more than 150 wildlife articles published in a variety of magazines in Southern Africa and around the world.)

My earliest experience with television work came about at a time when I was performing lectures and public reptile demonstrations at the Transvaal Snake Park in South Africa. At the time, in the mid-seventies, South Africa had just recently launched its first television station, and it was not long before a SABC (South African Broadcasting Company) film crew turned up at the park to record one of my public reptile demonstrations. This led to an offer to do a followup program at the Johannesburg SABC studios, bringing all my reptiles with me to appear on a program called *Compass*. This I did, with the show proving to be so popular that I was asked to return to perform two further shows.

However, it was only many years later, after I had relocated from South Africa to Namibia (South West Africa), that I first looked through the viewfinder of a 16 mm movie camera as I prepared to embark on a TV documentary film concerning the life of snakes. This I did for NDR (Norddeutscher Rundfunk; in English, "North German Broadcasting") Television in Germany and titled the film *Die Natur der Schlange* (*The Nature of the Snake*). The goal of the film was to document interesting behavioral patterns of some of Southern Africa's unusual snakes. And, to my delight, the film was nominated in the "First time film maker: Best documentary" category, at the Grenable Film Festival in France.

Moving with the times, I later changed to video format and spent seven months in the dunes of the Namib, where I tracked and filmed the secret lives of desert chameleons. Titled *Dragons of the Namib*, this film was aired on the National Geographic Channel and distributed globally.

Thereafter I was on numerous occasions contacted by international film companies to participate in a variety of film projects where reptiles were being featured, especially for UK-based companies. After completing work on a number of these programs, I was finally approached and asked if I thought it might be possible to do an interactive adventure episode involving venomous snakes. I said yes, that I thought this was possible, and the resulting dramatic film, *Seven Deadly Strikes*, became the catalyst that eventually led to Animal Planet's initiating the production of my first television series, *Austin Stevens: Snakemaster/Austin Stevens: Most Dangerous*. This was followed later by a second series involving dangerous mammals, *Austin Stevens Adventures*.

ৡ ৡ ৡ

My personal history with the Hartebeespoort Dam Snake and Animal Park reaches back many years, to the age of seventeen, when, with a growing sense of excitement, I read the snake cage "sit-in" challenge in the evening newspaper. The next morning saw me furiously pedaling my bicycle in the direction of the park, some forty kilometers away from where I lived on the outskirts of Pretoria. Hours later, exhausted but no less enthusiastic, I presented myself to Mr. Jack Seale, owner of the park, who was at the time locked in a snake enclosure with twenty-four venomous snakes, attempting to set a world record. The challenge I had read in the newspaper had come from Jack himself, daring anyone to have lunch with him in the cramped space he was sharing with the venomous snakes.

Thus it came about that I met Jack Seale for the first time and found myself now the subject of much media attention and a specific newspaper article that read, "Boy, 17, at ease with mambas." This was my first publicity article, with me in no way suspecting the many that would follow over the years to come.

Over a period of two days I spent some eight hours in the cage with Jack. We chatted, learning about each other and eating lunch amongst the serpents, a stunt that thrilled the gawking visitors and press personal alike as they gathered around the glass enclosure. It was time enough for Jack and I to establish a friendship that, unbeknown to us at the time, was to endure for more than forty years, to the present day. Little did we suspect that some twenty years later, to raise funds and awareness to the plight of the African gorillas, I would myself set a new world record of 107 days and nights spent in a cage with thirty-six of Africa's deadliest snakes. It would be the highlight of the many years I was to spend working at the park as curator of herpetology.

Jack had been fascinated by reptiles since his early childhood, his career beginning with a tiny snake park he constructed some twenty kilometers outside the Hartebeespoort area. At around this time, a small private zoo had begun to take shape right on the edge of the Hartebeespoort Dam itself, opposite the old Lake View Hotel. Jack later formed a partnership with the zoo owner, transferring his reptile collection to the new park. Shortly afterwards, Jack's partner grew tired of the operation, allowing Jack to buy him out and take over the business in its entirety, and the Hartebeespoort Dam Snake and Animal Park was born and still remains today.

The park began its design a hundred meters back from the water's edge, but as time passed and funds became available, further development was initiated with new sections being created for other animals as well as reptiles and soon these sprawled out along the waterfront. This created a unique setting enabling visitors to access the displays while at the same time offering a breathtaking view across the water, where colorful sailboats skimmed silently across the surface.

The park was Jack's dream, his passion, his life. It was all he ever wanted, and when he stood on the great turreted, stone-wall perimeter overlooking the dam, with his arrogant stance and thick walrus moustache jutting into the wind, he felt no less pride than a king surveying his kingdom.

When Jack offered me the position of curator of herpetology, it was to be the beginning of my professional career in the fields of herpetology and zoology, which in later years would progress to my interest in wildlife photography and documentary filmmaking.

Each evening the park closed its gates more or less as the sun was setting behind the Magaliesburg Mountains, which edged the northern perimeter of the Hartebeespoort Dam itself. At the western edge of the park, constructed high up on a steep incline surrounded by trees and with a magnificent view of the water, stood a rustic cottage built of natural stone—my home for the many years of my stay as curator of herpetology at the park. Here, each evening, as the last diurnal animal calls gradually diminished with the onset of night, to be replaced by the roars, grunts and howls of those of the nocturnal, I felt satisfied and at peace.

వ వ వ

Accepting my position at the park was a lifesaver in more ways than one. It enabled me to immediately become independent of my parents, while at the same time giving me a positive direction toward the fields to which I was obviously drawn. Despite my parents' wishes that I become a doctor (or at least a lawyer), I knew with some certainty that it would never happen. For better or worse, I was drawn in another direction. This was a natural compulsion I either obeyed or spent the rest of my life wondering where it might have led. I did then, and still do today, believe that being content in one's work overrides earning the "big bucks" in an unhappy environment.

My title as curator of herpetology in fact encompassed not only the reptile section but a wide variety of general work around the park. Under the supervision of Jack, as well as two other staff members in managerial positions, a large team of African staff were employed to do the daily maintenance, clean cages, and do the general animal husbandry. Though reptiles were my forte, with so many other animal species housed on the property, it was imperative to gain at least a general knowledge and experience concerning their well-being and keeping. Being a privately owned park, its design and construction had evolved somewhat erratically over the years as funds became available. The resulting outlay presented the visiting public with an interesting walk amongst a variety of species of mammals as well as reptiles, with a varying selection of each scattered along the way.

With the constant flow of visiting public passing through the gates each day, and especially the huge crowds on weekends, it was part of my job description to mingle and liaise, supplying information and answering questions. I was of course also responsible for the snake demonstration shows, which took place hourly from 10 a.m. to 4 p.m. on weekends and public holidays. These shows proved to be so popular that in later years, as the park grew in size, seal feeding and chimpanzee tea-party performances were introduced, the latter most often delivering unchoreographed, hilarious results, much to the delight of the audience.

Question-and-answer sessions were encouraged during public shows, and inevitably most questions were directed towards venomous snakes. Through widespread misinformation, bad publicity, and ignorance, people generally are raised to fear snakes, while at the same time experiencing a macabre fascination with them. Excited to view snakes from behind the safety of a glass window, people will otherwise often demonstrate an illogically exaggerated fear when confronted by one in the wild. By exposing the myths and presenting the facts at public snake-handling shows, parks around the world have always aimed to arouse a more accurate awareness of the plight of the snake—and reptiles in general—thus hopefully somewhat alleviating this misappropriated fear. Though research features high up on the agenda of any wildlife park, educating the public should remain a priority. Only through education can understanding ever develop, thereby creating the initiative to reach a compromise between human domination of the planet and the dwindling wilderness and wildlife that still remain.

CHAPTER 3

THE GABOON VIPER

Even the most idyllic of work situations experience their ups and downs, with people often posing the question, "Aren't you afraid of being bitten?" It's a logical question, I suppose. As curator of herpetology, I would hear it a hundred times a day, especially when found to be working inside a venomous snake enclosure. My answer is always the same: "As much as you are afraid of crossing the street in traffic, or driving your car. . . ."

Although the work I was doing may have appeared highly dangerous to others, I considered it no more perilous than crossing a busy road, providing you know the rules. It's all a matter of knowledge. In the case of the pedestrian or motorist, knowledge of the rules of the road is imperative. In my case, knowledge of the behavior, habits, and potential danger posed by the reptiles I am working with was all important. Of course, this does not totally rule out the possibility of an accident.

When Gabby, our large and beautifully colored Central African male Gaboon viper, developed an abscess close to his right eye, I followed the normal procedure of transferring the snake to our laboratory area, where I could surgically drain the abscess in a sterile surrounding. Within minutes I had administered a local anesthetic to the infected area while my assistant at the park at the time, Paul Hammond, controlled Gabby's writhing body, which was one and a half meters long.

The Gaboon viper is the largest viper species found in Africa, sometimes measuring up to two meters long and weighing up to ten kilograms (around twenty-two pounds). The snake is also known to have the largest fangs of any snake species in the world, the longest recorded being close to five centimeters in length. Although the species is considered fairly docile by nature, it will not tolerate interference and will retaliate with a lightning strike timed at seven meters per second, with the long fangs and connecting venom glands capable of delivering a huge quantity of a deadly concoction of nerve and tissue destroying venom. All in all, the Gaboon viper is a snake that even the most seasoned herpetologist should be wary of.

With the aid of a pair of thick leather gloves, Paul held down the snake's thick, powerful body, leaving me free to grip Gabby's broad, triangular head with my left hand while drawing the scalpel across the bulging abscess with my right. Because of the delicate maneuvering of surgical instruments required by the operation, it was necessary that my hands remain bare, other than for a pair of the usual thin, rubber surgical gloves. I felt no apprehension in doing so, as this was a simple operation, similar to many I had performed in the past. The scalpel pierced the tough skin, and instantly a dark brown pus oozed through.

"Got it," I exclaimed, imagining the relief Gabby must be feeling as the pressure around the eye was suddenly released, and carefully I began to clean the wound with a sterile cotton bud.

Consciously, I was making sure to do everything correctly. My eyes were focused rigidly on the massive, squirming head, still held firmly down by my left hand, and I was holding the cotton bud directly above the head, a safe angle and distance from those terrible hinging fangs housed in the roof of Gabby's mouth.

So how did it all go wrong?

In a split second and with a mighty effort, Gabby forced his head up and to the left, unhinging a fang far enough to slip past his bottom lip and hook my forefinger. There immediately came a fierce burning sensation, followed by a wave of shock as my mind struggled with the fact that the impossible had happened: I had been injected with a dose of powerful neurotoxic/cytotoxic venom; the worst, potentially most traumatic venom combination imaginable. But was it a lethal dose? Not wanting to believe it was, I stared at my finger as blood oozed from a tiny cut. Surely very little venom could have entered.

Paul's eyes were wide with shock, but thankfully he still had Gabby's writhing body under control, as I had his head. I quickly flushed Gabby's wound with antiseptic fluid, and together Paul and I transferred the reptile to a holding tank. Now for the first time I had a chance to properly examine my finger. It was obvious the finger was swelling fast, right before my eyes, and as it did, the amount of pain increased accordingly. The fang may just have pricked my finger, but it was already obvious that a serious amount of venom had entered my system.

Dear God the pain!

Silently, I cursed my stupidity. *How could I let this happen?* A dizzy spell swept over me and I felt the need to sit down. My mind raced over the basic treatment for such a snake bite: adequate intravenous polyvalent antivenom; replacement of fluid loss, especially whole blood in extreme cases; possible need for cardiac and respiratory support measures. But the real question was one I was unable to answer: Could my body cope with the Gaboon viper's terrible venom? Could I handle the excruciating pain I knew was coming? I knew of only one other recorded Gaboon viper bite, with the victim losing his arm below the elbow. Losing a limb is not uncommon where large adder bites are concerned, as their tissue-destroying cytotoxins (designed to digest the flesh of their prey) steadily devours the bitten limb until finally amputation is the only option to prevent gangrene poisoning . . . followed by death.

Opening the laboratory fridge, I grabbed the park's supply of antivenoms and other emergency paraphernalia.

"Call Jack on the radio," I ordered Paul. "Tell him to get down here quickly!"

Jack arrived minutes later, and together we began analyzing the situation. By now my hand felt as though it was on fire, and the swelling had spread to my wrist. My hand looked like a balloon. Seating me in a chair, Jack said calmly, "We both know the drill, but it's your life at stake. Do you feel you need serum?"

This was the crucial question. Looking at my rapidly swelling arm, I was sure that I did. Even though Gabby had just broken the skin, I knew that this was a lethal shot of venom, no doubt about it. But what if my body reacted negatively to the serum? Anaphylaxis is not uncommon in such cases, especially where the patient had received serum in the past. It is not uncommon to develop sensitivity to the serum. Such a reaction would be immediate . . . and potentially fatal. Yet Jack and I both knew that my best chance of survival lay in receiving antivenom injected intravenously as soon as possible.

"Yes," I said finally. "At least three ampoules." The serum was contained in 10 ml ampoules and I roughly estimated that 30 ml might suffice. It depended on how much venom had been introduced into my system: the more venom, the more serum was required. From the prick I had received from the fang, I suspected not a great amount of venom had entered my system. But, knowing that just one drop could be fatal, I was taking a calculated guess.

The best defense against an allergic serum reaction is to inject antihistamine into the blood stream ahead of introducing the antivenom. However, a quick search through our supplies revealed that we had no intravenous antihistamine in stock. We did find some oral antihistamine though, which would take longer to absorb into my system. But at this point, it was better than nothing. So I swallowed down half a bottle, about 10 ml. This done, Jack injected a small trial dose of serum under my skin to test for possible signs of a negative reaction. After ten minutes, there was no obvious negative reaction. By this time I was feeling dizzy and the pain in my hand was like a roaring inferno. I was also, for the first time, beginning to feel generally apprehensive. Time was running out. I was facing potential death from either the venom or the serum; it was not a happy situation, but there was little choice. With the venom in my system remaining untreated, I could be dead within a matter of hours. Better to take a chance with the serum rather than the certainty of the venom finishing me off.

"Jack," I said, "let's do it."

Jack sat in a chair opposite me, a syringe loaded with 20 ml of serum ready in his hand.

"You're sure you don't want to go to hospital?"

Going to hospital would mean a delay of at least an hour, an hour in which time the Gaboon viper's venom would have spread along my arm to an extent beyond repair.

"Do it!"

As the needle entered my vein, Jack, Paul, and I held our breath. A minute passed—an agonizing minute that seemed to drag on for an hour, until finally . . . no reaction! I was in the clear. I would have experienced immediate distress if there was to be any negative reaction to the serum. Jack and Paul sighed with relief, as Jack steadily emptied the syringe into my vein and prepared another. Three ampoules in all, 30 ml, a rough estimate of what was needed. I would possibly need more later, depending on my reaction to the treatment, but I was still a long way from home base. Unfortunately for me, the worst had yet to come. Not all the venom's properties would be neutralized, especially the cytotoxins, which would have to run their course. Once again it seemed I would live to fight another day . . . but at what cost? Painful memories of my puff adder bite while in military service momentarily surfaced in my mind. I pushed them aside. We were better prepared now, with the correct treatment being immediately administered. My chances were better than they had been when I was a teenager.

For the next four days I tossed and turned in bed. When the pain became unbearable, I paced back and forth, holding my arm aloft to somewhat relieve the pressure, as the pain and swelling in my arm raged like a fire all the way up to my shoulder. Back on my bed I thrashed about, almost crying in pain as a terrible dark-blue blood blister steadily grew out of my finger where the fang had punctured the skin. Destroyed blood cells were forcing their way to the surface, tearing the skin from my flesh. Double doses of powerful painkillers supplied by our local doctor seemed to have little or no effect against my agony. After the second day, I collapsed into delirium.

Twenty-four hours later I surfaced to focus on a smiling face looking down at me. It was Tanja, one of the park staff girls. She had been keeping an eye on me since day one.

"You look a mess," she remarked casually, concerned humor in her eyes. "Don't you ever wash or shave?"

She then looked at my hand. "Not a pretty sight."

I looked at it too. Indeed it was not a pretty sight. But something had changed. The pain had decreased considerably. The cytotoxins had run their course. The crisis was over. All that remained was to control the necrosis of the bitten area with suitable antibiotics and sterile dressings until the last remaining neucrotic tissue finally sloughed off.

Tanja helped me into the bathroom, where I stared shakily into the mirror. A pale, dark-eyed, hairy face stared back at me. I looked like someone who had been to hell and back . . . and it felt like I had.

I thought to myself, *is that not afterall what snakebite is—every herpetologists potential hell?*

And the time old question materialized in my mind:

Aren't you afraid of being bitten?

Yes indeed, all herpetologists are afraid of being bitten by a highly venomous snake, and most *are* bitten eventually. But one tries not to think about it and just gets on with the job as cautiously and skillfully as possible. Working with venomous snakes every day, though, does tend to up the ante somewhat, just as those people who swim in the sea are more likely to be bitten by a shark. I had just survived a near-fatal, excruciatingly painful experience from a snake bite, and for a while thereafter I must admit I was more nervous about handling a potentially dangerous specimen than usual. However, this feeling soon faded as day-by-day running of the snake park once more became the norm, and I promised myself that the experience would *never* again be repeated.

Little did I suspect at the time that this was a promise not to be kept.

CHAPTER 4

A WORLD-RECORD SNAKE SIT-IN

There had been numerous snake "sit-in" records claimed from various parts of the globe over the years since Jack Seale first established his record of twenty-four days all those years ago, when he and I first met. Some records claimed sixty days, others more, but it soon became evident that most were not verified. Some were found to have used only nonvenomous snakes, while other challengers had not remained in their cages overnight, making their claims to the record invalid.

My main motivation for attempting a world record venomous snake sit-in was to raise funds for the purchase of a mate for Kaiser, the Hartebeespoort Dam Snake and Animal Park's lonely gorilla. Kaiser was an adult-male lowland gorilla living in an enormous enclosure specially designed for his needs. Try as he might, however, Jack was unable to locate an eligible female for sale. The idea was not only to improve living conditions for Kaiser but to also attempt to breed these highly endangered animals. After much discussion and planning, Jack and I decided that a one-hundred-day sit-in might not only establish a once-and-for all, decisive claim to the ultimate world record for venomous snake sit-ins, but also arouse public awareness to the plight of Kaiser and African gorillas as a whole. Any funds raised during the sit-in would go towards the purchase of a mate for Kaiser, should one become available from an overseas breeding zoo. All this, of course, was assuming that I'd be able to survive the designated time in a cage of deadly serpents.

A special glass-and-brick enclosure was constructed on the lower level of the park grounds, opposite the primate and puma cages and close to the water's edge. The completed structure measured roughly three meters by four meters square and two meters high, and was stocked with thirty-six highly venomous African snakes. These consisted of six puff adders, six boomslangs, six black mambas, and eighteen snouted cobras. And as the starting date drew closer, the more unsure I became of my ability to go through with it. It would be bad enough being isolated in a glass cage for a hundred days and have to deal with hordes of public passerby's staring at me day and night . . . and then still to have to contend with venomous snakes all over the place. However, when the day finally arrived and the crowds of well-wishers and news reporters began to assemble, there was no turning back. So, I cautiously entered the cage of serpents. Unknown to me at the time, as matters were to develop, this would in fact become my home for an extended one hundred and *seven* days and nights—to say the least, a trying time of unusual conditions and proportions.

With the snakes constantly on the move in familiarizing themselves with their strange new surroundings, exploring every nook and cranny, the first weeks proved to be the most trying. I suffered periods of depression alternating with periods of frustration, alternating with periods of anxiety. This was possibly true for the snakes as well, as we all were forced to live together in the confined space of a cage. Territories had to be established, routines managed, all the while attempting not to get in each other's way.

Known for their lightning fast strike, large fangs, and terrible cytotoxic venom, the six puff adders—being heavy bodied and more sluggish— kept mostly to the floor, forcing me to watch my step at all times. The boomslangs, highly venomous but nonaggressive as they were known to be, spent most of the time perched on a small, dead branch planted in the cage for just this purpose. The six black mambas were the largest snakes in the cage, each almost three meters in length. The longest venomous snake found in Africa and known for their short tempers, nervous disposition, and powerful neurotoxic venom, they were the ones of which I was most wary. However, as matters turned out, these fearsome reptiles seldom bothered me, preferring to sleep under the bed most of the day to emerge only later at night, when they would crawl out over my sleeping body to explore their surroundings.

Of all the species of snakes housed in the cage with me, not surprisingly it was the eighteen cobras that were to provide the most problems, as they quickly discovered the warm confines of the bed and claimed it as their own, though they didn't mind sharing it with me as long as I behaved myself. In the early days of the sit-in this led to a constant battle for the bed, with me most often the loser, forced to sleep in the chair, especially on colder nights when the bed was most in demand. It was usually necessary for me to remove all the snakes from the bed with the aid of a hooked snake stick, then quickly settle myself on the bed in a comfortable position in preparation for their return.

Within five minutes the cobras would be back, nosing their way onto the bed to settle around my warm body for the night. It was in those first frightening weeks that I learned to sleep for only minutes at a time, training myself never to move while I slept, and to awaken ridged as I was, not moving a muscle until I had established where all the cobras were positioned. Most were usually pressed in tight along the length of my torso, while others were settled under my pillow. Sometimes, most frighteningly, a few might be snuggled up a trouser leg. This dangerous scenario I later prevented by sleeping with socks on and my trouser legs tightly tucked into them.

Snakes in general, even highly venomous species, will not attack simply for the sake of doing so. Provoked or hurt in some way, they will naturally defend themselves. Lying motionless, I presented no apparent danger. The cobras simply crawled and pushed their way in under me as though I were no more than a log in the forest. The essential rule of course was not to make any sudden movements, and in my particular case, not to accidentally squash any of them when maneuvering myself off and onto the bed. Those first weeks were terrifying; thinking back now, it is just simply a miracle that I was not bitten within the early period of that crazy adventure.

It was of course important that my attempt at a world-record snake sit-in be well publicized so as to generate as much interest as possible; thus I was forced to endure continuous bombardment from the media. One morning, still within the first weeks of entering the cage, I was greeted by the sight outside of a television crew laden down with what looked like tons of filming equipment. Fortunately I had completed my ablutions for the morning and had even managed to rush down a bowl of cereal while most of the snakes gathered together at the front of the cage, eager to absorb the early-morning rays as the sun slowly warmed the earth.

Gathering around the viewing area, the crew gaped at me in open-mouthed astonishment. Unimpressed, I stared back at them. Never at my best early in the morning anyway, that day I felt grumpier than usual, having just survived a night of dodging cobras in the bed, puff adders on the floor, and mambas and tree snakes on the chair, where I had eventually ended up dozing until sunrise in an uncomfortable, upright position. I estimated that I was averaging about two to three hours of broken sleep each night, and this particular morning I felt it in every bone of my body.

While I stared at the television crew, an urgent rattle came at the back door of the cage, followed by a voice: "Any snakes near the door?" I glanced briefly in that direction. "No," I called back, burying my face in my hands. Jack entered a second later, perky, freshly showered and shaven, making me feel all the more grubby, uncomfortable, and irritable. My little portable wash basin served rather inadequately as an all-in-one bathroom.

"Good news," Jack spoke excitedly, pointing at the crew outside the front window. His overly cheerful manner immediately aroused my suspicions. Still gesturing towards the team outside, he continued: "This is an international TV crew! They want to film and interview you right here in the cage to show the world exactly what you are doing and why."

I sighed. True, this was indeed good news. It meant that the fund might get a good boost once brought to the attention of an international audience.

However, I felt little enthusiasm, only fatigue. Jack beamed at me, a smile spread all over his face. My suspicions increased.

"Exactly what do they plan to film?" I asked slowly. I knew the newsworthiness of my venture all right, but an international film crew, weighted down as they were with equipment, did not come all the way from wherever it was just to film me sitting in a cage of snakes. Sensationalism was what sold news, and I knew only too well how Jack loved sensationalism. Certainly I would try everything possible to interest the public in what I was attempting, but there were indeed limits. After all, my life was at stake here. Jack viewed things differently however, and he let me have it all in one fast sentence.

"I told them you were prepared to drape mambas all over your body and hold cobras and puff adders with your bare hands while being interviewed and filmed," he said as he stared at me innocently.

"What?" I blurted out, shocked at his statement. Jack took an involuntary step backwards as I jumped up and got right in his face. "You know these snakes are still extremely nervous," I said. "Handling them now means taking risks that could end this sit-in a little prematurely."

Despite my icy tone, Jack remained unfazed and unrepentant, as though I had not even spoken. "Think of the news value," he responded. "Our cause will be broadcast around the world!"

I continued to protest, pointing out brutally that, with me dead, there would be only one big news item and *no* hundred days. Blandly unaffected by my statement and with a shrewd glint in his eye, Jack quickly responded: "This could mean the first big step to a mate for Kaiser." I felt all the wind drop out of my sails. If I was going to contest that, then surely I should not have agreed to start this whole thing in the first place. I went into this knowing there would be risks, and I had made the decision to go ahead, as I was the only one who could make this work. Obtaining a mate for Kaiser was in my hands, and it was something I very badly wanted to achieve.

So it came to pass that some forty minutes later I found myself perched nervously on the edge of my bed, gently cradling two snouted cobras and a puff adder across my arms while, from a safe distance away, using a long pair of snake tongs, Jack delicately draped a three-meter mamba around my neck. Jack was of course adept at handling venomous snakes, and I trusted him fully, as he did my ability to handle the situation. However, we were both acutely aware of the thin margin that separated ability from accident. One false move and all hell could break loose.

In the corner opposite me, squeezed back as far as was possible, was the cameraman, nervously preparing his equipment. Next to him, microphone in hand, was the director, carefully going over his notes before the take. With the aid of snake tongs, Jack had as best possible shifted all the more troublesome snakes to the far end of the cage, assuring the crew he would keep a constant watch on them while filming was in progress.

This was indeed a professional team; to risk the potential danger of snakebite in the line of duty was proof enough. Lights mounted on tripods were strategically positioned in opposite corners, ensuring that I and the entire cage were now fully illuminated. From outside the cage, other crew members operated a second camera that was directed at me through the glass. With me now covered in highly venomous and somewhat agitated snakes, filming was about to begin. The cameraman and director inside the cage were briefed on how to behave in these rather unusual circumstances.

"Make no sudden moves, no matter what happens." Jack told them emphatically. "You are in no danger as long as you remain quite still." Nervously they nodded, and the shoot began.

Having the snakes all over me was not a major problem. Keeping them on me was, as the powerful lights soon warmed their cold-blooded metabolism; I found myself desperately clutching at lithesome bodies as they continually attempted to remove themselves from my person. The more erratic my attempts to control the reptiles became, the more agitated they grew, and I could see a situation developing that was less than safe.

Eventually, having detected the source of the warmth, the snakes began to escape towards the lamps, some of them using the video camera as a handy bridge with which to span the distance. This came much to the dismay of the now wide-eyed, perspiring cameraman. I tried in vain to keep the snakes with me but within minutes found myself alone on the bed while the tripods and lights, as well as the cameraman, were surrounded by writhing reptile bodies—an unexpected turn of events. As we all stared in horror, one of the largest snouted cobras, a heavy-bodied specimen almost two meters long, made a final bid to position itself on top of the most accessible lamp, already laden with writhing bodies . . . and this proved to be one too many.

Jack, who meanwhile was vainly attempting to remove snakes from their close proximity around the petrified cameraman, realized what was about to happen, and dived forward, tongs outstretched . . . but it was too late. Top-heavy with the added weight, the lamp, tripod, and mass of writhing bodies came crashing down onto the floor with a resounding bang as the hot lamp exploded, showering sparks, shattered glass fragments, and snakes in all directions. And my original fears were realized as all hell broke loose! Considering what we were attempting, with so many snakes and people present in such a confined area, in retrospect, it was naïve to have expected that all would proceed smoothly. That some snakes would take to the lamps, however, was a scenario that I had not even remotely imagined.

On the way down, cables attached to the tripod snagged the camera lens, jerking it forward and prompting its operator to grab out instinctively to save it. Overbalancing, he stepped forward involuntarily, only to find himself suddenly, in mid-stride, feverishly back-pedaling to avoid the mass of startled, angry serpents below his feet. Until now the director had remained quite rigid, either with amazing self-control or pure fear. Transformed now, however, he leapt straight up into the air and with a piercing yell lunged for the doorway, where he connected head-on with Jack, who was desperately trying to redirect snakes that were escaping via the same route.

Within seconds his well-planned film shoot had turned to shambles, with enraged serpents speeding around the cage; confused, frightened, and eager to kill anything that moved. And if ever a snake had reason to attack something, this was it!

The terrified cameraman's feet meanwhile became entangled in the mass of cables jumbled on the floor. He toppled forward to crash down unceremoniously beside me where I sat on the bed with my legs held high in the air in the hope of avoiding snakes as I watched the pandemonium erupting all around.

The fast, erratic movements of the mambas attracted the cobras, who struck out randomly. This movement in turn caused the puff adders to flare up in anger, puffing and blowing, ready to unleash their long fangs with lightning speed. Terrified out of his wits and deciding that the bed was not safe enough, the cameraman lunged headlong straight out the door to land in a crumpled heap on top of Jack and the director, who were still struggling to disentangle themselves just beyond the opening, somehow managing to slam the cage door shut as they did so.

Oh bloody wonderful! This now left me alone, the only human resident in a cage filled with thirty-six highly venomous and extremely agitated serpents bent on revenge.

Suddenly, two cobras, one chasing the other, scrambled up onto the bed and came racing towards me. Still tilted backwards and holding my legs off the floor, I froze. One cobra slithered quickly over my chest, while the other passed directly between my legs where it stopped, head poised up high looking straight at me, as though seeing me for the first time. I held my breath. Suddenly my suspended legs felt impossibly heavy, but I dared not move. The serpent's glassy little eyes seemed to bore into my own, and I could not help but wonder what vindictive thoughts may be passing through its brain. Then, as if having considered the possibilities and deciding in my favor, the hood folded and the head turned sharply away, disappearing from my view. Slowly, I let out my breath and lowered my legs. From outside the cage came a small splattering of applause, drawing my attention to the all-but-forgotten fact that the outside crew had been rolling a camera all the while.

The cameraman, the director, and Jack now unanimously decided that all further filming would be conducted from outside the cage, from behind the safety of the glass. I myself remained on the bed, quite still, exhausted and praying that the snakes would soon settle down to their normal routine. Ten minutes later, Jack's head appeared through the doorway, a mischievous grin on his face.

"The film crew says they have some spectacular footage, but would you mind reenacting the part with the cobra between your legs?" And he ducked back out the door as I hurled a cushion at his face. I was not up for humor at that particular point in time. The recent incident could have ended in disaster, and I still had some ninety days to get through to achieve the designated new world record—plenty of time for more of Jack's harebrained publicity schemes to get me killed. I lay back and closed my eyes.

A few minutes later I felt the first nudge under my back. Soon there came another, followed closely by another. The cobras were back, come to once more lay claim to their bed, to snuggle up cozily beneath their "log in the forest." This was a sure sign that all was forgiven. I took another deep sigh and tried to relax.

Outside the film crew, after having collected their equipment, packed up and left, excitedly discussing the unique scenario they had captured on film (and the very fact that we had all survived it). The gap they left was soon filled by the first visitors of the day, who gathered around to stare in awe at the crazy man locked in the cage of venomous snakes, while beneath the bedcover the cobras relentlessly pushed and shoved their way in under my back as I thought to myself, *Oh Lordy, why do I let these things happen to me?*

As matters turned out, I eventually completed 107 days and nights in the cage, but not without a few close calls and one serious mishap. The latter occurred on day ninety-six, while I was doing a photo shoot for *National Enquirer* magazine of the United States. It was a time when I was close to exhaustion, having endured three months of living in the cage of venomous snakes with little sleep to speak of and the constant daily pressures of gawking visitors and the media. Of course this was all to be expected as part of the operation—and I accepted that—but this did little to ease the strain. Eating, sleeping, reading, writing, scratching, bathing—all were done in full view of the daily gathered crowds, with my only privacy being the few minutes I might spend each day hidden behind the tiny canvas enclosure that was my toilet. Even here everybody knew exactly what I was doing and, undaunted, waited expectantly for the "snake man" to return.

The *National Enquirer* photo shoot had gone well considering my state. Having completed a series of varying poses with numerous snakes, I was preparing for a final shot with a large snouted cobra, when, for reasons best known to itself—perhaps startled by a movement or the flash of the camera—the snake suddenly turned and struck at me without warning, both fangs penetrating my wrist, where they injected their deadly venom.

So close to achieving my goal of one hundred days, more than anything else, I remember experiencing emotions of shock and disappointment flooding through my thoughts. I had endured so much over such a long period of time. In spite of the severity of the situation, to give up now was simply unthinkable. Within minutes Jack was at my side, removing all snakes close to me with the aid of a hooked snake stick. After a quick discussion, it was decided that our stand-by doctor would be summoned to administer treatment right there in the cage of snakes, with the agreed understanding that I be removed and brought to a hospital only if matters deteriorated to a critical level. I could already feel the venom affecting my cardiovascular system, with my breathing reduced to short, sharp intakes. My eye focus began to blur, and I felt nausea setting in. Whether these early symptoms were brought about by a reaction to the venom or from shock was not immediately clear. I was acutely aware of the risk I was taking, but thoughts of my goal to raise funds for a mate for Kaiser loomed overwhelmingly, strengthening my resolve.

Fortunately, the antivenom, at the time produced by the South African Institute for Medical Research, proved to be a formidable product, and within minutes of its being introduced into my veins, I felt relief. In the case of snouted cobra, the venom is largely neurotoxic, with little or no cytotoxic effects to cause tissue damage, as is the case with adders. This made recovery much quicker, with less damage to my body. Two days later I was out of danger and declared fully recovered, though I was to be on the watch for any sign of returning symptoms.

A positive spin-off resulting from all the publicity that this little episode generated was reflected in the park attendance records, as the gate ticket sales soared to previously unheard of heights, with people streaming in to see the snakebitten "snake man" as he lay recovering in his cage. Such is the way of human nature. Prompted by this and rationalizing the opportunity, Jack was not shy to subtly point out the possibilities. And so it came about that I announced my intention to extend my stay in the cage to 107 days. This statement was greeted with astonishment and surprise by the press and general public at large. One would imagine that spending *more* time in the potentially dangerous surroundings of the snake cage would worsen my condition. But in truth, after having lived for over three months in the cage of snakes, it was actually the more familiar territory. The prospect of leaving the security of my protected environment and daily routine to once again face the crush of the outside world now loomed as frighteningly as the day I prepared myself to step *into* the cage. I am ever amazed at how the human body and mind can adapt and grow accustomed to even the most deplorable of situations or conditions.

Thus it came to pass, 107 days and nights after first stepping into the cage of venomous snakes, I finally stepped out to the tumultuous applause of thousands of well-wishers and a horde of media personnel. Needless to say, champagne flowed freely and a multitude of interviews appeared in newspapers and on television news around the globe. It was indeed a time to celebrate and remember but—I swore an oath—a time *never* to be repeated.

To this day my record remains unbroken.

CHAPTER 5

A COBRA IN THE BATHROOM AND A BLACK MAMBA IN
THE CAR

Reptiles—particularly snakes—are a greatly misinterpreted and misunderstood group, and it is largely a lack of knowledge that is to blame. Reptiles consist of a large collection of interesting, colorful, evolved species, most of which, contrary to popular belief, present little or no threat to humans. The fact that a small percentage of snakes are venomous has unfortunately precipitated the general condemnation of all the species. With just 10 percent of the roughly three thousand species of snakes occurring on this planet being potentially dangerous to humans, there is relatively little to fear. Of the thousands of lizard species on our planet, just two are venomous, with possibly a third, if one considers the toxic, bacteria-laden saliva of the Komodo dragon to be included. (The first two are the Gila monster, located in the southwest United States and northwest part of Mexico, and the beaded lizard, located in Mexico and southern Guatemala.)

In the southern regions of Africa some 160 species and subspecies of snakes are recorded, of which, again, roughly 10 percent are considered potentially dangerous to humans. Only in Australia does the percentage of venomous snakes reach as high as 70 percent, though the bites of many of these are not usually fatal to humans. In Africa, the puff adder is the main culprit where snakebites are concerned, as it is a well-camouflaged, slow-moving species with a lightning-fast strike and long-hinging fangs. Most cases of recorded bites by this snake come from rural areas, where they are plentiful and often stepped on by unprotected feet. In spite of this, however, it is the almost mythical black mamba that is by far the most feared snake on the African continent, and with good reason. These slender, graceful creatures may grow to a length of four meters (over thirteen feet) or more, of which almost half this body length can be raised off the ground when angered, from which position it is capable of striking out at great speed. Unlike most other species, one would not easily step on a black mamba, as a face-to-face encounter would be far more likely.

Many of the relatively few black mamba bites recorded have been situated high up on the victims' bodies, usually around the neck and chest areas. The long, needle-like fangs are situated far forward in the upper jaw to ensure an accurate bite. The venom injected through these fangs is a potent neurotoxin (nerve-affecting venom) and, in the case of a full bite, an adult human might feel the effects within just five minutes without treatment, death could occur within the hour. This presents a fearful picture indeed, but these are scientific facts only; there is another side to the story. Because they are agile and fast moving, there is little chance of a close encounter with a black mamba, unless you have it cornered—in which case it will readily defend itself with all of its formidable capabilities mentioned above. Known to be of a nervous disposition, the black mamba is often accused of attacking on sight. The mamba will not do this simply because, as is the case with most snakes around the world, humans are not considered prey and therefore are avoided at all costs.

The black mambas that shared the cage with me during the 107-day "sit-in" averaged around three meters long each. For most of the daylight hours they remained under the bed, presumably finding security in this less-illuminated area and showing little interest in my presence. At night, however, they became more active, often slithering across my chest and neck as they went about their exploration of the cage. Only once was I threatened with aggression from one of these snakes, and that was when I accidently stepped on one. This brought a quick reaction, with head raised high and mouth open, ready to strike . . . but the snake did not strike.

Instead it watched me carefully, swaying slightly from side to side, as though calculating if my action constituted a potentially retaliatory threat or not. The silver-white fangs gleamed against the background of an otherwise velvet black mouth, and I knew at that moment that my careless mistake had rendered my life in the balance.

Frozen on the spot, I was literally staring death in the face. But after a few minutes of this, the snake seemed satisfied that my stepping on it was not an intentional threat and it lowered its head and headed back to its secure area under the bed. Slowly straightening myself up from the cramped, half-crouched position I was frozen in, I breathed a deep sigh of relief. If this was not proof enough that the notorious black mamba did *not* attack without reason, then I have no other explanation for what had just occurred.

A different scenario completely, involving a black mamba, took place on a farm near the town of Mafiking (now known as Mahikeng) in South Africa. The snake had been cornered in the farmhouse kitchen and was angry as hell, causing great consternation amongst the staff and owners alike. I, along with fellow herpetologist, Peter Langley, happened to be on a field trip in the area at the time. The local African population is always on the lookout for making an easy buck, and would on occasion be enticed to inform us of the whereabouts of any recently spotted reptiles. If the tip paid off and we succeeded in locating and capturing the specimen, the informer would be rewarded according to the size and species. Black mambas, being extremely elusive in the African bush, were always on the top of our list, and hearing about one already trapped between four walls brought us running.

Together Peter and I entered the kitchen, much to the dismay of the terrified owners. The snake, a large female, was indeed agitated and struck out repeatedly as we brought our longest pair of snake tongs into play. We soon had her safely bagged, but the snake continued to protest violently, biting again and again into the fabric of her confinement and leaving wet patches of venom on the cloth. I secured the top of the bag with an elastic band and dropped it into the back seat of our car, where the furious snake continued to thrash about wildly. Back at the park, the snake would be measured and marked, have some venom extracted, and then returned to a safer area away from human dwellings. Thanking the relieved farmer, we headed for our bush camp some twenty kilometers outside the town.

The day was hot and dusty, and our nerves stretched from the excitement of capturing such a large and potentially dangerous reptile. In the back seat, the furious snake continued to wiggle around in the bag.

"I feel we deserve a little celebration," Peter said, wiping sweat from his brow. "How about a beer?"

"Damn right!" I answered immediately. I was sweating too. The mamba, cornered as she was, had been really angry. One wrong move and one or both of us could have been bitten. I recalled a recorded case where just such a specimen, cornered in an African village by the resident dogs, had defended itself against seemingly impossible odds. The snake eventually bit and killed eight of its canine attackers before escaping to freedom. An angry black mamba is not something to fool with.

Peter reached back between the seats, fumbling for the cooler bag. "I could do with a dozen," he laughed. Then, turning fully to face the rear, he suddenly froze, the laughter dying in his throat.

"What's the matter?" I asked, keeping my eyes fixed on the pot-holed gravel road ahead. "Bite your tongue?" There was no response from my companion, no movement even. Casually I glanced up into the rear view mirror and felt the blood drain from my face. I jerked my head around to verify what the mirror reflected. It was real all right, and it was raging mad! Small livid eyes darted from Peter to me, and I suspected strongly that this mamba was hell bent on delivering revenge upon those who had so unceremoniously stuffed her into the bag. Possibly the elastic band had snapped free, or maybe in my haste I had simply neglected to secure it well enough, but whatever the case, there was now a three-meter-long, enraged black mamba loose in the cab of our tiny, cramped motor vehicle.

Raising its rod-like body till its head pressed against the vinyl ceiling, the snake glared at us with venomous intent, its open mouth ready to strike, clearly displaying its deadly silver-white fangs. Peter's eyes were stretched wide open. "Holy cow!" he muttered involuntarily. My mouth opened to scream as I realized the snake was about to strike, but there was no time.

Like a bullet the grey head lunged towards us and as one man, screaming our terror at the top of our lungs, we threw open our respective doors and unceremoniously hurled ourselves from the car which was still cruising along at around forty kilometers per hour.

Connecting the hard gravel road with a terrible grating thud, I tumbled out of control, over and over, until being brought to a sudden bone-jarring halt by a barbed wire fence post at the side of the road. Scraped, bleeding, and bruised, I forced myself to my feet just in time to see Peter doing the same across the way, while on down the road trundled our car, both front doors wide open and nobody behind the wheel save a very angry, and by now frustrated, black mamba. Stumbling back onto the road, I ran as fast as my battered body would allow, chasing after the powerless car, which was now heading off the road directly towards a little wooden farm stall offering fresh fruit and vegetables for sale. Peter was close on my heels.

Two large-bodied African women minding the store noted with some surprise the driverless vehicle with open doors heading their way. Raising themselves from their seats, they watched intently as the vehicle shuddered and stalled just meters from their store. Curious, they strolled over to peer nonchalantly through the open door nearest to them. Still running and stumbling in my haste to avert further disaster, and still a good hundred meters down the road, I opened my mouth to call a warning, but once again, too late. Spreading their arms to the sky, the two women screamed, turned, and as one charged headlong for the supposed safety of the little wooden stall, the mamba in hot pursuit, seemingly determined to take revenge this day on whoever or whatever presented itself as a target.

By this time both John and I had reached the abandoned car, panting and wheezing, unable to take another step. From inside the store came the sounds of terrible carnage as bags of potatoes, oranges, tomatoes, and everything else on display came crashing off the racks as the two screaming women attempted frantically to create a back door where none had been before. Reaching into the car, I grabbed hold of the snake tongs and headed for the stall. Fruit and vegetables, boxes and bags were strewn everywhere as the two hysterical women continued their futile attempt to escape. Having obviously recognized the mamba for what it was, *the most feared reptile in all of Africa*, they were not about to surrender themselves quietly to their fate or even venture a glance behind them, for that matter. The entire wooden structure of the shop shook with the chaos.

The mamba, in fact, deciding it had had enough of people and having spotted its avenue of escape, streaked past me as I approached, not so much as affording me a sideways glance before disappearing into the surrounding bush, never to be seen again. The two women, unaware of this change in the state of affairs and still in a state of blind, superstitious panic, continued their frantic efforts to put distance between themselves and the nonexistent mamba. And it took some effort between Peter and me to eventually calm them down and reassure them that the danger was passed. What astonished me most was that nobody had been bitten throughout the whole episode. Surely, if ever there was a time when somebody should have been bitten by a black mamba, this should have been the time. There was absolutely no explanation for it . . . other than blind, unadulterated luck.

"Not a good day," Peter commented as we limped back to the car.

"Not a good day indeed," I muttered in return.

Battered and bruised, with nothing to show for it, we climbed back into the vehicle. Starting the engine, I pulled back onto the road and headed towards camp.

ی ی ی

There are numerous species of cobras found in the Southern African region, but by far the most common and widespread is the Egyptian cobra (later re-named the snouted cobra). These snakes are of course highly venomous and can attain a length of over two meters. Like most snakes, they will avoid contact with anything too large to eat, and thus are of little threat to humans. But if cornered or angered, these cobras will rise up the first third of their bodies and spread their ribs to display an impressively long and slender hood as a warning not too approach too closely. From this hooded position, the snouted cobra will usually exhale a powerful blast of air, further presenting itself as a potential danger not to be fooled with.

On a particularly warm and humid midsummer day, Jack had just put down the extension phone as I stepped into the breeding laboratory. "There's a cobra trapped in somebody's bathroom in a house not far from here," he told me. "Seems it's a big one too, so take a pair of tongs with you."

"I'm on my way" I called back, collecting the address from the front office as I stepped out.

This was by no means an unusual occurrence. The park received hundreds of such calls throughout the year, especially during the hot summer months. The Hartebeespoort area particularly, being a farming district surrounded at the time by endless acres of scrub bush, boasted a wide variety of venomous and nonvenomous snakes, some of which occasionally found themselves unintentionally entering human abodes. People tend to create areas that attract such creatures as rodents and frogs, be it a rubbish pile or a fish pond. As snakes are, after all, designed to prey on these animals, they will pick up the scent and come slithering along innocently to help themselves to a nice treat. Unfortunately, people are not usually sympathetic to this practice, and any snake—whether venomous or harmless—spotted near a home is likely to be destroyed. Sometimes the snake will manage to escape, causing even greater consternation, as its unknown location looms as an ominous, perpetual threat over the household. Although most people do not like to see a reptile on their property, once they have seen it, they are even more perturbed when it disappears. It is usually about this time that an urgent call is made to the snake park in the hope that the "experts" will know what to do. Of course, the snake park will react as quickly as possible if it means saving the life of the reptile; and, if it is feasible, these captured snakes are released back into the wild, safely away from human habitation.

As I drove the few kilometers up the road to the address I'd been given, I hoped I was in time. I pulled up outside the house and knocked loudly on the front door. Instantly the door was flung open and there stood a woman, young and lovely, and dressed only in a skimpy towel.

"Are you the man from the snake park?" she gasped, fidgeting agitatedly with her hands and hopping from one foot to the other as though she was standing on a hot tin roof. Without waiting for my answer, she continued: "Oh, I'm so glad you're here! It's so big! I saw it! It slid right past me and my taps are still running." All this, and all I could do was stand and stare like the village idiot. She jumped up and down. "Please," she cried, "do something, or the house will be flooded!"

Caught off-guard by this unusual call to capture a snake, I was struck dumb. The woman was exquisite, and as she continued nervously to bounce up and down in front of me, I battled to concentrate on the matter at hand. Finally focusing my eyes away from her, I stuttered uncertainly; "Uh—um—show me where it is," and off she bounced down the hallway. The bathroom door was closed, and from within came the sound of gushing taps. There was indeed a good chance that the house might become flooded, as I noticed my boots splashing in the water that streamed out from under the door. Apparently the woman had been about the step into the bath when suddenly the cobra had appeared, scaring her out of her wits and sending her racing out of the bathroom, slamming the door behind her.

"I'm not afraid of snakes in the bush," she explained apologetically, "but I don't want to bathe with one."

I couldn't help smiling. She was quite lovely, and in her present attire I guess any man would have tackled the cobra for her with his bare hands. Cautiously I pushed open the door and entered the bathroom, which was now about a centimeter deep in flowing water. No sign of the cobra. I checked around the room, turning off the taps as I did so. The woman, secure now in my presence and keen to follow my progress, pressed against me from behind, peering over my shoulder, her closeness distracting me terribly. Together we moved over to the open washing basket, filled with dirty clothing. This was an obvious place to search for the elusive serpent. The woman remained tight against me, as though she felt safe with my body to protect her.

Slowly and delicately, I lifted the top item of clothing from the basket, all the while keeping my eyes peeled for any sign of movement. The woman squeezed even more tightly against me, causing a fluttering of butterflies in my stomach. Curiosity getting the better of her, she leaned over me, peering intently into the basket as I removed further items from it.

At first I did not register the source of the sound. Possibly I imagined it was the geyser topping up its water supply or the cistern ball-valve shutting off. But the sound grew in volume, and as the towel I was lifting from the basket cleared the opening, there came an explosive hiss, like steam escaping. And like an erupting volcano, clothes flew in all directions as a tower of pure fury came shooting up out of the basket. It was the largest snouted cobra I had ever seen in all my years as a herpetologist.

I jumped back in sheer fright while from behind me came a terrified scream. Turning quickly, I was just in time to glimpse a white, towel-less bottom disappearing out of the door heading at top speed for a safer place.

In spite of its powerful display of aggression, I had little problem in securing the cobra. Once I had it safely tucked, and finding no trace of the woman anywhere in the house, I went outside . . . and there I found her, standing stark naked on the lawn with her arms clasped as securely as possible over strategic places in a futile attempt to cover herself.

Unable to suppress my smile, I apologized profusely for her fright before resolutely turning my back and heading for the truck parked outside the gate. I smiled all the way as I negotiated the winding road back to the snake park, quite unable to get the woman's image out of my mind. And I thought to myself, *what a body!*

The most frightening and somewhat catastrophic encounter I have ever experienced with a snouted cobra was in no way of my own doing. The blame here I rest squarely on the shoulders of my long-ago friend, Gerald Nelson. Gerald was not your average amateur herpetologist; he was a man possessed with a passion for reptiles unequalled by any other. It might be safe to say that Gerald had a love affair with reptiles, and his private collection included exotic species from around the globe, both venomous and nonvenomous.

Gerald also owned a Mini Cooper, his other passion in life. Naturally this was no ordinary Mini, but a "souped-up," extremely modified Cooper S, rebuilt from the ground up with loving care by Gerald himself. The motor had been treated to every modification known to man in order to almost double its original power output. Gerald loved speed, and the highly-tuned engine of his Mini seldom operated below 8,000 rpm, way past anything registered on the dial. This resulted in constant overheating, blown head-gaskets, and the occasional seizure. But Gerald could make that car fly.

Tall and skinny, with boney knees and elbows and a beak-like nose, Gerald's appearance belied the fanatical enthusiasm that was boiling away inside of him. When he was squeezed in behind the wheel of the Cooper, his lips would part as he ran his long pink tongue across them, his bulging eyes glazed over in ecstasy and anticipation of the power about to be unleashed. *My greatest fear in life was to have to ride with Gerald in his beloved Mini Cooper S.*

The episode with the cobra began on a day when my own car was in for service and Gerald happened to be visiting me at the park. Gerald insisted I accept a lift home with him, as he was heading in the same direction and, unable to conjure up a quick excuse, I reluctantly accepted. Soon we were cruising at low altitude with the Cooper just barely following the road as Gerald feverishly pushed for peak revs. Frozen in terror, both feet up against the dashboard in a pointless attempt to brace my body in preparation for the catastrophe I felt was imminent, I inwardly cursed my stupidity for allowing myself to be trapped into this situation. Negotiating a right-angled bend at fearsome speed, the Cooper roared off into the sand at the edge of the road. I was just about to let fly with a string of verbal abuse when suddenly, not thirty meters ahead of us, a large cobra with head raised proudly, sailed smoothly and speedily across the road into the underbrush.

Incredibly, without any change of facial expression, nor any reduction in speed, Gerald threw the steering wheel a full turn to the right to follow in the direction of the disappearing reptile. Instantly my body was hurled violently against the door and the air was rent with a tortured, wailing screech as all four tires strove to adapt to the sudden change in direction. The cab filled with the pungent smell of burning rubber as the Cooper's body and suspension buckled under the terrible strain, still traveling in its original direction but now turned at a ninety-degree angle to the open stretch of tar road ahead. I almost bit my tongue clean in half as, impossibly, Gerald crashed the gear lever down from fourth to second without bothering to depress the clutch. Unperturbed, the powerful little motor never missed a beat but roared deafeningly in response, all but shattering my ear drums in the process.

We were still screaming sideways when I spotted the oncoming car. I was about to yell a warning when Gerald floored the accelerator to its maximum, precipitating a forward surge as the spinning front wheels pulled desperately at the road, with clouds of white smoke billowing from the screaming tires. The fast-approaching driver, with an expression of shock and astonishment on his face, slammed on his brakes, swerving dangerously to avoid us, just as the Cooper gained full power and roared off the side of the road and ramping a sandy embankment. Still at full throttle, we were now momentarily airborne, heading roughly in the direction the cobra had disappeared to only seconds before.

My mouth dripping with blood, I clung to my seat with all my strength as the Cooper touched ground again and tore through the tall grass, over rocks, and into a plantation of wattle trees. Through all this Gerald had not uttered a word nor changed expression, his eyes fixed rigidly ahead, but for the life of me I could not see any sign of the snake. Nevertheless, we kept right on going at full throttle, swerving amongst the trees until suddenly there appeared before us a fallen tree stump, raggedly sprawled across our path.

The Cooper slammed into it with such force that our bodies were hurled unmercifully against the windscreen, our faces squashed flat in a splattering of blood and twisted flesh.

With no more than a grunt, Gerald dived from the car and disappeared into the bushes. I could hear the sounds of a scuffle and saw sticks and stones scattering in his wake. Moments later he reappeared: torn and tattered with his nose still bleeding from the crash. In one out-stretched hand was a large snouted cobra suspended by the tail. I was speechless. My body ached all over, my nose was broken and bleeding, and the fool just stood there grinning! I closed my eyes and shook my head, convinced that this could not be happening. But when I opened them again, he was still there, smiling broadly and proudly, displaying his prize. Unable to control myself, I burst into laughter. Gerald joined me, rocking on his heels, and together we stood and roared with laughter. And the pain in my face was terrible.

The Cooper's radiator was squashed all over the engine block, and steam gushed out noisily. Tottering clumsily in our somewhat mutilated state, we headed back towards the road, where we planned to hitch a ride back to the snake park.

Motorists passing along the old Hartebeespoort road that evening were treated to the somewhat unusual sight of two young men with broken noses and blood splattered clothing thumbing for a ride at the side of the road with a live, two-meter snouted cobra in tow. Not surprisingly, perhaps, no one stopped for us. After a while I suggested to Gerald that he hide the cobra. This he did by wrapping it around his waist, under his shirt, while holding the head securely with one hand. He now looked like a skinny Napoleon Bonaparte in the midst of Waterloo, with bloody nose and bony knees, but the very next car stopped to offer us a ride.

She was a kindly lady of about sixty years old, well spoken, neatly dressed, and driving a Volkswagen Beetle. She was very sympathetic and terribly shocked to hear of our accident in the Cooper. She also hoped Gerald's covered hand would soon heal.

At last heading safely back towards the park, where we would house the cobra overnight, we were chatting away amiably when suddenly Gerald gave a yelp and there came a flurry of activity from the back seat. This was immediately followed by another yelp, and the next thing I knew there was a snouted cobra dangling over my shoulder, gazing intently into my face, as Gerald had obviously lost control of the creature. Our Good Samaritan still blithely chatting away, she took her eyes off the road for a moment to look at me. For a second or two she seemed not to focus as her mind battled with the unlikelihood of what her eyes were seeing. Then in mid-sentence, her mouth dropped open and with a piercing yell she rose straight up into the air and dived for the back seat. Not being quite as athletic as she might have once been, she landed head first, legs up over the back of her seat, the screaming now slightly muffled. The Beetle meanwhile careered across the road and I was obliged to ignore the cobra and grab for control of the steering wheel. Thankfully the snake showed no malice whatsoever, but seemed rather to be enjoying the ride (though was probably more intent on finding an avenue of escape). With the vehicle swerving dangerously from left to right, I fought desperately from the passenger seat to gain control. The difficulty here was further increased by our driver's wildly kicking legs, which sporadically connected with my already-battered face. She continued to scream hysterically and, try as he might, Gerald could not dislodge her head from behind the back seat.

And that was how the traffic officer found us some minutes later as the stalled car bumped and shuddered to a halt a few meters off the side of the road.

Neatly parking his motorcycle, the officer strategically adjusted his sunglasses, swiped a finger across his moustache, pulled out his pen and ticket book, and strutted importantly up to the car. He was in an aggressive mood, and he shoved his head in through the open window to see what all the commotion was about. "Haai! Wat gaan hier aan? [Hey! What's going on here?]" he blurted in a heavy Afrikaans accent. But any intended further aggression quickly turned to blind panic as he came face to face with the cobra. For a split second the officer's eyes bulged before frantically back-peddling. The cobra, having now seemingly decided that enough was enough, darted like an arrow out the same window right where the officer's head had been a second before, slumped to the ground, and darted for the surrounding trees.

Gerald and, I meanwhile, were trying to calm the distraught woman enough to untangle her and remove ourselves from the little two-door car. This finally achieved, we were amazed to find our officious officer of the law heading speedily for his motorbike. Jump starting the machine, he called out in Afrikaans, "Julle Engelse is almal blerry mal! [You English are all bloody crazy!]" and sped off at speed without as much as a backward glance. Considering his earlier aggressive attitude, I suspected that he was experiencing a bad day, and having a snake lunge at him from inside a car was the final straw. *Nothing like a cobra in your face to initiate reconsidering your options.*

There was no sign of the cobra, which had most likely curled up under a log somewhere in the surrounding bush, glad to be away from all the chaos. Our lady friend, calmer now but still panting and wheezing heavily, seemed dazed and remained motionless where we sat her, propped up back behind the steering wheel of the Beetle.

Gerald and I looked at each other, unanimously deciding without the need for words to walk the rest of the way before she recovered enough to demand an explanation or before the traffic officer changed his mind and returned. Setting out at a fast pace, we arrived back at the park an hour later, painfully exhausted. The following weeks saw Gerald and myself with bruised noses and black eyes but otherwise little the worse for wear. The Mini had been towed and garaged in preparation for extensive repairs. The fact that nobody had been killed, bitten, or at the very least arrested that day remains in my mind one of life's great mysteries. Testimony enough that snakes do not attack humans unless provoked; or sometimes, even when provoked.

CHAPTER 6

ON LOCATION WITH JULIE AND SLIMY

As funds became available, Jack poured everything possible into the further construction and improvement of the reptile and mammal housing conditions at the park. However, as the years passed, it became painfully obvious that takings at the gate, no matter how constant, could just barely support the conditions at that time. Besides the obvious costs incorporated in such a conglomeration, there were further expenses to be considered. The purchasing of certain species for the purpose of further propagation thereof, for example, played an essential part towards the future diversity and feasibility of the park. One could not simply expect to replace lost animals from nature, as though available on a store shelf. Many species were already becoming endangered, emphasizing the necessity for breeding programs.

However, the costs involved in the purchasing of compatible specimens, and especially breeding pairs from already established programs, locally or overseas, were enormous, sometimes running debts into the hundreds of thousands. And being a privately owned business as was Hartebeesport Dam Snake and Animal Park, no outside funding or government grants were forthcoming. Thus the takings at the gate were stretched to the limit, with barely a cent to spare.

Another consideration was the enormous feeding bill. Here the big cats (the lions, tigers, pumas, leopards) and a further assortment of smaller meateaters claimed a large slice, while the apes, monkeys, wild pigs, and birds took their share in fruit and vegetables. The snakes, too, though not necessarily fed every day, as was the case with the other animals, consumed large numbers of mice, rats, guinea pigs, and rabbits, which in turn consumed volumes of vegetables and specially formulated compressed food pellets. Now take into account salaries, electricity bills, and all the other general financial absorption typical of any business dependent entirely on the takings at the gate . . . dependent, in other words, solely on public support. It was a narrow fence to walk!

However, matters were to take a turn one day, when a casually dressed, soft-spoken man introduced himself to Jack as Jamie Uys, filmmaker. In fact the man needed no introduction, as he was already becoming known locally and internationally for his presentations, which for the greater part conveyed humorous episodes of typical early South African-type conflict between the British and the Afrikaner, forced into mutual, if somewhat reluctant, coexistence.

In parts of Africa people live in close proximity with wildlife, especially in rural areas. Jamie's idea was to script sequences of human encounters with wild animals into his stories. These would mostly be humorous interactions. (One of these films, *The Gods Must Be Crazy*, was to later become a worldwide hit.) Having received favorable reports about the large variety of African and exotic reptiles and mammals housed at the park, and especially the mention that many of the animals were hand reared (therefore to some degree adjusted to human contact), he decided to pay a visit.

It was the beginning of a new era, with improved mutual financial gain for all concerned, as the wonderful world of moviemaking came to Hartebeespoort Dam Snake and Animal Park. Working with wild animals on location was a whole new ballgame for me, and there was much to be learned and experienced. No matter how big or small, how tame or how docile the animals, they remained wild animals, with little or no inclination to do anything more or less than they pleased. Adult lions, tigers, bears, and other potentially dangerous animals were always more than a handful and often had to undergo long periods of basic training in preparation for a particular scene. Even this, however, did not guarantee absolute cooperation.

Another important factor for consideration was the preparation and basic training of the actors expected to perform in close proximity of, or sometimes in direct contact with, the animals. And as the business progressed, the demand and variation grew by leaps and bounds, from companies asking for brief animal appearances to others with hardcase directors demanding if not the impossible then something dangerously close . . . with *dangerous* being the operative word.

It was up to Jack to either accept or reject a project. Simply having the animal in demand was not reason enough to blindly attempt any scripted scene that was submitted. And if indeed the animal was available and suitable, there was still the matter of travel relocation, housing, feeding, and in the case of potentially dangerous animals, safety precautions and qualified staff able to assist.

Eventually, to more easily deter those more impractical and somewhat illogical celluloid miracle makers, Jack upped his prices drastically so that only the serious would approach for animal work contracts. Jack did not promise the impossible, but rather guaranteed satisfaction for the client once a script had been accepted. And this strategic move paid off, with the Hartebeespoort Dam Snake and Animal Park becoming well known and respected over the years to come—both locally and internationally—as *the* professionals in the business of wild-animal rentals for commercial advertising, television, and film.

Snakes were always featured high on the wanted list, and in spite of the obvious difficulties and dangers of working with venomous species, they presented little problem, were easily transported and housed, and needed no feeding for days at a time. And in all the dozens of scenes designed to portray the serpent, never once, I am glad to say, did there ever develop a life-threatening situation for either handler or actor.

However, live reptiles on location, however safely housed, remained a matter of some disquiet amongst most film personnel, actors and crew alike. But the day I was called upon to conduct a scene that scripted the brief appearance of a four-meter African rock python, little did I imagine the consternation that would arise from this usually simple task.

The snake selected for the movie was named Slimy, a four-meter African rock python of calm disposition who had been bred and reared at the Park. Some eight years old at the time, Slimy was already a powerfully muscular creature, who feverishly attacked and devoured anything furry thrown his way.

However, when otherwise handled, Slimy was the purest example of a "friendly snake" and was a favorite amongst kids and adults alike, especially on weekends, when he would be liberated from his cage to pose with visitors for photographs. It seemed that Slimy loved the activity as much as those excitedly gathered around him. And having considered the facts, everybody concerned agreed, Slimy was the obvious choice for the film role in question.

A two-day shoot was scheduled on location in Northern Zululand, where an American/Canadian team was completing the final footage for an African adventure series. The python scene had been reserved for last, with the director not wishing to expose his actors to the "stress" of working with a live snake until all else was completed. Thus, two days later, after an eight-hour drive across the country, my unusual "baggage" safely and soundly asleep in the back of the Nissan Cruiser, I arrived at the location in Northern Zululand, where a temporary bush camp had been erected for the purpose of the film scene. Here I was introduced to all those taking part in this particular segment of the shoot.

The scripted scene was a simple one, as was the part for Slimy to play. The actress, an exquisitely beautiful young British woman named Julie Gooding, was to be pictured struggling for her life against the suction pull of quicksand, while the hero, Dave Duncan, a tall Canadian, was prevented from immediate rescue by the presence of a large python, which threatens him as he attempts to get near. No heavy heroics, nobody getting swallowed or "crushed" . . . simply a battle of wills, set against time, as the hero prods the great snake with a pole in an eventually successful attempt to get the reptile to retreat rather than attack.

At first sight, Julie Gooding—with her long, flowing, almost-snow-white hair hanging loosely around a lovely face, accentuated by cherry-red lips, chiseled nose, and sparkling blue eyes—seemed no less than a goddess, and

I imagined immediately to be frantically in love with her. That is until she opened her mouth to speak to me for the first time.

"Make sure that *Slimy* creature stays the hell away from me at all times!" she almost spat at me, ignoring my greeting and self-introduction. "It's bad enough I have to tolerate this festering jungle, but if that . . . that *creature* so much as comes near me, your head will roll!" And with that she turned and stormed away, as though in some way I had aroused in her all the anger she had obviously collected over the years.

"Don't mind her," a voice sighed from close behind, and I turned to face the director, Buck Mitchell, a middle-aged American with shoulder length gray hair, as he now shook his head somewhat apologetically. "She goes off at everybody, mostly for no good reason other than maybe her hair won't curl today, or her nail is split. She's amazingly beautiful, knows what effect she has on men, and has grown accustomed to their squirming at her feet for attention. She hates everybody and everything outside her dressing room." A slight frown wrinkled his brow. "She is also a damned fine actress and always in demand. In other words, mostly we let her have her way, just so she keeps up the good work. That's why we even let her bring that damn yappy mutt all the way up here with her." He rolled his eyes. "Won't go anywhere without the furry beast. Even takes it on set at the studio. *Yap! Yap! Yap!* Damn critter drives me crazy; but anyway . . ." he took my arm and led me towards his tent. "This will only be your problem for a few hours. I have to live with it. She's my wife!"

In the tent, over a cool glass of orange juice, we discussed the strategy to be employed for the python shoot. Outside the dense foliage reverberated with the shriek of cicadas and a multitude of other equally energetic invertebrates. The heat was humid and stifling, as it invariably is in tropical regions, and I can well imagine the actress's discontent in this world so far removed from her own. However, everybody else seemed in high spirits, excited, while at the same time nervous about the handling of the pending scene. A huge python, after all, was not something one worked with every day.

With the details discussed and finalized, the actors and crew were called in for briefing. Julie presented herself last, bringing with her little

Fifi, cradled in her folded arms and yapping irritatingly at everyone and everything around.

I smiled at her, noting once more just how truly beautiful she was. She in turn ignored me totally while Fifi, your typical Maltese/poodle/lap dog, glowered at me, baring its miserable array of tiny teeth and rendering a chorus of yap-yaps in my face.

All matters finally discussed, I led the party out to the Nissan, where Slimy was dozing contentedly, still in his carry-cage lined with comfortable sacking material. Julie, however, shunned the demonstration, strongly reminding us all that, though she would be in close proximity to the snake, she would herself be occupied with the quicksand, and had therefore no need to otherwise concern herself with *"that slimy creature."*

Having briefed the team on the basic do's and don'ts of python handling and having assured them of this particular specimen's favorable character, I now produced Slimy in the flesh. And true to his usual way, the giant snake took to the handling as though with relish, sliding gracefully from neck to quivering neck as each in turn buckled slightly under the weight of the huge reptile. And within seconds, all were amazed at the cool, soft feel of the shiny body-scales, astonished that the snake allowed itself to be so easily handled, showing no distress or any inclination to bite.

In the same vein, the shoot went well, with minimal fuss and retakes. Slimy quickly becoming the star of the show as he easily, and almost it seemed, eagerly, performed as was desired of him. Julie too, with total disregard for her obvious discomfort, played her part in the swamp with typical British gusto, delivering a performance as realistic as the scene demanded. And at the end of a day spent in sweltering heat and somewhat demoralizing swampy conditions, covered in mud and decaying vegetation, we all returned to base for showers and an African-style barbeque supper to be served under a crimson sky as the glowing ball in the West gracefully slipped from view. A perfect end to a perfect day. However, the night was still to come, and with it, drama beyond my wildest dreams.

With my job done, my plan was to leave at the crack of dawn, when the air would still be cool before the later onslaught of the day's heat. But for now the night was young and warm and friendly under the African sky. Drinks were served after supper, and everybody gathered around the cooking fire to discuss further the film saga now finally completed with the shooting of the python scene. Only Julie seemed not to be affected by the events, even declining to participate in a champagne toast to the success of the show. Instead she somewhat isolated herself off to one side, where she sat brooding, with little Fifi snuggled on her lap.

"She's not the party type," her husband confided in my ear as he noted my occasional curious glances in Julie's direction. "Seldom accepts a drink and does *not* enjoy jolly people." He pulled a face with a lop-sided grin. "Prefers the company of that yappy mongrel. Damn thing even shares our bed! But let me say one word, and it's *me* that gets put outside!" He took a sip from his glass. "But this is not your problem; have another drink." And throwing his head back, he downed the remainder of his still half-full glass of champagne.

The party continued into the starlit night, with the volume of it ever-increasing as bottles of good-quality champagne were liberally distributed for relentless consumption. And as the fever pitch grew, so the "happy-snap" instamatic cameras appeared all the more frequently to record the occasion. Indeed, I myself was feeling rather flighty, even to the point of seriously considering approaching Julie for conversation. These thoughts were quickly laid to rest as her scowl of disapproval at my approach blasted the air from my sails, and I allowed for discretion to prevail over valor.

Later, when the suggestion was made that Slimy be liberated from his confinement to be included in the "happy-snaps," my initial reaction of caution was heavily frowned upon by all inebriated around me, until finally the champagne bubbling merrily through my veins tumbled the last remnants of resistance, and I conceded.

And there came a roar of approval from the team as Slimy finally made his appearance at the edge of the circle, draped smartly around my neck, his head held high as though in anticipation of the new experience of being invited to a party. Everybody rushed up to greet the gentle snake, stroking him and tickling him as though he were a cuddly kitten, their earlier fears long forgotten. The sounds of "oohs" and "ahs" and giggles resonated as Slimy slid from neck to neck for respective photographs, while all about the dense forest was alive with the sounds of insects and frogs. The fire and gaslight flickered shadowy forms against the trees and along the leafy floor, as the stars glittered above in a cloudless sky. And as the cameras flashed and excited voices rose in delight of the moment, I thought, *What a perfect ending to a wonderful evening.*

Then Jenny, the makeup artist, who by now had consumed somewhat more than her fair share of champagne, claimed Slimy for herself, draping him voluptuously around her neck and shoulders as she slowly, sensuously, gyrated her hips as though a belly dancer from the Far East. Happily Slimy swayed with her to the rhythm, his head held ever high, his eyes staring, as though in trancelike rapture. And all about, the party took on a new and increased volume as in unison the team clapped and cheered to the undulating movements of the woman, faster and faster until beads of sweat glittered down her cheeks and neck.

Julie meanwhile had not moved from her position outside the circle of activity, where she viewed the proceedings with irrational distaste. She had stayed quiet for the entire night until Jenny, still gyrating to the rhythm of the clapping hands and sweating under the weight of Slimy (who now seemed to have slipped into a hypnotic sleep) ceremoniously and sensuously started to remove her clothes, to the loud approval of all present, inebriated and otherwise. This now apparently being the straw to break the camel's back, Julie lunged to her feet, almost toppling little Fifi upside down as she did so, and with black rage in her eyes she shoved her way through the crowd to confront Jenny.

"What the bloody hell do you think you're doing?" she challenged through pursed lips, with little Fifi yapping from her position, cradled under Julie's right arm. There was a moment of stunned silence as all clapping suddenly subsided and all cheering waned, to be replaced now instead by startled looks of dismay.

"Do you think this is a friggin' freak show for lowlifes?" Julie continued to vent her pent up frustration at Jenny, who sweating and breathless, too, now stared in dismay. Fifi continued to yap in all directions, as though in support of her owner's harsh condemnation of the light-hearted activities that had just been brought to a crashing, unceremonious halt. *Yap! Yap! Yap!*

Next to me where I stood closest to the scene (from where I had kept a close vigil on Slimy), I heard Buck release an exaggerated sigh, as though he had seen it all before. As if to confirm my thoughts, he slumped his shoulders, shook his head, and muttered under his breath, "Oh boy, here we go again," and taking a step forward as though to intervene, he reached out to take Julie by the shoulder, but pulled back quickly as little Fifi reacted to the movement with a noshing of tiny teeth and a harsh series of yaps.

Buck's face now flushed with sudden anger and his reflex getting the better of him, he slapped out at the irritating little mutt, connecting with it accurately on the snout. *Hooowwwllll . . . Yap! Yap! Yap!* The irritating little animal vented its frustration at its attacker. *Hooowwwlll . . . Yap! Yap! Yap!*

Violence erupting in her face, Julie turned to face Buck, just as at that very same moment an angry Jenny swung round, almost tumbling under the weight of Slimy as she ventured to launch her retaliation at Julie. The air was rent with the sounds of vocal battle while, all about, astonished mouths dropped open in further dismay.

With words being exchanged by Julie to Buck and Buck to Fifi, Jenny now stumbled drunkenly into the attack. With Slimy still swinging heavily from about her shoulders, she lunged for Julie, grabbing for her long, beautiful hair. Pivoting around to face the attack, Julie unwittingly brought Fifi around with her. And from where I stood, somewhat shocked into immobility, I saw Slimy's head jerk erect as though having received an electric shock and his senses fixed rigidly on the furry little animal now rendered so tantalizingly just inches from his nose! *Hooowwwlll, Yap! Yap! Ya . . .*

CHOMP!

And Slimy, no longer the meek and mild exotic pet, transformed once more into predator extraordinaire, struck out with instinctive and deadly accuracy.

And, with that chomp, total pandemonium shattered the night!

Clamping his huge mouth down hard on the furry tidbit so thoughtfully presented to him, Slimy now pulled back in an attempt to draw the morsel into his coils so that the erratic, frantic squirming of the dog might be rendered immobilized under pressure. But rendering a horrific scream, more of startled surprise than of fear, Julie clutched at Fifi's hindquarters, while at the same moment Jenny wrenched her body backward in an awkward attempt to keep her balance, upset now by the outstretched tugging motion of the heavy-bodied snake.

And for one split second, the scene before my eyes materialized as ludicrous as any I might ever imagine: on the left, a screaming woman with a huge python draped around her neck, leaning back against the outstretched pull of the reptile as it determinedly held fast onto the head of a squirming little furry animal, whose hindquarters were in turn being fiercely tugged in the opposite direction by another screaming woman!

And with quiet inner resignation, I thought, *Oh Lordy, my life is over!*

For one split second in time everybody gawked, seemingly frozen to the spot. Then chaos, as suddenly the entire team moved in at once. There was shouting and screaming and tugging and tumbling and a whole lot of cursing, as everybody tried to do something but achieved little as they all tumbled over one another in a frenzy of uncertainty. Both Julie and Jenny continued to scream, all the while tugging frantically at little Fifi, who was about to be torn in two, as Slimy diligently pursued the very reason for his existence, to indiscriminately devour anything furry that would fit in its mouth.

The sudden dawning realization that my very immediate, and indeed far-reaching future, was precariously balanced on the final result of the unfolding catastrophe before me, spurred me into action. Lunging forward just in time to avoid the tumbling crush, I grabbed Slimy behind the head with one hand while simultaneously encircling Julie's outstretched arms with my free arm. My priorities were clear: first prevent the mutt from being ripped in two by the opposing forces, then dislodge those forces and free the mutt.

However, simple as this analysis of remedy seemed, there were detrimental opposing factors involved, the first becoming painfully evident as a frantic and hysterical Julie blindly mistook my interference as a further threat to her beloved Fifi and turned to direct the full force of her frustrated, fearful anger in my direction. Screaming still, now directly and accurately into my right ear, and never slackening her grip on Fifi's ever-stretching hindquarters, she lifted her knee to my crotch, to render me quickly and effectively doubled over in open-mouthed, breathless agony. And for good measure, as my head dropped down past her mouth, she clamped her teeth down hard on my ear . . . and held on.

Good grief, the agony of it, as desperately I tried not to release my grip on either her arms or Slimy's neck, convinced still that the demise of the mutt would depict similarly my immediate future. Fighting back the terrible nausea creeping up into my throat, the flashing, dazzling lights exploding behind my eyes, and the terrible crunching of my ear, I twisted my body, to reverse my elbow into Julie's stomach! With a forceful expulsion of air from her lungs, she relinquished her excruciating grip on my ear, as did she her grip on the somewhat elongated Fifi. Unceremoniously she crumpled to her knees, all fight gone out of her. It was a desperate gamble, but I saw no other way out.

Free to move now, I screamed to the disorganized crowd around me: *"Grab the python's body! Grab the python's body!"* And suddenly there came a surge of activity as Slimy was at last pulled off from around the shoulders of the still-shocked and screaming Jenny and cradled safely in the many willing, if uncertain, hands of the crew. My left hand, still gripped fiercely around Slimy's neck, prevented the giant snake from re-coiling, thus preventing the process of constriction. Not deterred, however, Slimy's highly flexible jaws were already in operation, working left to right in turn, to quickly draw the now unrestricted, kicking, and squealing Fifi further into those dark depths of no return. There was only one way to stop the process: unhesitatingly, I jammed the fingers of my free hand into the lips of Slimy's upper jaw and tugged upward with considerable force.

Pythons are of course nonvenomous, killing their prey by constriction (suffocating the animal by constantly tightening pressure from its coils). However these sometimes large snakes are very powerful and have as many as a hundred long, needle-sharp teeth fixed within their jaws. A number of these now punctured the tips of my fingers as I desperately tried to loosen Slimy's relentless grip on his tasty prize.

Soon my arm was crimson with blood, which must have looked frightening to those around me, but I knew that the effect was comparable to that of slight razor cuts, and the wounds were in fact very minor. However painful the operation, considering too that my crotch and ear still throbbed ceaselessly, I knew I could not stop now. Slimy struggled, twisted, and hissed his disapproval at me, but with strict instructions to those handling the body to *"hold on for dear life,"* I finally ripped the pup's tiny body from the jaws of death, upon which the terrified little animal gnashed out viciously—*Yap! Yap! Yap*—and successfully managed to nip me on the wrist. Obviously the mutt was little the worse for wear, other than a few needle-like tooth puncture wounds visible through the skin on its head.

Relief flowed through my body, and I breathed a huge sigh and gratefully took Slimy from the arms of my "assistants." Slimy was unimpressed and showed his disgust by squirming and wiggling in an attempt to free himself, presumably to pursue his recently stolen prey. Then, with a shock, I suddenly remembered Julie and turned to where she kneeled doubled up on the ground.

Thankfully, her husband and a few others were already attending to her, as were others to Jenny, who sat now in silence, her eyes staring as she sipped absentmindedly on a stiff shot of something alcoholic.

I quickly delivered Slimy safely back to his holding cage in the Nissan before hurrying back to the scene to find Buck. I apologized to him sincerely for Slimy's attack on Fifi and for personally striking his wife, promising to take full responsibility for the events. *What did I have left to lose? My life was over anyway, as was my career at the park when Jack got the report . . . not to mention what Julie would do when she recovered!*

To my total astonishment, however, Buck grinned a huge grin and draped his arm around my shoulder.

"My dear boy," he said, "think nothing of it. We were all to blame, but you least of all. You saved the day, and unfortunately, the life of that nasty critter as well." He reached for a half-empty bottle of champagne left unattended on a table. "Let's have a drink." He raised the bottle to his lips, then offering the same to me.

"But what about Julie?" I protested meekly. "I should apologize to her." Buck looked at me now with humor in his eyes, the slightest of smiles creasing his lips.

"Between me and you, lad," he said, lowering his voice slightly, his eyes shifting from left to right as though expecting to be overhead, "best thing that's ever happened to her. Can only do her good. Don't give it another thought!" And with that, he downed the rest of the bottle in one long gulp. And I thought to myself, *These bloody movie people are crazy!*

By morning, Julie had recovered sufficiently to be heard across the bush camp as she relentlessly hurled abuse at all who dared to come close, and it was with some relief that I turned the Nissan key and headed for home, six hundred kilometers across the country, back to Hartebeespoort, where the air was fresh and the people sane. Each finger of my right hand was adorned with small band-aids, stemming the flow of blood from the multitude of razorlike cuts inflicted by the python's teeth. My ear, too, was similarly decorated, and I could just imagine the look on Jack's face when I arrived back at the park to report that *all had gone well.*

CHAPTER 7

THE DRAINPIPE PYTHON RESCUE AND SHOTGUN MAN

S nake-handling demonstrations remained a popular attraction on weekends and public holidays for the Hartebeespoort Dam Snake and Animal Park. Husbandry of the reptiles, however, by far absorbed most of my time. Work involving reptiles, especially venomous snakes, needs to be very precise, as there is little room for error. Keeping reptiles in captivity can be a fairly complicated affair, depending on the specimens being housed. There are some three thousand species and subspecies of snakes recorded around the world, and just as many lizard and frog species. Each species acts and responds differently, and it remains the task of the herpetologist to know all creatures as well as possible. Contrary to popular belief, reptiles are fragile creatures, and because they are "cold-blooded" (ectothermic), specific heating and humidity conditions are required. A cold reptile most often will not feed or digest well, while too high a temperature is likely to kill the animal. Temperatures need to be correct, so naturally reptiles from different regions of the world need different temperature and humidity considerations to ensure they not only survive, but thrive. Plus, if a successful breeding program is to be established, there is the seasonal factor to be considered as well, necessitating the appropriate temperature fluctuations.

Many reptiles, like the cobras and mambas, for example, lay eggs, as do turtles, crocodiles, and a variety of lizard species. Other species, like the rattlesnakes, give birth to live young. In the latter case, the female retains the eggs inside her body until the young are fully developed before giving birth. The young emerge enclosed in a thin, clear membranous sack from which they immediately break free. With the exceptions of the pythons and the king cobra, snakes generally do not assist with the incubation of their eggs, thus eggs produced in captivity are most often removed from the cage to be placed in an incubator for controlled hatching.

Proper housing is essential when keeping reptiles. Some need more space than others, and, depending on the species, it is also important to supply ground material and foliage that is as close as possible to that of their natural habitat. Some species must be supplied with large water bowls, while others need no water bowl at all. Some desert adders, for example, require only to be sprayed with a fine mist of water every couple of days, as they drink the moisture that collects on their bodies. If they are not sprayed, they will die of dehydration, even if a water bowl is present in their cage. Other species, such as the tropical anacondas, spend much of their lives submerged in water, so a large container of water would be essential in their living area.

Naturally, food is of utmost importance, with some reptiles' needs being very specific. Many snakes survive on rats, mice, lizards, and frogs, while others are adapted to eat only specific foods. A good example of the latter category is the African egg-eating snake, which consumes nothing but eggs, its system being designed solely for this purpose. Protruding through the roof of its throat are a number of extended vertebrae against which the egg is forced, cracking the shell and allowing the contents to drain into the snake's body, after which the shell is regurgitated. There are other snakes that eat only fish, while others eat only insects. There are also cannibalistic snakes that prey on their own kind (king snakes). Some species of snakes prefer insects or lizards when they are young, but change to a diet of rodents when mature. Large monitor lizards are known to eat just about anything available, including snakes, small mammals, eggs, birds, crabs, and even newborn crocodiles.

Technically speaking, the only two species of venomous lizards are the Gila monster and its close relative, the beaded lizard, of the American southwest and Mexico, as I mentioned in Chapter 5. These ungainly and sometimes brightly colored lizards have a number of grooved teeth in their bottom jaw along which venom is stimulated to flow by a chewing motion when clamped onto a victim. These teeth are used mainly to immobilize the small rodents and fledgling birds on which the lizards prey. Strangely, despite this venomous weaponry to disable living prey, Gila monsters and beaded lizards are most partial to eggs.

When feeding snakes in captivity, it is preferable for a number of reasons to feed them prey that is already dead. Dead mice and rats, for example, can be stored in a deep freeze in great numbers, thus disposing of the problem of their housing, feeding, and maintenance. A major drawback to using live rodents, especially rats, is the potential danger they pose to the snakes. This may seem ludicrous to those who may not be familiar with the keeping of snakes, but, improbable though it may seem, many a valuable specimen has fallen victim to the powerful incisors of a rodent.

Occasionally one comes across a snake that refuses to eat in captivity, under any circumstances, and here "trick feeding" may be the only answer— other than to release the animal back into the wild. The largest venomous snake in the world is the king cobra of Asia. These snakes can reach a length of six meters and are known to be cannibalistic, feeding solely on other snakes. Needless to say, this presents something of a problem under captive conditions. One such specimen housed at the Hartebeespoort Dam Snake and Animal Park, measuring four meters in length, refused to eat any of our local species other than mole snakes. Because we were not able to supply the number of mole snakes necessary to satisfy the appetite of such a sizeable reptile, we introduced "trick feeding." This involved attaching together, head to tail, a number of more readily available larger species (collected over the years and stored in a deep freezer) with a single mole snake secured up front. The cobra would instantly grab the offered mole snake end and then proceed to swallow the entire attached string of defrosted serpents, none the wiser but all the more satisfied thereafter. There is much to know and learn where the successful keeping of reptiles is concerned.

The ability to handle venomous snakes comes only with patience, learn- ing, and caution. Each specimen reacts differently to being handled, and, in captivity, the less a snake is handled the happier it is. A highly venomous snake can be kept successfully in captivity without ever being touched by hand, unless it has to be treated for some medical reason, in which case it is necessary to secure the head safely before proceeding.

The potential to receive a dangerous bite from a snake is not restricted solely to the venomous species. Larger specimens of non venomous snakes, endowed as they are with about a hundred needle-sharp teeth comprising six rows (four in the upper jaw and two in the lower jaw), could certainly inflict a nasty wound. Nonvenomous snakes are generally constrictors, using these rows of teeth to secure the prey animal with a firm bite before encircling it with body coils. The snake then applies pressure to suffocate the prey before swallowing it down whole.

The longest snake in the world is the reticulated python of Asia, which is reputed to reach a length of around nine meters. A serpent of this size would certainly have the strength to constrict an adult human being and possibly even be able to swallow them whole. However, few of the giant constrictors grow large enough to present any danger to humans, other than the prospect of a nasty bite should anyone be silly enough to fool with such a specimen. Besides the reticulated python, there is the green anaconda of South America, the Burmese python, and last on the list, the African rock python. Smallest of the group, the African rock python has been known to reach close to six meters long. This species has been protected for many years in Southern Africa, where it is held in high esteem by farmers because of its capacity to eliminate vast numbers of crop-destroying rodents. This species is particularly useful in the cane fields of Zululand, where the giant cane rats are known to wreak havoc on the yield.

ර ර ර

On any given day, the park would receive a half-dozen or more calls to remove snakes from surrounding properties. The park advertised this as a free service so as to encourage the practice. This not only saved the caller in question from a possible snake-bite, should the species encountered prove to be venomous, but also offered the opportunity to rescue and relocate the snake. The Hartebeespoort Dam area being a rural region at the time, surrounded mostly by uncultivated African scrub bush, was a reptile haven, providing refuge for a wide variety of species. These included a multitude of harmless species, such as the common house snake, mole snakes, grass snakes, and bush snakes. Venomous species included the boomslang, black mamba, puff adder, and two species of cobras, the most prolific of these being the snouted cobra—or Egyptian cobra, as it was known at the time. All these species and more we encountered on a weekly basis, especially after a heavy rain, when frogs and small mammals were on the move, inciting snakes into a frenzy of activity as they instinctively sought out their prey. Snakes do not intentionally enter human abodes, but may be attracted to rodents and amphibians that reside on properties. This sometimes leads to human confrontation, at which time the snake park is called in to help. I have over the years removed a variety of snakes, venomous and nonvenomous, from bathrooms, kitchens, lounges, ceilings, cupboards, drains, garages, and even from motor vehicle engines.

An unusual confrontation with a snake I remember vividly occurred when the Jackson family returned home one day to find their recently acquired pet Wirehaired Fox Terrier missing. This brought about a thorough search of the property, which revealed no sign of the dog in question but did bring notice to something large coiled up in the stormwater drain directly in front of their rural property. Warning his wife and their two young sons to keep clear, Mr. Jackson went inside to call the snake park. I happened to be nearest the phone in the office at the time and took the call.

"Hello, snake park?" Mr. Jackson asked with a shakiness in his voice that reverberated in my ear. "I think there is a large snake stuck in my stormwater drain, close to the gate at the entrance to my property." He hesitated, seemingly unsure of how to explain. "It's dark in there, and I can't be sure what it is, but it looks like a big snake . . . and our dog is missing." Another insecure pause. "Can you possibly come have a look?"

The Jackson's ten-acre plot was some twenty kilometers away, further than I would usually travel to remove a snake, but because Mr. Jackson considered the snake to be so large as to fill the opening of a storm-water drain, and in mentioning that their dog was missing, I suspected that

Mr. Jackson was coming to a similar conclusion to that which was forming in my head. It would not be the first time that somebody's pet had been taken by a large snake, which, under the circumstances, could only be a rock python. Feeding on a wide variety of warm-blooded animals, such as birds, rats, rabbits, and even small deer, a large enough African rock python would not differentiate between a wild animal and a domestic one but instead take full advantage of any opportunity, as that is how nature designed the snake.

Having noted directions to the property, I assured Mr. Jackson that I would arrive within the hour. Grabbing a couple of snake bags, a pair of snake tongs, and some leather gloves, I climbed into the park's Nissan Cruiser and headed out onto the main road. Negotiating the final few kilometers of a rutted gravel stretch of road, I finally arrived at the gate of the Jackson property, where the whole family was gathered in nervous anticipation. As I exited the vehicle, I noted that the younger of the two boys was teary-eyed, possibly having been warned by his parents that there might be more than just a snake down the drain, as there was still no sign of the family pet.

"Thank you for coming out," Mr. Jackson greeted me with a handshake. "We have had numerous snakes on the property before, but never anything so large as this." He indicated the torch in his hand. "It's dark down there but I can clearly see the skin pattern. It's definitely a big snake."

Mrs. Jackson, meanwhile, stood back, keeping the boys close to her side. She was calm enough but obviously not keen on allowing herself or her two sons to get too close. The younger of the two had now dried his tears, becoming more curious as to what I was about to do than concerned about the potential whereabouts of their pet dog. Bringing his mouth close to my ear, Mr. Jackson whispered the question that was obviously current on his mind. "Is it possible that the snake ate the dog?" He peered at me through a light-weight pair of glasses balanced precariously on his nose. "I have prepared my kids to realistically expect the worst, just in case. Seems too coincidental that the dog has disappeared same time as we discover the snake." It was a statement more than a question. Taking the offered torch from Mr. Jackson's hand, I responded cautiously. "There is the possibility . . .

depending on the size of the snake." I turned to look towards the storm-water drain at the side of the road. "We'll know for sure if I can get the snake out."

Heading over to the storm-water drain, I peered into the gloom. The pipe was about eighty centimeters in diameter, buried about a meter underground, with a square, concrete junction housing a narrow slot into which runoff water from the road could flow when it rained. Mr. Jackson stayed close to me, while his wife and kids looked on from their safe position a few meters back. Bending down, I switched on the torch and directed the beam into the pipe. The torch was a small two-cell model offering weak illumination of the interior but enough to confirm Mr. Jackson's earlier conclusion. The dark, scaly skin glistened dully in the light, interspersed with brighter yellow chevrons spaced inches apart. The coils I could see were impressive, and as I pushed the light in further for a clearer look, for just a second I caught the reflection of an eye, while at the same time a long, slow, forceful hiss, enhanced by the hollow pipe, emanated from the drain. This was indeed a big snake, and well entrenched in a most difficult of places.

Standing back I considered my options; there was really only one . . . I had to go in there, secure the head of the snake, and gently coaxed it out. Judging by the thickness of the tightly wrapped coils, I estimated the python to be at least four meters long, maybe five. I also knew that the only way to get a grip on the snake's head would be to entice a strike . . . not an inspiring revelation. Being wedged into a close, claustrophobic pipe, and trying to entice a large python to defend itself with its huge jaws, which sports a formidable array of centimeter-long teeth, was not anybody's idea of fun. From past experience, I was familiar with the strength of a large African rock python. Wedged in the drainpipe as this one was, I knew this would be an almost impossible task. The only other option was to leave the snake to come out in its own time, but if indeed the snake had fed on the Jackson's pet wire-haired terrier, it would be weeks before it emerged, after slowly digesting the meal. Fearing for the safety of the snake, I felt strongly that to remove and relocate it to a safer area was crucial. Having thus decided, I unwittingly set myself on a path of self-destruction.

Collecting the snake bags from the Cruiser, I passed them to Mr. Jackson. "Please hand these down to me once I have maneuvered myself into the drainpipe. I'm going to need them as a buffer." Taking the bundle of bags from me, the look on his face reflected the obvious question . . . so I elaborated. "I plan to attract the python's attention by waving the bags in its face in the hope of enticing a strike. If all goes well, the snake's recurved teeth should then get firmly embedded in the bags, giving me a split second to grab for the neck. Once I've got a grip around the neck just behind the head, I can safely coax the rest of the body out of the drain." Mr. Jackson looked at me in astonishment, his face reflecting disbelief and his jaw moving slightly from side to side as though weighing up whether I was joking or not.

In fact, it was a standard maneuver employed by herpetologists when working with large, aggressive, nonvenomous snakes. Enticing a strike towards a bag, the recurved teeth invariably get caught up in the soft material of the bag, temporarily immobilizing the head, and allowing time for the herpetologist to get a grip on the neck before the snake manages to free itself. The problem with the particular scenario I now found myself confronted with, was how to achieve this in the dark confines of an eighty-centimeter storm-water drainpipe. Even assuming I was able to secure the head safely, there remained the question of the four or five meters of attached muscular body that I knew would immediately move into defensive mode by attempting to coil around me, the aggressor. Getting tangled up in the coils of a python while stuffed into the confines of a storm-water drainpipe was a one-way ticket to one of the numerous herpetologist's "worst nightmare" scenarios. Softly, I sighed to myself; there was no way around it, and projecting a more positive confidence for the benefit of the watching and expectant family than I actually felt, I began the uncomfortable process of squeezing my body through the opening slot and into the mouth of the drainpipe.

Upon my entry, a loud hiss immediately came from the darkness—a darkness that was now intensified as my body blocked out the last available light from the outside. I was basically entombed in a concrete pipe with four meters of powerful muscle supporting a head and mouth armed with six rows of needle-sharp teeth, ready to defend itself. *Who said herpetologists don't have fun?* Quickly I extended my right arm back out the concrete slot, where Mr. Jackson was ready to hand me the cotton snake bags and the little torch. "Good luck," he said, and then disappeared from view. I was on my own.

With cotton bags bundled up and dangling from my hand, I switched on the torch . . . and instantly it all went wrong. Ignoring all the rules, the giant snake took the advantage by striking out immediately, not randomly for the decoy bags, as was the accepted norm, but *over* the bags and straight for my face . . . with deadly accuracy! *Aaaarrgghh!*

Involuntarily I screamed my shock, dropping the bags and torch as I did so and grabbing desperately with both hands for the terrible mouth that was now attached across my face! In spite of my shocked panic, I knew above all things that I must get a secure grip on the snake's head before the dozens of recurved teeth imbedded in my skin ripped my face off. The pain was instantaneous, sharp, and terrible!

In semi darkness now, as the torch lay abandoned on the floor where it had fallen, I wrestled desperately with the terrible head filled with teeth, feeling the power of the snake as it attempted to pull me deeper into the pipe. Having long, recurved teeth, especially designed to secure prey animals with furry bodies, I knew that I had to somehow force the jaws forward, deeper into my face, before I would be able to unhook the teeth and release the head back again. I also knew that, with so many teeth embedded in my face, I was not going to manage this without multiple lacerations. I clearly remembered an incident some years earlier when a herpetologist was bitten on the arm by an Asian reticulated python, the resulting wounds requiring forty-six stitches. *What would a similar bite do to my face?*

All this ran through my mind in no more than a few seconds, as in final desperation I jammed the fingers of my right hand into the front of the snake's upper jaw, feeling the teeth penetrate my fingers as I did, and forced the jaw up and out of my face. The pain in my fingers was terrible, but preferable to that experienced in my face. With the top jaw now dislodged, any further control I had mustered evaporated, allowing panic to prevail.

With little thought for the consequences, I ripped the snake's bottom jaw free, breaking off the last remaining embedded teeth as I forced it away. Blood streamed from multiple lacerations running down into my neck and shirt. I was free but still a long way from safe, as the head now clutched feverishly in my blood-soaked hands pushed and squirmed to get free. To lose my grip now would be disastrous, as I had little space to maneuver and the snake was steadily uncoiling and pushing towards me.

I had to get myself and the snake out . . . and now!

Obviously, this was easier said than done. My blood-slippery hands struggled to maintain their grip on the neck as I shuffled backwards towards the concrete junction entrance. I would have to do it all backwards, dragging the python with me. I dared not lose my grip on the head and I dared not allow any body coils to get around my neck. Desperate now, I called out to Mr. Jackson, who by now must have been wondering what was going on and probably feared the worst after hearing my first scream of panic.

"Mr. Jackson! Can you grab my legs and pull?" I tried to sound as calm as possible as I maneuvered myself onto my back and shoved my legs through the drain opening. My eyes were full of blood, the snake was pushing and twisting in my sticky hands, and I was about to exit the drain upside down, legs first, hopefully dragging four meters of angry python with me. All in a day's work for me . . . but not so for Mr. Jackson, who hesitated when first I stuck my legs out the drain opening. I could sympathize with his confusion, but had little time to explain. "Pull me out by my legs. Quickly! My hands are full of snake!"

Fortunately for me, Mr. Jackson caught on quickly and proved to possess considerable strength as he grabbed hold of my protruding boots and tugged with all his might. I felt the skin scrape off my back as I attempted to assist his efforts by wiggling and maneuvering myself steadily over the rough concrete edge of the drain entrance. Finally my head emerged, and there came an audible intake of breath from the whole family, as for the first time they were exposed to my head and shoulders, which were covered in blood. Face and head wounds are known to bleed profusely, usually looking worse than they really are; however, I must have really looked a mess because the younger of the two boys clutched at his mother's dress and burst into tears. Everyone else just stared in horror as I steadily emerged, bloodied and battered, with a giant gaping head in my hands that continued to writhe, push, and hiss.

Until this time I had not even been able to wipe the blood from my eyes, and the sticky blindingness of it brought fears that one or both of my eyes may have been punctured by the python's teeth. Once free from the drain, I unceremoniously dragged the rest of the giant snake out onto the surrounding open ground and was finally able to release its head. Quickly wiping my eyes with the back of my hand, relief flowed through me as my vision cleared. At the same time, the now-released snake made a lunge at my legs, determined to seek revenge. With the whole snake now exposed on the open ground, and my no longer being confined by the drainpipe, I was back in control and easily side-stepped the strike.

Meanwhile, the Jackson family all stood huddled together a good distance away, watching the scene with some trepidation, their eyes rigidly fixed on the python. Suddenly the elder son now also broke into hysterical tears, followed closely by Mrs. Jackson, as Mr. Jackson made futile attempts to console them all. *Good grief! Just how bad did I look?* Not fully comprehending at first, I turned to look back at the snake, and all became clear. Strategically placed right where the reptile's tummy would be located, was a large lump. Could this be the Jackson's pet terrier? Another resounding howl emanated from Mrs. Jackson and the two boys, while Mr. Jackson continued his futile attempts to console with soft words and hugs.

As if the day had not already been traumatic enough for the family, the giant snake now began to writhe its body from side to side while at the same time contracting its length into a concertina shape. I recognized the maneuver immediately. Any snake that has recently swallowed a large meal will quickly regurgitate it if disturbed, thus affording it a better chance of escape. This snake had been seriously disturbed, having being dragged out of its hiding space by the neck, and was now about to disgorge its meal right in front of the watching Jackson family. It had been stressful enough coming to terms with the fact that a giant snake had eaten their pet dog without the need to see its squashed, slime-coated body being regurgitated from the snake's mouth right before their very eyes.

Quickly I stepped over to where the Jackson's stood huddled together. As one they stepped back, horror etched on their faces. The boys clutched even more tightly to both parent's legs, a fresh bout of tears bursting from their eyes. I had momentarily forgotten how bad I must have looked, my face, chest, and hands all covered in sticky blood. Urgently signaling Mr. Jackson over, I whispered in his ear. "Take the family inside quickly. The python is regurgitating its food. They don't want to see this." Somewhat confused, he stared at me uncomprehendingly . . . then suddenly his face registered my meaning. The soon-to-be-materializing pet wire-haired terrier was not going to resemble anything as cute and cuddly as they last remembered it.

About to follow my suggestion, Mr. Jackson turned to his family to usher them away when at that very moment there came a gurgling, scraping sound from behind me. As one we all lifted our eyes in the direction of the sound, just in time to see a large, furry, unrecognizably slimy object spurt from the gaping jaws of the snake.

"Bwwwaaa." A renewed burst of uncontrollable tears flooded from the boys, while Mr. and Mrs. Jackson stared stricken at the regurgitated object, as if unable to fully comprehend what they were witnessing. Rationalizing the predicament, I chose to ignore this renewed onslaught of hysteria, directing my attention instead towards the snake, which was already heading unerringly back towards the storm-water drain. I *could not* and *would not* face another episode in that drainpipe!

Sprinting forward, I made a desperate lunge for the snake, grabbing it at mid-body with both hands, just in time to pull it back from the edge of the storm-water entrance chute. The constrictor naturally took offense to this handling and effectively retaliated with an open-mouthed reverse lunge at my body, striking me squarely on the thigh. Once again needle sharp teeth penetrated my flesh. Taking advantage of the action, I released the mid-body and instead fastened both hands behind the snake's head. Secured now, it remained only for me to fight the rest of the body into one of the large snake bags that lay scattered on the ground. But I needed help.

"Mr. Jackson," I called out hopefully, "could you give me a hand please . . . if you don't mind?"

Mr. Jackson stared across to where I stood, gripping the head of a giant, wriggling python attached to my now bloody thigh. What was I thinking? *Of course he minded!* Mr. Jackson would rather stick bamboo shoots under his fingernails than help the crazy man covered in blood with a giant, wriggling python attached to his thigh! It was not that he was unwilling, just that he correctly estimated that, if he walked away now, he may still have a chance to live a long life and see his boys grow to maturity. Having witnessed the results of my two encounters with the enraged snake, there was no way in hell Mr. Jackson wanted to come near me.

Surprisingly though, after some hesitation, Mr. Jackson did slowly move closer and, under my instruction, successfully helped stuff the great muscular body of the python into a bag, while I kept the deadly head well secured between my bloody hands. Finally bagged and sealed, we both breathed a sigh of relief. I ran a shaky hand over my face, both sticky with drying blood. Pinpricks of pain indicated the incidence of numerous fractured snake teeth embedded in my forehead and chin, but the bleeding had basically subsided, as was usual with sharp, razorlike cuts. There would be time to clean up for proper examination later; right now there remained the matter of the regurgitated pet terrier. This would have to be disposed of as discretely as possible to avoid the family being further traumatized. I suspected that already the nights to follow would be riddled with nightmares and more crying.

Turning our attention for the first time to where the regurgitated animal lay in a sticky mess on the sand, we were surprised to see the eldest boy standing over the carcass, a look of euphoria growing on his face. "Dad, that's not Moppet . . . that's . . . something else." And the realization suddenly dawned on me that we had all gotten so wrapped up in the whole business that we automatically assumed that their dog, Moppet, was indeed the cause of the bump in the python's body. I bent down to examine the mystery prey animal and was quick to realize that this was not a dog but rather a large, grey wild hare, common in the area. The snake had after all fed on its natural prey, and the fact the dog was missing was no more than a coincidence. Smiles and jubilation broke out amongst the family, as just on cue, as though planned by a higher power, a car rolled up to the gate. "Hey Jim," a man's voice called out from the open passenger side window. "Got Moppet here with me. Found him way down the other side of the plots. There's a bitch in heat down there somewhere; dogs all over the place. Better tie him up for a while." And with that, Moppet, the wire-haired terrier I had yet to meet, nimbly hopped out the window and ran over to examine the interesting, smelly, freshly regurgitated scrub hare that had until then been the source of our fullest attention. Needless to say all attention was now quickly transferred to Moppet, the wayward terrier, who lapped it up with wagging tale. And general happiness prevailed, with earlier traumas placed securely in the past.

As for me, after splashing my face and hands with some water from an outside tap, I bade the Jackson family farewell, tactfully declining their offer to stay for coffee by stating the need to get the snake back to the park. In reality, this had been one of the most difficult snake extractions I had ever undertaken and I really needed to get back to examine all the damage to my person. As matters turned out, with the aid of some flat-edged tweezers, I eventually removed eleven broken needle points of python teeth from my face and scalp, leaving another three deeper tips embedded. These I knew, from previous experience, would fester out over the following days or weeks. The numerous lacerations otherwise inflicted healed without the need for stitches but did leave a few scars that would be slightly visible on my face for years to come. *Just another typical day as curator of herpetology at the Hartebeespoort Dam Snake and Animal Park.*

After measuring and notching a few of the python's ventral scales (for identification purposes in the event it be encountered again in the future), and knowing we had no need for pythons at the park, I released the snake back into the wild, a good distance from human habitation. It goes without saying that, on being released, the unforgiving reptile further pursued its attempts to rip my face off with a series of vicious strikes . . . but who can blame it after my dragging it from its hiding place and causing it to lose its hard-earned meal. Unable to explain to the snake, I knew, however, that had I not removed it from the area, it would in all likelihood sooner or later have turned up on someone's property, where it might have been killed by a less-conscientious property owner than Mr. Jackson.

All's well that ends well.

ಕ ಕ ಕ

While some calls for snake removal play out in a similar fashion to the story above, an incident reflecting the extreme opposite manifested itself one particular morning. Shortly after the python episode, an urgent call came through to the park that a man was "trapped" in his house by a dangerous snake. Knowing how people often overreact to the presence of a snake, I was skeptical. Managing quite easily to locate the property, I drove up a long, grassy driveway to the house, where I parked the car close to the front door. As I stepped out, a thunderous roar came from within the house, followed almost immediately by another. The entire building reverberated with shockwaves, sending me diving behind a low stone wall. Another two explosions followed. Then suddenly the front door burst open, and what seemed to be a half-crazed person with blazing eyes and hair standing on end rushed out onto the veranda brandishing a twelve-gauge pump-action shotgun.

"I got him!" The man cried hysterically, punching a fist at the sky. "I got him!" And turning swiftly, he charged back through the open door. I decided that where I was, safely hidden behind the stone wall, was as good a place to be as any. Absolutely furthest from my mind was any idea of approaching the house at this stage of the game. If I was going to die prematurely, it should at least be from snake-bite, not a shotgun wound! I waited. Five minutes passed. No further sounds came from the house. I decided to call out. Raising my head cautiously above the wall, I peered nervously in the direction of the open door.

"Anyone at home?" I called out, and then ducked back down just in case. "I got him!" the same hysterical voice screamed from inside. "You can come inside. I got the monster!"

Slowly I stood up and, still nervous of what to expect, headed for the house. Pausing in the doorway, I peered into the gloom. The strong smell of cordite burned my nostrils as my eyes adjusted to the dim light. Then I saw the man. He was perched on a couch in the living room area, loosely pointing the shotgun towards the floor, his gaze fixed intently on one spot. Lamps, a television set, side tables, couch pillows, and even paintings lay crashed all around him, all riddled with bullet-holes. Even the chandelier, walls, floor and ceiling, were peppered with lead shot.

Without getting off the couch the man gestured with the shotgun. "I got him!" he said triumphantly. "He's there under the carpet. I'm just waiting for him to move again." The carpet was an expensive one, I noted, now too ruined by lead shot.

"Please point the gun away, sir, and I'll see if I can find the snake," I said as politely as my quivering nerves would allow. Unsteady as this lunatic was, I was not planning to venture inside while he still brandished the shotgun. Jerking his head upright, he looked for the first time directly at me, then screamed, "Are you mad?" His eyes blazed. "Are you totally insane? That's a rinkhals under there. Keep away. When it moves, I'll blast it to hell!" He hoisted the gun to the ready position.

Well that was that as far as I was concerned. There was no way I could see getting around this one. It was very obvious the man harbored a more than average fear of snakes. I looked at him one more time. His eyes were blinking rapidly and his mouth twitched as he stood in the ready position, waiting for the slightest sign of life from beneath the carpet. A bad case, I decided, a real phobia. Quietly I stepped back from the door and headed for the car. This one, I told myself, was above and beyond the call of duty. I was better left out of it. Leaving as I had come along the driveway, I reached the main road just as two more explosions rocked the house. I put my foot down and headed back to the park, my thoughts a mixture of confused emotions.

Examining a beautifully marked puff adder. This snake has a powerful tissue destroying venom and is responsible for about 80 percent of all African snake bite casualties.

Exposing the hollow, needle-like hinging fangs of the African puff adder. The fangs fold back up into the top jaw when not in use, as do all adders.

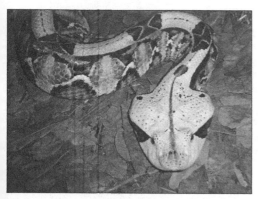

The Gaboon viper/adder is the largest viper in Africa with fangs measuring up to 5cm (2in). The venom is nerve and tissue destroying, resulting in respiratory failure and possible gangrene poisoning.

FRIDAY 21st DEC. 1990.

Hy oorleef Gaboen-adder se pik – 3.

Mnr. Austin Stevens wys sy regterwysvinger wat deur 'n Gaboenadder gepik is.

Gabon viper may cost snake expert a finger

By STEPHANIE HULL

THE curator of the Hartbeespoort Snake and Animal Park and world record-holder for a snake sit-in, Austin Stevens, may lose a finger after being bitten by a Gabon viper.

Mr Stevens, 33, was bitten by the snake while operating on its eye after it was bitten by a rat it was eating.

"I am positive I'll be fine," said Mr Stevens, whose arm was badly swollen and discoloured yesterday.

"He was very lucky — the snake was under local anaesthetic and therefore not at its most venomous. Otherwise Austin could have been killed," said park owner Jack Seale.

The Gabon viper is very poisonous

and has the longest fangs of all snakes.

Mr Stevens gained international fame several years ago when he spent 107 days and nights with hundreds of snakes at the park.

"The last time I was bitten this badly, I spent three months in hospital. And, ironically, it was on the same finger."

He spent Friday night pacing his bedroom to make sure he would not lose circulation.

"I have been treated with serum from Zululand and I'm under the supervision of two doctors. So all we can do now is wait and see what happens," he said.

Austin Stevens's badly swollen hand Picture GARTH LUMLEY

Just a scratch from one fang of a Gaboon viper introduced enough venom into my system to cause this amount of swelling and tissue damage to my hand and finger.

Being interviewed by phone in the snake cage during the 107-day world record sit-in. One curious cobra tries to "listen in" as others lay claim to the bed.

Potentially Africa's deadliest snake, this black mamba poses defensively, ready to strike.

A beautiful and rare banded snouted cobra with hood spread in defensive warning.

With this Egyptian cobra's attention being diverted elsewhere, the cameraman moves in for a rear-end close-up.

The rock python is the largest snake in Africa, reaching a length of 6 meters (20 feet). Though nonvenomous, its mouth is rimmed with sharp teeth capable of inflicting a nasty bite.

The colorful Gila monster is one of the only two lizard species in the world that have evolved venom glands for aiding in the killing of prey.

Approaching a desert chameleon on a sand dune during the making of the documentary film, *Dragons of the Namib*.

An accommodating rock monitor lizard located while on film location in Namibia, displays no fear of being handled.

Washed down almost to the Namib coast by inland desert flooding, this huge black mamba was eventually relocated back to its more typical habitat.

Feeding on desert lizards and geckoes, this slender and beautifully marked Namib sand snake is totally adapted to the harsh desert conditions.

The most common of the cobra species found in Southern Africa, this snouted cobra displays its typical defensive pose, ready to strike.

One of the only two back-fanged snakes considered deadly, the male African boomslang (tree snake) is often green while the females may be black or brown.

Incorporating the use of a 6-meter (20-foot) collapsible crane to enhance scenic cinematography while on location in Sudan.

My campervan amongst the great sand dunes of the Namib, home to a variety of desert adapted reptiles.

A dusky sunset over the Kinabatangan River while on film location in Saba, Borneo.

Catching and filming venomous banded sea kraits in the shallow coral reefs around the edge of Snake Island in Borneo.

Dodging the whipping tail and powerful bite of a water monitor lizard while filming on Survivor Island, Borneo.

Filming and photographing one of the worlds largest and most aggressive reptile species, the reticulated python, proved to be a difficult and daunting task.

An aerial view of the beautiful Komodo Islands, home of the largest living lizard species on the planet: the Komodo dragon.

Tall palm trees greet the dawn through a misty sunrise in the Komodo Islands.

A moment of overwhelming exuberance prompted me to take this dive into the sea after a fast swimming sub-adult Komodo dragon.

Swimming at full stretch I managed a touch the tip of the reptile's tail, prompting a sideways glare, followed by a burst of speed that left me floundering in its wake.

Known to consider humans as potential prey, this sub-adult Komodo dragon seemed keen to prove the fact as it enthusiastically pursues me up a tree.

Facing the ultimate snake, the awesome king cobra. Largest of all the worlds' venomous snakes, the king cobra can reach 6 meters (20 feet) in length.

With twelve SLR cameras, two mini DV cams, and a 16 mm high-speed film camera, all focused on a central point, the set is prepared to secure a time-slice effect as the king cobra strikes.

Using the length of the digital HD camera body and lens as a buffer, the cameraman edges in for a super-wide close-up sequence.

CHAPTER 8

THE HELMSTADT SNAKE REMOVAL

At the time it had seemed logical. I had spent my youth as an amateur herpetologist studying reptiles and amphibians and later turned professional when accepting the position of curator of herpetology at the Hartebeespoort Dam Snake and Animal Park in South Africa. During my years spent at the park, I had published numerous articles concerning reptiles and other animals, supported by my own photography, established a World Record for spending 107 days and nights in a glass cage with an assortment of Africa's deadliest snake species, and later published a book about my experiences. Was there any doubt then that a movie had to follow?

Well, be this indeed as it may, had I the slightest inkling at the time of exactly what such an endeavor might entail, I dare say I might never have attempted it. Though I had become well practiced in the art of still photography around the snake park, from where I collected images for my published works, I would now be drawn into the far more complicated world of the movie camera—a very different proposition all together. As it happened, this proved to be the least of my problems to emerge; the first being simply to find a second-hand professional 16 mm movie camera and accessories within a very limited budget . . . my life's savings.

This matter resolved itself when a long-time friend, Jurgen Hergert, owner of a small reptile park in Germany, asked for my assistance in renovating and redesigning his park to accommodate an increase in reptile displays. I had helped design and bring the park into operation some years earlier, and Jurgen and I had remained in constant contact thereafter. Though I had many fond memories of the Nordharzer Schlangenfarm (Nordharzer Snake Farm) and the people I came to know in Germany, the cold climate and lack of wildlife and wilderness areas did not fit in with my long-term plans. Nonetheless, Jurgen's offer now provided me with an opportunity to spend time in a country that was well known for its documentary wildlife programming, as well as for dealings in new and second-hand cameras and other paraphernalia used in making documentary films.

Taking leave of my life and position at the Hartebeespoort Dam Snake and Animal Park was not a decision taken lightly. However, there was restlessness inside of me—a feeling that there were other avenues still to explore—and once the idea to make my own documentary film became established in my head, there was no turning back. It is ironic that to do this I would first have to travel to a country far removed from the wildlife and wilderness that is Africa, the very wildlife and wilderness I now wished to capture on movie film. But such is the way of the world. With the cost of new 16 mm film cameras far out of my price range and my being unable at the time to find reasonable second-hand equipment in South Africa, the offer of work at the snake park in Germany, which included a place to stay, would at least pay me a salary while I searched for what I needed. Within a few weeks I was packed up and on a Lufthansa flight to Germany.

I had first met Jurgen many years earlier while employed as assistant curator of the Transvaal Snake Park, and later, on a return visit to South Africa, he had looked me up and come to visit at the Hartebeespoort Dam Snake and Animal Park, which had become my permanent home. Fascinated by all the animals and reptiles on show, the public demonstrations and the crowds of visitors, Jurgen asked if it would be possible for him to spend some time at the park, working closely with us, to learn the basics of reptile husbandry and the general running of a park of this nature. I conveyed the request to Jack, who agreed on one condition, that I take full responsibility for Jurgen while at the same time did not neglect my usual duties.

Jurgen had explained to me at that time that he had begun construction on a snake park of his own, in the northern Harz mountain area of Western

Germany, where he hoped to duplicate our style of display and demonstration. Probing a bit further, I soon came to realize that Jurgen in fact had little knowledge of herpetology other than what he had gleaned from brief visits to other parks. The bug had bitten, however, and knowledge or not, he was determined to succeed in his dream venture: the establishment of the first open-air snake park in all of Europe. I remember my mind reeling at the multitude of complications such a venture might entail, the cold climate being just the tip of the iceberg. But the fact that he had already begun construction of the building was proof enough of Jurgen's determination, and for this I admired the man. I felt that the best I could do for him was to take him, step by step, through the basics of running a snake park.

Over the weeks that followed, Jurgen became my shadow, following me everywhere I went, studiously jotting down notes in German. He attended and watched with enthusiasm each and every public show I performed, furiously scribbling in his notebook and afterwards bombarding me with questions. Working closely with me in the venom laboratory, he learned how to feed the variety of species being housed and, later, how to perform the venom-extraction process. No teacher could have wished for a more attentive student. With Jurgen drilling me for information every step of the way, after many weeks of this rigorous educational training I was exhausted, as I believe Jurgen was, too. Much had been achieved in a short time, however, rendering Jurgen a very happy man, as he waved goodbye from the Lufthansa international terminal in Johannesburg. Little did I imagine at the time that I would, in years to come, find myself working side by side with Jurgen at his very own "Schlangenfarm."

The Nordharzer Schlangenfarm, as Jurgen's park came to be known, is situated some two kilometers outside of the little tourist town of Schladen, in the northern Harz mountains. A popular tourist destination, Schladen is one of a cluster of small, Gothic-styled villages to which tourists flock every winter to ski the gentle mountain slopes and skate the many naturally frozen lakes in the surrounding area. In the heart of winter temperatures here sometimes reach below –20°C (–4°F). The region is lush green with forests of pine and fir, while the red and orange, steeply sloped and pointed roofs of the towns sparkle gaily at the foot of the mountain slopes.

Life at the Nordharzer Schlangenfarm was in many ways similar—and yet very different—from that at Hartebeespoort. The everyday running of the snake park was similar, as the daily needs of reptiles housed anywhere in the world are similar. But the park was much smaller and the surroundings and climate very different. Germany is not a country known for its great outdoors or wilderness. It is cold and small and cramped, with massive overpopulation, as most European countries are. However, I had a goal in mind and settled into the routine, while at the same time every day scouring newspaper and magazine ads for the 16 mm movie camera equipment I desired.

The first few weeks at the Schlangenfarm were chaotic as I busied myself with general reorganizing of everything that I found unsatisfactory to my way of thinking and experience. Familiar as I was with the park, having worked with Jurgen in the early years of its conception, there were now numerous additions to the building, with still more planned for the immediate future. The park now housed more exotic species, which brought about the need for more glassed enclosures so that the specimens could be displayed for the public. At this time, much of the collection was being housed in the laboratory, out of view of the general public. The huge number of smaller cages housed in this area were collectively temperature controlled as one, the entire hall being heated by hot oil radiators mounted on the walls. The larger outdoor public exhibition cages were also heated by oil radiators, but these were positioned under the floor so that the reptiles inhabiting the cages could self-regulate their body temperature simply by alternating their proximity to the subterranean heat source. This was an essential part of the park's design, as the winter months in the Harz region were known to be bitterly cold.

The very first cage to be viewed by the public as they entered the park was the Asian cobra display. The cage was beautifully decorated with a formation of rocks, drift wood, and a natural-looking pond; but of the snakes advertised, there was no sign. Taking note of this and the telltale mounds of sand deposited in little heaps around the radiator area, I was quick to realize what was going on. By scraping sand aside with their necks, the snakes had burrowed their way in under the radiator. From experience I knew these snakes, having settled themselves in comfortably out of sight, would never again be seen by the public, coming out only at night when nobody was about. A totally unacceptable situation, which I set about to rectify.

Swinging open the large front window of the cage, I cautiously peered inside. All clear, definitely not a snake in sight. Carefully scraping away all the loose sand around the floor radiator, I probed underneath with a hooked snake-stick. This proved to be an awkward task, forcing me to crawl further into the cage in order to be able to force the snake stick under the radiator, which just cleared the concrete base by a few centimeters. In no time a crowd of curious spectators had gathered outside the open cage to watch intently as the crazy man probed around with his bare hands in a cage marked Asian cobra. Looking briefly over my shoulder, I called out, "Stay back, please! Keep well back from the door! There are venomous snakes in here." Quickly I returned my attention to the potentially dangerous task at hand. I could not afford to be distracted.

Suddenly there came a hiss from under the radiator. I had located the missing cobras. Jurgen had told me there were two in the cage. I probed again. Another hiss, louder than before. The watching crowd, totally ignoring my instructions (or, in retrospect, having not understood properly my English) pushed closer, craning their necks for a better view. Suddenly a head popped out from beneath the radiator and I pulled back slowly as the rest of the body eased its way out. Cautiously I moved back towards the open window, calling a warning to the crowd over my shoulder: "Stand back, please! Stand back." And everyone pushed closer to get a better look. I repeated the instruction more sternly: "Stand back, please!" There was a shuffle of movement. I backed up further, keeping my eyes firmly fixed on the cobra. Suddenly my rear end came up against something solid. I looked around anxiously, only to find that I was neatly trapped in the cage, the window having been forced shut by the crowd, now smiling at me safely from outside the glass door. The onlookers had closed me inside, and as this nasty fact dawned on me, there came another more forceful hiss from beneath the radiator, followed by yet another, and out popped two more cobras, irritably come to investigate the disturbance in their cage. *Jurgen had said there were only two cobras in the cage!*

Quickly I tried to turn my body, but the movement attracted the closest snake, which immediately reared up, spreading an impressive, threatening hood. This in turn startled the others and within seconds I was face to face with three angry cobras in a closed cage two meters by two meters in size. *I had a definite sense of déjà vu!* Glaring defiantly at me, the menacing cobras swayed slightly from side to side, poised to strike at the slightest provocation. Desperately I pushed against the closed window, and as if by prearranged signal all three cobras struck out determinedly. With a Herculean shove, I threw my weight against the glass door, forcing the crowd back, as I dove headlong into their midst.

Suddenly all the smiles disappeared, as the crowd registered the seriousness of the situation, and three angry cobras, no longer hindered by the confines of their cage, came slithering out close at my heals. And with their escape, the air came alive with a chorus of "Mein Gott!" as one and all galloped off towards the park exit, where there were a few desperate moments as twenty people attempted simultaneously to pass through the turnstile. This left me lying alone on the ground where I had landed, the wind knocked out of my lungs, faced with the problem of three escaping cobras. Ignoring the lack of oxygen in my lungs, I forced myself up, grabbing for another snake stick that I had fortunately left outside the cage. Within a short while I had everything back under control, with the snakes safely bagged. I was now freely able to work in the cage without further danger of being killed. Curiosity getting the better of them, slowly, one by one, the nervous crowd gathered outside the park, popped their heads back in around the entrance way. *Cowards,* I thought to myself, still fuming from their behavior. Ignoring them, I proceeded to get on with the task at hand.

The German people display some great interest in wildlife. They can be found in group tours around the world in even the most remote of regions. Wild animals, especially of the African variety, seem to hold a special fascination to them, and many top-quality film documentaries on the subject of wildlife in Africa are produced by German camera teams every year. Some of the world's most prestigious wildlife magazines too, are based in Germany, *Das Tier* (which unfortunately ceased publication in 2010) and *Geo* being two good examples. On the whole, it can be said that the German nation strongly supports wildlife and the conservation thereof. However, the law in Germany concerning the keeping of venomous reptiles is quite plain. It states simply that no venomous reptiles of any description are to be kept by any private member of the public.

Catching up with some paperwork in the laboratory one day while Jurgen was away on business in Hanover, the phone from the front office rang, redirecting to me in the laboratory because of Jurgen's absence. My German being as basic as it was, I preferred not to answer calls myself, as from experience I knew the simplest discussion could quickly become confusing. The phone rang again. Reluctantly I picked up the receiver.

"Guten Tag," I said. The response was immediate. "Herr Stevens? Polizei, Schladen . . ." followed by a tirade of rapid-fire German delivered in a guttural tone of which I was only able to catch a word or two before the voice declared "Alles gut!" and the phone went click in my ear. "Alles gut" indicated that everything had been discussed, worked out, and a time set. Of this I had caught only my name, the time—2 p.m. that same day—and the fact that the Schladen police wished to discuss a matter with me. They would be collecting me at the park; no further information was offered and no questions asked. I broke out in a cold sweat. Had I unknowingly broken some sinister Schladen law, or passed through a speed trap? The insecurity of being in a foreign country where I was barely able to converse loomed menacingly in my mind.

My thoughts flashed back over the past few weeks since arriving in the Harz. Sure, I had had a few rowdy "beer nights" in one or two pubs with Jurgen, but everybody did that, with the Germans making more noise than most. It had to be something else. My mind reeled with illogical scenarios. Maybe Jurgen was involved in something illegal and had now fled the country, leaving me to face the music. He never did disclose to me from whom he had purchased all his exotic reptiles. I dismissed the thought. Jurgen loved his park. He would never do anything to jeopardize it. My mind roamed for further possibilities. There was of course the incident a while back when I accidentally dropped a cobra at the feet of some diplomats while doing a snake demonstration . . . but that had been all smoothed over and apologized for. No, it had to be something else, but for the life of me I could not imagine what. I just had to sweat it out.

In no time at all 2 p.m. arrived, and with it, promptly, as is the German norm, a Schladen police green and white VW Golf arrived. A few minutes of discussion brought relief as it was explained to me that I was to accompany the police to assist them on an unusual mission to investigate a house in the little town of Helmstadt, some forty kilometers away, where it was reported that a man had been bitten by a red diamondback rattlesnake. He had injected himself with his own serum supply but was later rushed to hospital, critically ill. Naturally, the police were informed and a full investigation into the matter was called for.

On entering the victim's premises, the police discovered what seemed to be no less than a small reptile park. The collection housed species from around the globe, venomous and nonvenomous alike. Either the man was a keen collector or was dealing in sales of exotic, live reptiles. Whatever the case, it was an illegal operation. Not knowing anything about the reptiles in question, the police called for an expert to accompany them to identify and remove the snakes. As matters turned out, I was to be the expert.

The police were most apologetic for taking me away from my work, while I in turn expressed my gratitude for the opportunity to save the reptiles, which would surely have been destroyed otherwise. I was informed that the reptile owner would in due course be charged with illegal possession of venomous reptiles. I would then be asked to testify in court as to the accurate description of the species involved.

We arrived at the residence within the hour. It was a small house positioned high upon a slope. I went inside and was immediately confronted by numerous glass-fronted wooden cages piled one on top of another, each housing far too many snakes . . . proof enough in my mind that the man was indeed a dealer and not a collector. On closer examination I found most of the animals to be in rather poor shape, somehow surviving in atrocious conditions with little evidence of cleaning. This angered me, and I felt within my rights to confiscate the specimens to relocate and house them properly at the snake park.

Accompanying the police were two reporters who busily made notes and took photographs as I began to extract snakes from the various cages. A few minutes later, more police, members of the veterinary department, and more reporters arrived on the scene. This little incident was obviously making big news in the Harz. I was constantly bombarded with questions as I worked, while flashguns flared in my face. The room now seemed to be chock full of people, and, as I extracted each new specimen from its cage, there came a resounding chorus of *oohs* and *aahs* and flashing lights continuing to explode in my face. Half the time I couldn't see a damn thing I was doing!

Steadily the flow of people increased as nosy neighbors now joined the throng, eager to get a piece of the action. Numerous times I politely asked everyone to stand back, to allow me room to work. This they did, apologizing profusely for their intrusion, only to crowd in again as soon as I reached for the next snake.

Amongst the specimens were a number of young boa constrictors and pythons, but the rest were venomous, some highly so. I was surprised to see medium-sized black mambas in one of the cages and decided to leave these for last, as their size, agility, and nervous disposition made them the most potentially dangerous of the collection. The man was running a big show here, probably supplying snakes to buyers across Germany and most likely beyond its borders. I counted about seventy specimens in all, and after a while the floor around me was covered with wriggling snake bags.

Reporters continued to shoot film and take notes as I tried to explain something of interest about each species. One thing was certain: I was going to make headlines somewhere in the German news, and I wondered if German TV might not get wind of it as well. As if by command, a new face popped through the doorway, followed by an enormous tripod onto which was attached a video camera. Then came a jumble of cables, lights, and various fittings. German TV news had arrived, and just in time for the grand finale—the removing of the four deadly black mambas.

Quickly I allowed a short interview and explained that the bagging of the mambas was going to be more difficult and dangerous than had been the case with the other snakes. I suggested everybody should leave the room as a safety precaution. This statement was met with a chorus of negative groans, but I was adamant. These snakes were a different kettle of fish altogether. One does not mess with four adult black mambas confined in a cage too small even for a single specimen. *All I needed was an angry mamba streaking out into the crowd.*

And two minutes later, that is exactly what happened.

Reluctantly, after much pressuring and against my better judgment, I agreed to allow only the TV crew to remain in the room, at a safe distance from where I was to work with the snakes. Then, using the longest snake tongs, I slowly and gently lifted the first snake and gradually coaxed it towards the entrance of the cage and the waiting bag. The animal glared at me distrustfully, with open mouth, in typical mamba fashion. These snakes had probably been tossed around quite a bit since leaving Africa and, nervous as they were, could be expected to attack at the slightest provocation.

There came a hushed murmur from behind me, accompanied by the continuous hum of the video camera. As the first snake cleared the cage door, balancing critically in the light grip of the tongs, I reached out to slide the glass door closed for fear of the others escaping. A specimen closer to the door than the others watched nervously with raised head and slight hood, but made no move to strike as I moved extremely slowly, extremely smoothly.

At this point, from somewhere behind, came an illuminating series of flashes triggered by eager photographers craning their necks from the doorway and hoping for a glimpse of the action. Simultaneously, there came an almighty crash as an overenthusiastic viewer, perched on a chair, overbalanced and careered forward into the group of tight-pressed reporters. Together the entire lot came tumbling into the room, a shower of bodies enveloping the TV crew and their cameras and other equipment.

Startled out of my wits, I almost dropped the mamba, and the sudden activity was just the excuse it was waiting for. Lunging at incredible speed, the mamba's deadly head flashed forward. Instinctively I ducked my head and body to one side as the gaping black interior of the mouth, with gleaming white fangs, reached out for my face. Over balanced, I collided with the still-open glass cage, which toppled over, creating terrible panic amongst the three remaining mambas still inside. Within seconds the room was alive with scrambling bodies, tumbling camera equipment, four angry black mambas, and me, suspended upside down over the fallen cage, my legs waving in the air. Total pandemonium! And from somewhere from the back of the room, a single flash illuminated the scene. I clambered off the cage and looked around frantically. People were still scrambling out the door with yells of alarm, the last one slamming it shut with a resounding bang.

Oh bloody wonderful! I fumed. Now that all the action had been stirred up, with lots of nice pictures taken, guess who had been left behind to sort out the mess. *It was the snake sit-in camera-crew scenario all over again!* I hurled the snake tongs at the closed door and screamed at the top of my voice, "AND STAY THE BLOODY HELL OUT OF HERE, YOU MORONS!" No answer came, only nervous shuffling noises from down the passageway. The thought came to mind to throw open the door and set all four mambas after them, but I dismissed the idea. I was already in enough trouble as it was.

I gazed around the room, cluttered with hastily discarded cameras, tripods, and other paraphernalia, and marveled that nobody had been hurt or bitten in the incident. More astonishingly, the four mambas had all gathered together in a nervous group near the window, where they seemed content to remain, heads raised, staring at me suspiciously. It was my move, and as soon as I made it, the four heads reared up towards me, daring me to come closer. *Here we go again*, I thought. How to convince four frightened, angry black mambas that I mean them no harm.

Considering the situation for a minute, I decided that the old "dark corner" trick would be my best bet. It was as good a chance as any to save what was left of the day. Most snakes will head for the closest dark opening when trying to escape. Often one can coax a snake into a bag in this way, which makes catching the animal that much easier and safer. I had no heavy, dark-interior type bags with me, but a quick search in a linen cupboard yielded a blanket, which I decided would have to suffice. I spread the blanket out on the floor as close to the mambas as they would allow without causing too much panic. Then, reaching out at full arm's length, I carefully raised the end closest to them by means of a meter-long snake tong. To my surprise, with barely a second's hesitation, the snakes rushed for the offered dark refuge, obviously relieved to escape the bright light and probably the sight of me. I now had four highly venomous black mambas tucked under a blanket, in a stranger's house, somewhere in the northern Harz region of West Germany, in a little town called Helmstadt, about thirteen thousand kilometers from my home in Africa. Who would argue that herpetologists don't have the most fun?

The next stage of the operation provided little problem as the blanket enabled me to extract one snake at a time, sliding each straight into separate, wide-mouthed bags. Twenty minutes later I stepped out of the room and announced to the nervously waiting crowd that all was under control. This statement was met with a great cheer of "Wundebaar!" and cameras clicked and notebooks reappeared. Soon after I was being transported back to the snake park by police vehicle, the trunk and back seat of which was laden with bags of wriggling snakes.

The following day, Jurgen arrived back from his trip. Bristling with excitement and an arm load of bundled newspapers, he called my name. "Austeen! Austeen! Where you . . . Austeen?" With this heavily accented English, Jurgen pronounced my name with a double "e" instead of an "i." When I appeared, he ran over and would surely have hugged me had it not been for the newspapers in his arms.

"Austeen! I read everything! You make my park famous!" He was bursting with pride as he searched for more English words with which to express himself. "You do goot job for us, Austeen. You picture in all newspapers." He pushed one of the bundles over to me. I unrolled it and there I was, slap bang on the front page of the local Harz news, with both legs straight up in the air, the rest of me dangling ludicrously over the up-ended mamba cage, with snakes disappearing in all directions and the headline read, "Schlangen experte aus Africa zeigt wie es gemacht ist. [Snake expert from Africa shows how it's done.]" I stared at the picture in disbelief, feeling my face flush. Of all the dozens of pictures that were taken, they had to pick that one! And I thought to myself; *These Germans drive me crazy!*

CHAPTER 9

SULTAN THE CROC AND OTHER STORIES

Sultan was a two-meter Australian saltwater crocodile that lived in a large glass hothouse in the center of the German park's open-air arena. This he shared with an aquarium full of piranhas, another containing three American turtles, and one with Asian water snakes. Jurgen had always worked this area, which included scrubbing out Sultan's pool when algae began to grow. Jurgen had told me that Sultan was quite docile, and that one simply had to shove him aside with a broom when scrubbing the pool, so as to gain access to all the corners and edges. I remember thinking briefly how unusual that was, as I recalled reports from other parks about how bad-tempered saltwater crocs usually are, even smaller specimens like Sultan. Largest of all the world's crocodiles, the saltwater crocodile can reach over six meters in length and are known to attack and eat humans, should the opportunity present itself.

Thus came the day when Jurgen was away on business and no less than five busloads of tourists were booked for a visit. The weather had picked up somewhat over the previous days, with more than the average sunshine drenching the Harz area. I noticed algae was gathering thick and fast on the sides and surface of Sultan's pool, where the flat green surface was broken only by a pair of scaly nostrils and two glowing yellow eyes. Not wanting to present an example of neglect to the expected public, I decided for the first time to tackle the cleaning of the pool myself. It was early morning, and the day promised to be warm with plenty of sunshine bursting out between the low cloud formations. I decided this was the day to get better acquainted with Sultan, while at the same time rendering him more visible to the visitors.

There were no visitors in the park as I entered the hothouse, and I was hopeful of getting the job completed without interruption. Working in an enclosure with animals always draws a crowd, which can easily distract one's attention and in turn cause a potentially dangerous situation, as was the case with the Asian cobra incident, still fresh in my mind.

The two yellow eyes peeking out through the film of green surface algae watched me with interest as I exchanged my regular shoes for a pair of gumboots (slang for rain boots). Taking up a long-handled broom, I cautiously stepped into the water. The eyes remained where they were, so I began to scrub away vigorously at the algae. The temperature in the glass house was just below 30° C (86° F), and within minutes the sweat was pouring down my face and arms, soaking into my shirt. The algae was proving to be stubborn, resisting my attempts to remove it, eventually forcing me to sit down on the side of the pool for a breather. Just as I sat down, I felt a gentle nudge against my right boot. Looking down I found myself staring straight into a pair of almost luminous golden eyes. Sultan was inspecting the new arrival. He seemed quite calm, and with Jurgen's words fresh in my mind, I lifted the broom to give the crocodile a gentle shove with the brush end . . . *and all hell broke loose!*

With a tremendous bellow, Sultan raised his head clear of the water, lunged at the broom with lightning speed, snapping it in two with one mighty chomp of his jaws. Momentarily paralyzed with fear, I stared at the splintered handle in my hand. Immediately Sultan lunged again, this time fastening his gleaming jaws around my right gumboot, and one powerful twist later I found myself toppled upside down on my back in the green slush—all this in a split second. As my head sank below the surface, I envisioned the headlines: "South African snake man killed by docile Australian crocodile in Germany!" What a way to end it all!

Twisting my body around, I lifted my head for air, at the same time clawing at the side for a hold, but finding none. Viciously, the crocodile twisted again, and I allowed my body to go limp, knowing instinctively that, if I resisted, my leg would go the same route as the broom handle. Crocodiles are known to break up and drown their prey in this fashion. Thankfully the pool was not too deep, which allowed me the chance to break the surface for air. Frantically then, in panic, I began to kick and pull with all my strength until I finally managed to free my foot from the gumboot. With my breath coming in short, sharp gasps, I scrambled out of the pool, throwing myself clear onto the side. Mentally I cursed myself. *How could I have been so stupid? With all my years of experience!* And still I let Jurgen's words lull me into a false sense of security, resulting in my almost being dismembered by his "docile" crocodile.

Sultan glared at me defiantly from his green pool, the gumboot still clasped firmly between his powerful jaws. I glared back, suppressing an urge to beat him over the head with what remained of the broom.

When somewhat angrily relating this story to Jurgen on his return to the park a few days later, he burst out laughing. "Oh Austeen, he do that to me first times also. He always do that when he in water. You must first let water out. Then Sultan climb out and lay on side. He docile when *out* of water." He was shaking all over with mirth. Placing both hands on my shoulders, he said soberly, "I lose many gumboots this way." Disgusted, I contemplated beating him over the head with a bloody gumboot, but he turned away, still chuckling, leaving me fuming to myself.

Sometime later, when nobody was around, I slipped into the hothouse to test Jurgen's theory for myself. It seemed unlikely, nothing like what I had ever experienced with captive crocodiles in the past. Quickly I pumped out the water, and lo and behold, once the water was drained, out climbed Sultan. He perched himself neatly on the far side of the pool, allowing me complete freedom of movement. Somewhat astonished, I watched him as I scrubbed at the still-stubborn algae, and his toothy jaws opened slightly into a hideous grin. I could have sworn there was a twinkle in his eye.

Though I encountered many a keen amateur herpetologist during my stay in Germany, some proved not to be knowledgeable enough when taking on an exotic animal species as a pet. In Germany, at the time at least, as in many other parts of the world, it was a simple matter to purchase, virtually over the counter, even such animals as lions, tigers, or pythons. Reptiles especially need expert attention as well as daily monitoring. Also, their diet is very specific and temperature control is of the utmost importance.

In Germany I came across some of the most unusual reptile problems ever experienced in my career, most of them due to carelessness and the lack of knowledge on the part of the keeper. After a show one afternoon at the park, a young woman approached me and rattled away excitedly in German about having a friend who bred African ball pythons. She went on to explain that she herself had in fact chosen and paid for an egg and was waiting for it to hatch any day now. Having just watched my show, during which I had allowed the audience to handle a ball python, the woman expressed how much she was looking forward to doing the same with her own snake, once the egg had hatched.

In return I explained that ball pythons are sometimes problem feeders, and I advised that correct temperature and humidity would be crucial to the successful raising of such a snake. Furthermore, I explained, a newly hatched snake would require especially good care to ensure it fed well. To all this she nodded vigorously, assuring me that her friend had supplied her with all the necessary information. It seemed she knew it all, and I felt pleased that this would not turn out to be another case of a pet snake's death due to lack of knowledge. I then asked by way of conversation when the paid-up egg was expected to hatch and when she hoped to collect her specimen. It is not uncommon for breeders to accept payment in advance for as yet unhatched eggs of sought-after species. Responding to this question, the woman's face lit up, and, plunging her hand into her pocket, she proudly produced a wrinkled, semiputrid, oblong object that only slightly resembled a snake egg. Stroking the smelly object lovingly, she explained that she was keeping it close to her body for warmth, as her friend had advised, and that she expected it to hatch any day now. With this she popped the egg back into her pocket and strolled off to gaze raptly into the ball python cage, leaving me dumbfounded, grappling to fully comprehend what I had just witnessed. I did not pursue the matter . . . there seemed no point.

On another occasion, a woman came rushing into the park carrying a baby basket. Inside, covered with a little pink blanket and surrounded by little fluffy toys, was an obese-looking juvenile boa constrictor. The woman was almost in tears as she gestured insistently towards her snake and then to me. It was obvious there was something terribly wrong, but for the life of me I could not make out what the problem was. Boa constrictors are amongst the most common harmless snakes kept as pets, and this young specimen look fine and well fed. The woman rattled on so fast, almost hysterically, that I could not make out a word and was forced to call on Jurgen to translate. Having somewhat calmed the woman down, Jurgen listened to her explanation and finally translated to me. It seemed there were two boa constrictors. Oh, I thought, the *other* must be sick. Quickly I pulled back the little pink blanket. No sign of the other snake. Must be under the bottom blanket, I mussed, and soon I had removed everything from the basket. Still no sign of another snake. Turning to the woman I candidly pointed this fact out to her, and with a heart-wrenching howl of anguish she dropped her head on my chest and burst into a fresh spasm of tears.

I began to suspect there was some sort of misunderstanding here and looked again to Jurgen for help. Once more he took the distraught woman in hand and slowly coaxed her through the story one more time. At last he turned to me with a broad smile. Apparently the poor woman had kept a pet boa for many years. Then one day it took sick and died. She had raised it from a young snake, in the same baby basket now lying before us. She had been heart broken by the loss until one day she decided she was ready to get a new pet boa. But this time, to prevent any further heartbreak, she decided to purchase *two* snakes. In the event of one dying, so the logic went, she would still have the other to console her. She had no experience with the keeping of more than one snake, however, and unwittingly introduced two dead mice into the basket for her new babies to eat before nipping off to call her neighbor over to see her new babies enjoy their first meal. On their return, however, instead of two small boas, they found only one rather larger boa with a tail protruding from between its jaws. What had happened was clear. Obviously both snakes had latched onto the same mouse at opposite ends (a common occurrence when feeding more than one snake in a confined space), and the more aggressive specimen had simply swallowed the mouse as well as the snake attached to it. This explained the healthy, well fed boa I held in my hand at that moment.

Again the unfortunate woman burst into tears, this time flinging herself onto Jurgen's chest. Jurgen looked helplessly to me for assistance. There was absolutely nothing I could do about the eaten snake, so instead I made some coffee to calm her down and practically pointed out that one snake was far less trouble than two, and that her plan had after all been successful, as she now still had one snake instead of none. At this Jurgen rolled his eyes, while the woman sobbed more loudly than ever, leaving me with no further comfort to offer.

It was a stark reminder for promoting the importance of research before acquiring an exotic pet. This is especially the case when dealing with something far removed from the usual domestic pet menagerie. Reptiles, amongst other exotics species, require specific and detailed attention if they are to live a long and comfortable life.

ಠ ಠ ಠ

Word had gotten out that there were daily snake "milking" demonstrations taking place at the park, and to most Germans this was something new. Nowhere else in Europe could one actually witness the handling of highly venomous snakes, not to mention the 'exciting' venom extraction process. The Germans picked up the new phrase quickly. They called it "schlangen melkung," and I was amazed at how many visitors would ask when the "schlangen melkung" show was to begin, making up-and-down cow-milking movements with both hands. I suspect that, after watching a demonstration of venom actually being "milked" from a snake, many people were quite surprised, perhaps even disappointed. One person went so

SNAKEMASTER

far as to ask if snake milk could be consumed by humans, and if so, what price it might fetch in a store. I soon became accustomed to this type of question, displaying little surprise, instead patiently explaining the basic facts concerning "schlangen melkung."

One day I became involved in a discussion with a couple who badly wanted to purchase a special snake to keep as a pet in their home. They were a genuine couple who had done their homework. They knew exactly what they wanted and how to look after it, having gleaned all the available facts from all the literature on the subject. Good common sense told them that purchasing a snake from a dealer was not in their best interest, as there was no telling where the animal had come from or whether it was internally healthy or not. On that day I had displayed a young African ball python and had allowed individuals to handle it, as I often did during shows. This was when the couple approached me and expressed their desire to purchase such a reptile. As it happened, six ball python eggs had been successfully hatched at the park a few months before, and the youngsters had quadrupled in size since then. Jurgen had wanted to sell off four of the specimens, as our collection already numbered eight. The couple was ecstatic, and begged to be allowed to purchase a pair immediately, despite the hefty price of DM300 (roughly the equivalent of 150 euros) each. (The average price at the time for captive-bred, good feeding juveniles)

As we were negotiating the deal just outside the laboratory entrance, another couple stepped forward from the watching crowd. They were a Chinese couple and asked if there were a possibility of them purchasing the remaining two specimens. I was amazed. Seldom did I have the opportunity to sell four exotic, expensive reptiles all in the space of one hour. Jurgen would indeed be pleased. Mr. Chang spoke perfect English, assuring me of his knowledge of reptiles, and without further ado he produced a large wallet, from which he extracted six one-hundred-DM bills. Minutes later two very happy couples left the park, their newly purchased pets snugly housed in warm woolen bags for transport.

Two weeks passed by, during which time the first couple telephoned periodically to report on the progress of their pet snakes, which by all accounts were growing in leaps and bounds.

"No trouble at all," the proud father exclaimed enthusiastically.

"Better than having babies," the proud mother chimed in.

I wondered how the Chinese couple were making out with their pair of youngsters. As if in answer to this thought, just four days later, while shopping in the town of Goslar, some forty kilometers from the park, I spotted the Changs walking along the crowded main street some distance ahead. I called out to them and waved wildly to get their attention. Mrs. Chang recognized me first and quickly pulled her husband over towards me.

"How are you? I asked. "And how are the ball pythons?"

Smiling brightly, Mr. Chang nodded vigorously. "Oh very nice!" He said. "Very nice! We will buy from you again. Every few months we have family come visit from Hong Kong, and it is always nice to serve something special for dinner."

CHAPTER 10

THE ASIAN COBRA INCIDENT

T he daily routine at the German park naturally called for the handling and working with highly venomous snakes. Though my duties included doing snake handling shows for the public, it was on a much smaller scale than what I had been doing in South Africa, and so proved to be of little potential danger to my person. Working with the off-display laboratory specimens was another matter, however, as the large majority of these were housed in a variety of small glass cages. The daily cleaning of these cages was difficult, as each reptile had to be removed from the cage before cleaning could commence. This meant that every reptile, venomous or nonvenomous, had to be handled with every cleaning, the confined space making any other method potentially dangerous. Ironically, it was not the cleaning and handling of the snakes that saw my downfall, but the *feeding*.

The snake in question was a very irate and permanently bad-tempered Asian spitting cobra. A juvenile, at just sixty centimeters long, I had always made sure to handle this specimen with snake tongs and keep my eyes protected against the spray of venom the snake relentlessly threw in my direction. I have seldom encountered such an aggressive reptile, and on this fateful day, my last at the park before my flight back to South Africa with all my collected camera equipment, I stupidly decided to feed this little monster one more time before I left.

The feeding technique simply involved placing a freshly killed laboratory mouse into the snake's cage. I did this with the aid of a pair of forceps which were thirty centimeters long making sure my hand came nowhere close to the open cage door while doing so. On this day, as usual, the little cobra raised its head threateningly as I approached, watching my every movement. Sliding the glass door open carefully, I pinched a dead mouse from the feeding tray with the forceps and, as gently as possible, threw it into the cage. Usually the snake would immediately attack the dead mouse, striking and biting into it with determination, "killing" it again and again to its own satisfaction. . . but not this time. With a perfectly timed lunge, the little cobra flung its body out the open door and all the way over the forceps to accurately jab both fangs into my thumb . . . and there it hung suspended, injecting venom into my hand with gusto.

I simply could not believe my eyes as my heart sank. This could not be happening to me. *Not again!* Quickly I grabbed at the snake's body, which was whipping about in the air, and gave it a powerful tug. No time to worry about breaking its fangs; every second meant more venom being injected. I had to get the snake off my hand, and immediately! The tug pulled the snake loose, streaks of blood materializing as the teeth and fangs raked across my flesh. With a quick flip of the wrist I flung the cobra back into its cage and slammed the door closed.

I was shaking all over with shock and disbelief. This was to be my last day in Germany. I was all packed and ready to leave, cameras in hand, excited to begin work on my new project in Africa. With painful resignation, I suspected that I would not be catching my flight. Even if I were to survive this, I was going to be in Germany for a while . . . unless I did something fast!

I hurried my way to the laboratory fridge, where all the medical equipment and medicines were stored. Blood from my bite wounds splattered over everything as I frantically searched through all the serums for something that might cover the Asian cobra species. It took me just a minute to go through the lot, locating a variety of serums for just about any venomous species on the planet, but nothing specifically covering Asian cobras!

Bloody hell! What was Jurgen thinking? It was important that we carry serum for all species housed at the park. Time is always of the essence where a snake bite is concerned. The sooner the serum is administered, the better the results. And this is what worried me about the spitting cobra. Back home in South Africa, where spitting cobra research had been conducted, some evidence had been accumulated to show that the terrible necrotic effects of the Southern African spitting cobra venom could be avoided if specific serum was injected intravenously within at least thirty minutes after the bite. It was just possible that the same might apply to the Asian species. I desperately needed to get the specific serum. Finding nothing in the fridge, I ran from the laboratory out across the park to the main building, where Jurgen was working in his office.

Barging through the door, my heart pounding, my hand dripping blood all over the place, I almost shouted, "Jurgen. I've been bitten! I need spitting cobra serum. I can't find the right serum." And I held my bleeding hand aloft for him to see. I knew I was doing all the wrong things, getting my heart rate up instead of taking everything slow and easy, but in my desperation I felt that, if I was to prevent a long and painful recuperation period, I needed to get that serum into me as fast as possible.

Like a startled rabbit, Jurgen jumped up from his chair and rushed over for a closer look at my hand.

"Austeen! This bad! You need doctor," he cried in his usual heavily accented and broken English. "I call doctor now!" And he dived for the phone on his desk and frantically began to place a call to medical services. His stating of the obvious infuriated me.

"I know I bloody need a doctor, Jurgen," I blurted out in frustration, "but I need to get the correct serum immediately, or I'm going to have necrosis problems later." Like most Germans, Jurgen was not accustomed to handling such emergency matters himself, having been taught by the book. And the book said such matters as snake-bites were to be handled by doctors only. The making of decisions amongst Germans relies on precedents, and when a situation is unprecedented, people are uncertain how to behave.

So there I was, myself an expert in the treatment of snake bites, expected to await the distant arrival of a German doctor, who, living in a country that had no highly venomous snakes to speak of, in his whole life had more than likely never seen a single snake-bite, least of all a bite from an exotic species from another continent, to help me. *Holy mackerel!*

By this time my hand was swelling and in pain, all the worse from all my activity. Frantically I lunged at Jurgen and pulled the phone from his ear, forcing him to look into my face.

"Jurgen! You can call the doctor later. Right now I need to know if we have any serum for Asian cobras! I need to know this *now!*"

Shocked at the anger in my voice, and probably the vision of my bleeding hand splattering blood all over his neatly arranged desk, Jurgen stared at me with wide, frightened eyes. The last thing he wanted was a dead "Austeen" on his hands.

"Do we have serum, Jurgen?" I repeated, almost shouting into his face, forcing him to come to his senses and help me directly. There would be plenty of time to phone the bloody doctor later, but there was no time to waste right now if I was going to save myself from a repeat experience of the terrible necrotic effects of snake-bite poisoning. If there was any serum about, I needed to get it into my veins immediately!

"Ja . . . ja! I have many serum in van for snake transport." Jurgen finally managed, his eyes focused rigidly on my face, his mouth quivering as he spoke. "I have all for Austellung [exhibitions]. I get it." And he ran from the office. I should have thought of it myself. Transporting snakes around the country for display and public shows, Jurgen naturally kept serum available in the transporter van. I just hoped he had what I needed.

Carefully I replaced the fallen telephone receiver and waited, making a conscious effort to calm down. An increased heart beat meant a speedier circulation of venom, venom that right now was coursing through my body in search of the most efficient way to destroy all my living systems. My blood, my nerves, my tissue—all of it would die in a very short while if I did not get the correct serum. Outwardly I calmed down, but inside I was shocked to my very core that I had somehow allowed this to happen to me again.

Within seconds Jurgen reappeared with a large emergency medical case in hand, retrieved from the truck. I grabbed the case from his hands and wrenched it open. And there it was, ampoules of serum for various species of venomous snakes . . . including Asian cobras! My heart leapt. (Not a good thing for someone with snake venom in his system, but my relief was great nonetheless.) On the down side, I could find no antihistamine. I would have to take my chances without it.

Quickly I ripped open a 10 ml syringe and fitted a needle. Next I snapped off the tip of the first ampoule of serum and sucked up the life-saving fluid. I knew I needed at least three ampoules, probably more. I just felt it—more later, possibly, but an immediate three ampoules right now if I was to survive. Jurgen watched me as though in a trance, not believing that I was actually about to inject myself with antivenom. He had been taught that, under no circumstances, was one supposed to do anything without a doctor present. Great in theory . . . not so great when knowing I probably had more snake-bite experience than most doctors and also knew that their first advice would be to wait for symptoms to appear, by which time it might be too late. If my suspicions were correct and Asian spitting cobra venom did produce a similar cytotoxic effect to that of the South African species, I needed to cover myself quickly.

So transfixed was Jurgen with what I was doing that I now had to remind him to phone for the medical assistance he was so keen to call for earlier. I had the serum in hand, but I was treating myself, so any further assistance would be most welcome. And without further ado, I plunged the needle into a prominent vein in my left arm . . . and slowly pressed down on the plunger as I did so. The shock of it made me dizzy and I felt myself stagger. This was not a time to go weak at the knees. I needed help.

"Jurgen, get over here."

Quickly he obeyed, shock written all over his face as he stared at the needle in my arm. Twenty minutes had passed since the bite. *Borderline!* I knew it may even be too late, but there was no turning back now. It was a race against time to get that serum into my system. Anaphylactic shock was a real possibility without the antiallergic properties of an antihistamine being injected first, but I had never shown any signs of negative reaction to serums in the past and so was willing to take the gamble. Risky, when I think of it now, but such was my fear of necrosis setting in. I just did not believe I had the strength to live through that again. I was in a strange country with strange people who I feared might not have the experience necessary in this field, so I wanted just to take care of myself to the best of my ability. It was about this time that I began to feel myself slipping away, and slowly I slid off the chair I was occupying to lay down on the floor.

"Jurgen," I whispered through a veil of dizziness and steadily progressing pain, "Please don't let me die. Give me all the serum we have." My life was now in his hands . . . and I knew it was the worst thing I could do to him.

It is said that the true character of a person can best be judged when faced with a difficult or even life-threatening situation. This is when a person's "true colors" are revealed. And going against all his carefully cultivated instinct and all he had been taught by a protected society to leave matters to others better qualified, Jurgen now rose to the occasion, believed in what I asked of him without fully understanding, and proceeded to take over the job of getting the remaining ampoules of serum into my vein—something he would never have believed he was capable doing of just a few short minutes earlier.

"Slowly, Jurgen," I said . . . "slowly." It was important that the serum be administered at a slow, regular speed, so as not to further shock my already-traumatized system. All I wanted was to get the serum circulating in my system; thereafter, I would be happy to receive any further medical attention advised by a doctor.

Doctors do not like being told what to do, and I can understand that, but I was not going to get into a lengthy explanation concerning the potential postenvenomation effects of Asian spitting cobra venom if serum was not administered as soon as possible. There are many doctors and herpetologists alike who still advise not to introduce antivenom until symptoms are beginning to manifest themselves. And that's fine; they are welcome to their opinion on whatever grounds they base them. But at this point in time, my life was at stake, and I was making the call according to all the experience and knowledge *I* had gained over many years in the snake business. As a studied and experienced person in the field of herpetology, I felt it was my right to decide on the method of treatment.

I will never forget an incident some years earlier in South Africa when a venomous boomslang (back-fanged tree snake) I was rescuing from a flooded ditch struck out at me, just managing to imbed its front teeth into the palm of my right hand. Instinctively I jerked my hand away, leaving behind a few bleeding puncture marks. I felt fairly confident at the time that the rear fangs housed on each side of the snake's upper jaw had not penetrated my flesh. However, prudent thinking suggested that I admit myself into a hospital, where an overnight vigil, including blood counts, would confirm whether I had indeed been envenomated or not.

A doctor "specializing" in snake-bite treatment was notified and presented himself at my side at the hospital in question and closely studied my bitten hand for some minutes before finally concluding that, in his "expert opinion," this was not the bite of a venomous boomslang. It was a case of mistaken identification. I was quick to explain that I was a herpetologist and, without question, could identify a boomslang when I saw one. Visibly bristling at my doubting his "expertise" and self-proclaimed knowledge on the subject, the doctor then refused to admit me even for overnight observation, stating that I would be needlessly occupying a bed required by someone who was *really* sick!

Holy cow!

I could not believe my ears, and it took some argument and numerous frantic phone calls to friends and associates able to confirm my status as a qualified herpetologist before I was finally, and somewhat reluctantly, admitted for tests and overnight observation, the doctor in question all the while still insisting that he had seen boomslang bites before, and this was *not* a boomslang bite.

As matters turned out, overnight hourly blood counts confirmed that no venom had entered my system. I had been lucky, but my confidence in so-called medical "experts" in the field of snake-bite was somewhat shaken. I could have been left to die . . . or at least forced to wait for symptoms to manifest themselves. In the case of the powerful hemotoxic effects of boomslang venom, the damage to my body might have been irreversible.

Suddenly the air was alive with the irritating, wailing sound of an ambulance siren as it pulled up in a screech of rubber just outside the snake park. This was followed by an invasion of paramedics and a full-blown doctor, who immediately pounced on Jurgen as he was withdrawing the needle after administering the last ampoule of serum into my arm. Sternly he reprimanded Jurgen, insisting that no treatment should be administered until snake-bite poisoning be positively established by the occurrence of symptoms. I sighed inwardly. *Thank you, Jurgen, for getting the job done before the arguments began.*

I felt mentally exhausted, but alive. No matter what treatment would follow, I had received the serum I needed. Nothing more to do but hope it was in time to prevent serious local tissue damage by the potential cytotoxic properties that I was not even sure occurred in Asian spitting cobra venom. Only time would tell, and I lay back in submissive acceptance of things to come.

The ride to the hospital was something to remember, as the vehicle sped along narrow streets with the siren going full blast. Some cars were forced off the road, while others skidded to a halt to allow the emergency vehicle to pass. Curbs were mounted, stoplights ignored, and pedestrians forced to dive for areas safe from the speeding emergency vehicle. Obviously this was a life-and-death situation of the most grievous nature.

Strapped down on a gurney in the back of the vehicle with a 500 ml saline drip filled with a concoction of treatments emptying into my body at a frightening rate while being fussed over by half a dozen very concerned-looking medics as the ambulance jostled and lurched and swerved its way towards the hospital, the thought occurred to me that death by motor-vehicle accident might be the more likely outcome of this experience.

When I arrived at the hospital the chaos continued, as more enthusiastic German nurses, doctors, and any other available staff appeared, transferring me from ambulance to a hospital ward at full emergency tilt. Exotic snake-bite cases were a rare occurrence in Germany, and it seemed the entire medical fraternity wanted a piece of the action. Not surprisingly, considering the fuss and noise of the whole operation, television press arrived with cameras rolling as I was hurriedly wheeled down a corridor to the emergency room. With luck, and if I lived through it all, I might catch myself on the 7 p.m. news. And I thought to myself . . . *these bloody Germans are crazy!*

Swollen now to its maximum, my arm was extremely painful to the touch—different, though, from that of a viper bite. There was none of the terrible burning sensation at the site of the bite, no oozing of fluid, no sign of blood-filled blisters. Of course with cobra venom, a powerful neurotoxin, one has to be prepared for the unexpected, and after some discussion with the doctor in charge, a tall blonde-haired woman of serious disposition, it was agreed that at least two more ampoules of serum be fed gradually into my system via the saline drip. Hopefully this would be enough to continue the battle against the venom. Continual monitoring of my system was now all that remained to be done. In spite of strong painkillers, it proved to be a night of little sleep.

The next day, however, found me feeling stronger and more comfortable in spite of my painful and swollen arm. I believed I was out of danger, that the serum had done what it was designed to do. There was no sign of necrosis at the sight of the bite and no discoloration anywhere along the length of my arm. My gamble had paid off. I was alive and on the mend.

My diagnosis did not impress the doctor, though after a close examination she reluctantly agreed that my condition seemed not to have deteriorated overnight. This was all the encouragement I needed, and I immediately announced that I wished to leave as soon as possible, as I had a plane to catch back to South Africa. This statement was first met with stares of astonishment by doctor and all staff present but slowly evolved into patronizing smiles of disregard.

"This not possible," the doctor said, voicing the general consensus, and everybody nodded in agreement. She focused a stern look towards me. "After such traumatic und life-threatening experience as venomous snake-bite, vun must obviously remain hospitalized und under observation for some days, und thereafter take it easy for an extended period. International flying is something not even to be considered for some time to come. Ja!"

Jurgen, who was forever trying to convince me that his park in Germany should become my home, did not want me to leave anyway, and so agreed whole heartedly with the doctor's prognosis. But I was adamant. My Lufthansa flight was scheduled for 9 p.m. that night, and I was going to be on it one way or another. Admittedly it would not be an easy task. My arm was painful and swollen to twice its size, reducing carrying or any other traveling activity to one arm only. Most importantly, to my way of thinking at the time, I had a packed collection of cameras and other painstakingly purchased equipment waiting. I had an idea in my head, a film to make. I was going home . . . *tonight.*

There followed further justifiable argument on the part of the doctor, but finally she capitulated, unhappily producing a German version of an RHT (refuse hospital treatment) form for me to sign. This I did, and, after sincerely thanking her and all the staff involved for all their efforts on my behalf, I left the hospital with my arm in a sling, a bottle of painkillers, and a letter from the doctor describing my condition, should there be any questions at the airport. I knew I was again taking a chance with my life, but such is the way of youthful enthusiasm. I had a goal set in my mind, and all else seemed irrelevant.

A very unhappy Jurgen drove me to the airport. "I'm sorry, Jurgen," I muttered, somewhat unsure of how to express my inner emotions. "I just simply have to be on that flight home to Africa." I tried to explain how I felt but saw by the confused look in his eyes that I was not having much success. I could imagine and sympathize with his confusion. I was hurt and potentially still in danger for my life, yet still insisting on leaving immediately, while he on the other hand was offering me a permanent position and job security in Germany. To Jurgen, the Schlangenfarm and Germany were the be-all to end-all of life. And though I could understand this, sometimes even tempted to submit myself into the security of it all, I simply could not do other than to follow my heart. I had an idea in my head that I was striving towards—a feeling that there was something I had to do back in Africa, and nothing could change my mind. This was simply the way it had to be. I could not properly understand it myself, so how could I explain a personal, driving emotion to someone from a vastly different background?

Reluctantly Jurgen saw me safely to my terminal, wishing me well as he did so, with the promise that his door would always be open should I ever wish to return. "I never forget you, Austeen," he called as I turned and waved before passing through the gate. And I knew we would be friends forever.

My arm in a sling promoted much attention, and I was not short of people offering help with my heavy hand luggage full of camera equipment. I was about 20 kg overweight, but I was sent on my way without so much as a suspicious glance. (The good old days, before the threat of international terrorism.)

My aching arm rendered the flight uncomfortable but otherwise uneventful. I dosed myself with pain pills and tried to sleep. My arm was not getting worse, but I knew there remained still the danger of possible relapse if the amount of serum introduced into my system proved not to be sufficient and had not neutralized all the cobra venom. Though I had not advertised this to anyone, I carried the last two ampoules of serum available at the park in my jacket pocket. I also carried a syringe loaded with a sterile needle. I could just imagine the chaos should I experience a relapse on the plane and need to be treated. *Oh lordy!*

When I think of these things so many years later, I am astounded at my daring stupidity. As matters turned out, I arrived back in South Africa feeling well enough, collected my Land Rover from storage, and headed out into the wilderness on a twenty-five-hundred-kilometer trip across two deserts—the Kalahari and the Namib—to a little town on the Skeleton Coast of South West Africa called Swakopmund. From here I would attempt my first solo documentary film. Little did I suspect at the time that this would become my base and home for the next twenty years of my life.

CHAPTER 11

FILMING IN AFRICA

In returning to Africa with all the camera and film equipment, my plan was to secure some interesting wildlife footage with which to tempt a production company to allocate funds that would allow me to proceed with my envisioned project. My first idea was to make a film about unusual species of snakes and other reptiles native to the Southern African region and record any unusual behavioral patterns. First I chose to work with those species closest to where I lived in the middle of the great golden-desert sand dunes located along the Atlantic Coast. These included the elusive side-winding adder, two species of legless lizards, the little-known golden mole, and the prehistoric-looking Namaqua desert chameleon.

It was in fact a Namaqua chameleon that I encountered first with my camera, as it strode purposefully across the dunes at a hurried pace. This reptile is an amazing example of desert adaptation, surviving extreme conditions in a waterless realm of heat, dryness, and blowing sand, armed only with the ability to camouflage and a long, sticky tongue housed in a toothy set of jaws. As with all chameleon species, the desert chameleon's eyes swivel individually. After several weeks of following the reptile, I was able to bring the camera very close, though even when hunting I noticed one eye remained ever-watchful, given my close proximity.

I spent many weeks in the dunes with this one particular female chameleon, who I named Rosy because of the beautiful mottled pink color she adopted when directly exposed to the harsh rays of the desert sun.

During this period, Rosy led me on a merry chase over a large area of her desert territory. Gradually, her daily routine was exposed to me. I witnessed Rosy snap up hundreds of dune-dwelling beetles with her lightning-fast tongue, along with a few large locusts, numerous other insect species, and even a dune lizard.

To my astonishment, Rosy one day tackled a side-winding adder that had surfaced close to where she was perched amongst the fleshy leaves of a dollar bush. In an attempt to defend itself, the little adder desperately lashed out with vicious, venomous bites to Rosy's head, but soon succumbed to her crushing jaws. Interestingly, I noted that the little adder's venom seemed to have no obvious effect on the chameleon whatsoever. After about an hour of struggle and complicated swallowing, Rosy waddled off down a dune, her stomach dragging in the sand, stuffed with snake. I was fortunate to have caught the whole episode on film. My perseverance was beginning to show dividends. Now at last I felt I had something to offer the world of wildlife documentary making.

As it turned out, Germany's NDR Television liked what they saw and was interested in financing the completion of the proposed film. Thus I was, for the first time, introduced into the complicated business that exists behind the making of a wildlife documentary. Unceremoniously, I was thrown in at the deep end. Not only was I expected to find and film unusual behavior amongst the reptiles I might pursue, I needed to record sound to match, transfer all my 16 mm footage to video, edit the video into an acceptable rough-cut version, and take it all across the world to Germany. There, with the aid of a professional editor, I would be allocated a studio where, for a period of some two months, I would work the film up to an acceptable standard for network release. An exhausting task, as I was soon to find out.

However, for the most part this all lay in the future. With the security of an allocated budget in my pocket, I was free to roam Southern Africa's wilderness areas, cameras at the ready, in search of the interesting footage I imagined may be lurking out there. Cobras, like sharks or lions, always excited documentary viewers, so as a start, I set out in search of one of these predators, the African snouted cobra.

For some weeks I searched the rocky regions and dried riverbeds hundreds of kilometers inland from the coast without success. One can never find a snake when one needs one. Instead, I came across a large male rock monitor lizard, which one day entered my camp and helped itself to everything edible that was available, including much of my stock of raw eggs. Presumably recognizing a good thing when he saw it, the giant lizard decided to stay. Munchy seemed as good a name as any for my newfound hungry lizard friend, and with an inspired change of filming schedule, I now turned to following Munchy all over the surrounding countryside, recording the daily activities of one of nature's most interesting reptiles.

Coincidentally, one day this included sniffing out the elusive snouted cobra I had so long desired to find. As I was to learn over future projects, staying with one animal will often lead to interesting interactions with others. The snouted cobra in this instance was quick to defend itself against Munchy's attack, raising its hood menacingly and striking out, its fangs loaded with deadly venom. Apparently familiar with the scenario, Munchy did not for one second hesitate, instead lunging forward with open jaws. Grabbing the meter-long cobra at mid-body, quickly spinning as he did, Munchy hurled the cobra across the ground. Quick as a flash Munchy followed up, and, fixing his powerful jaws over the stunned cobra's head, he crushed down with all his might. He then proceeded to bash the writhing body from side to side till satisfied no life remained in it. After some ten minutes of this activity, Munchy began to swallow the snake down whole. As astonishing a feat as any I have ever witnessed, and, once again, I had caught the whole action on film. My project was now moving forward nicely thanks to my hungry lizard friend.

It was not long after this incident that Munchy disappeared back into the bush, never to be seen by me again. Not even my cracked raw eggs, strategically placed at night, produced any results. It was almost as if he had come just to show me the way and, with this achieved, was once again free to roam the wilderness that was his home. It is not unrealistic to imagine such things when one is spending long days and nights alone out in the bush. Immersed in empty, sweeping landscapes by day, replaced each night by a darkened canopy of overwhelming, starlit heavens. It is as though one is gradually absorbed into the surrounding majesty of it all. Never am I more acutely aware of my connection with, yet insignificance in, the overwhelming vastness that is our universe than when lying on my back on the sandy floor of a desert, staring up at the wondrous night sky above. This is my time of greatest peace and wonder; it is all that keeps me sane in an ever-increasing world of insanity.

Before leaving the area I scattered about a dozen raw eggs as a goodbye and thank-you gift, should Munchy by some chance return to the area.

As the winter months grew to a close, to be replaced by warmer spring air, I began to find more evidence of snakes and was fortunate enough to film various species in action. This included such scenes as a venomous tree snake raiding suspended nests of weaver birds while the birds launched a daring attack on the reptile in an attempt to save their chicks; black mambas in mating combat, their bodies entwined and raised high in the air; a black mole snake stalking, attacking, and constricting a mouse; a side-winding adder demonstrating its undulating body motion and burying ability in the dune sand; and a pair of puff adders mating in the grass, their tails entwined and joined in amorous display.

This latter scene reminded me that most adders deliver live young. In the months that followed, though I came across many male puff adders, it was only towards the end of the year that I finally located a female whose body appeared swollen enough to convince me that she was within days of producing her young. Not wishing to lose the opportunity and knowing that the snake might easily elude me in the field, I placed her in an empty apple box that I kept in my vehicle where she could remain safe until it was time for her to give birth. Thus having the snake under my constant observation, I was sure to be ready with my camera when the time approached. Naturally, matters do not always pan out as one might expect.

Three days later at about 4 a.m., my female snake, who I chose to call Mum, feeling the time to be near and obviously not satisfied with the location I had provided, somehow managed to force the lid of the box open. She slithered out and over my body as I lay sleeping in my truck, to give birth to no less than twenty-eight healthy, wet, and venomous offspring. And it was with some bewilderment that I was awakened not to the patter of tiny feet but rather to the slithering of tiny scales as the little reptiles explored their new and exciting world. Needless to say, never before in the history of wildlife filmmaking had a vehicle been so speedily vacated, rendering me wide awake, scantily clothed, and freezing in the glow of dawn. Staring at the Land Rover from a few meters away, I considered what exactly to do next.

In fact, it took an hour by torchlight to locate about half the tiny snakes, which huffed and puffed their indignation at my attempts to capture them. This was by no means the end of the matter, as for the next week the tiny adders kept turning up, usually at the most inopportune times: One in a cup as I was about to prepare some tea, another under my pillow where minutes before I had been dozing. One even crawled between my bare toes while I was driving, almost causing me to have a heart attack and veer dangerously off the path. And I will not go into detail about the one wedged comfortably inside a toilet-paper roll, to be discovered one dark night, when spade in one hand, toilet-paper roll in the other, I went to answer the call of nature! All in all, it was about two weeks before I was relatively certain that my vehicle could once more be considered a "snake-free zone."

Though disappointed at having missed the opportunity to successfully film the birth of these tiny snakes, they otherwise certainly provided me with some nervous entertainment, as I was forced constantly to be aware that one might suddenly appear out of nowhere at any given time. Though small in size, new-born puff adders are miniature replicas of their mother, their tiny venom glands and fangs capable of delivering a venomous bite. Live-born snakes leave their mother immediately after birth to fend for themselves, thus it was no problem for me to release these individuals back into the wild as they appeared.

ﻞ ﻞ ﻞ

While most front-fanged snakes recorded around the world are considered dangerously venomous, only a very few of the back-fanged species may be potentially lethal to humans. Of these few, two are proven to be deadly, both being found in the Southern regions of Africa. They are, in order of toxicity: the African boomslang (tree snake) and then the African twig or vine snake. The latter is so named because of its unique ability to make itself look to take on the appearance of tree bark. The snake relies on this camouflage when it lies in wait for prey, blending in perfectly with the surrounding branches. Remaining motionless amongst the dry branches of a bush, the slender snake extends its orange-colored tongue as a lure to attract lizards and small birds on which it feeds.

The boomslang grows larger than the twig snake and varies in color, with the females often being of a brown or black coloration, while the males generally are bright green. The venom apparatus of the tree snake is primitive compared with those of the mambas, cobras, or adders. A number of grooved teeth situated halfway back in its upper jaw are used to direct the flow of venom into the wound inflicted by the teeth. Venom is not forcibly "pumped" into the wound, with the result that tree snakes are generally inclined to hold onto their prey, chewing continuously while allowing the venom to penetrate into the wound. There have been a number of tree snake bites recorded (by me, among others) where envenomation has not occurred simply because the snake has been pulled off quickly, allowing it no time to chew the back fangs into the flesh.

Few cases of tree snake bites are recorded as the snakes are shy, elusive, and nonaggressive. They spend most of their time well out of reach of humans, high up in the foliage of trees, where they hunt birds and chameleons, their prey of choice. Their only human victims are usually handlers and catchers. The venom of the boomslang, though slow acting, is extremely toxic, with just a scratch from a fang being enough to kill a human. The boomslang is considered by many herpetologists to be, drop for drop, the most venomous snake in the world; in other words, needing the least amount of venom to cause human fatality. Falling victim to the bite of a boomslang, one would suffer massive hemorrhaging throughout the body over a period of forty-eight hours or longer before fully succumbing to the effects. On the positive side, this provides a good length of time for the victim to reach professional medical attention. A specific monovalent serum (designed to act against a specific antigen) is produced specifically for this snake, which is only made available to hospitals on positive confirmation of a bite, as the product is generally in short supply.

Needing to get some footage of Gaboon vipers to complete the tropical section of my film, I traveled to Zululand on the north-eastern coastal region of South Africa, where these snakes were still known to occur in the dense undergrowth of the tropical Duka Duka forest. The largest and heaviest-bodied adder in the world, the Gaboon viper is recognized by its beautiful camouflage pattern specifically designed to blend in with forest floor vegetation, where it lies in wait for prey animals, such as large rats and rabbits. The broad head and mouth houses huge fangs, often over three centimeters long and capable of delivering a lethal dose of a virulent cocktail of neurotoxic and hemotoxic venom. These snakes are rare and elusive, their perfect camouflage making them all but invisible in the undergrowth. I knew it would take some searching and a lot of luck to capture one on film.

Because of the lush tropical conditions of the region, numerous other species of snakes could be encountered. These included the forest cobra, both the black and green species of mambas, puff adders, twig snakes, and the boomslang, to name but a few. One day while exploring for a potential Gaboon viper habitat, I was attracted by the excited chattering of a group of African cane cutters, heads upturned, gathered around the foot of a large wild fig tree. Curiosity getting the better of me, I approached closer to investigate. The cane cutters greeted me cordially as I stepped from the bush to join their circle. Enquiring as to the reason for their excitement, they pointed upwards into the overhead branches in an attempt to guide my eyes.

"Up there, mister . . . you can see it?" The calloused finger of an old man pointed roughly towards the network of branches, high up near the top. "Mamba!" he exclaimed with certainty, and, as one, the entire group echoed the name—"Mamba!"—as though in awe of a god.

I knew that most snakes the local people encountered in these rural areas were referred to as "mambas," but as both the green and black mambas do occur in the region, I did not doubt the possibility.

"You see it, mister?" The old man continued to point. Shading my eyes from the streams of sunlight penetrating the leafy canopy, I peered up into the branches. Then I spotted it. A safe distance from the ground, the snake was lying relaxed on a thin branch, its head directed downward, apparently interested in the activity below. The beautiful green body was long and slender, and any novice might easily mistake it from this distance, with the bright light as a backdrop. I noted immediately, however, that it was a large male African boomslang. From where I stood it looked like an exquisite specimen for some photography, but I knew any attempt to get near would startle the reptile into flight.

Observing my longing gaze, and taking note of my camera suspended by its strap over my shoulder, the old man spoke again: "You want heem mister? I knock heem down with my stick." And from his belt he pulled a meter-long stick, worn shiny smooth from much handling, with a carved knob at one end. A *knobkerrie* (traditional African club), I thought without enthusiasm. Although the Zulu people are well known for their prowess in handling this centuries old traditional weapon, I could not imagine how he intended to get the snake down with it.

"I get him for you, mister!" the old man repeated, and, like a boomerang, he spun the stick upwards into the branches, where, unbelievably (I will never know whether by chance or expertise), it hit the poor, unsuspecting reptile squarely on the head, bringing it down to land with a thud, virtually at my feet, and sending the old man and all his coworkers scampering off in superstitious fright. I was dumbfounded! The snake lay motionless on the matted cane leaves. I bent down to examine it carefully without touching it. Then, satisfied that there was no sign of life, I lifted the limp body in my hands. I had of course not for one moment imagined the old man would actually kill the snake, or I would never have allowed him to try to dislodge it.

Seeing me handling the dead serpent, curiosity overcame fear, and slowly, in dribs and drabs, the men approached, until they were all there again, the whole lot crowding around me, all talking at once and gesturing at the lifeless body of the snake. The old man rubbed his hands together with glee. "I get heem good, hey mister?" he grinned.

"Yes," I answered reluctantly with a sigh, deciding there was no point in spoiling his delight. "You get him good alright."

As they all pressed tightly around me, some of them reached out nervously to touch the smooth, shiny underbelly as I turned the reptile over in my hands and like children with a new toy, they ogled, "oohed," and "aahed." I reached for the head and was about to examine the mouth when suddenly, as though shot through with a jolt of electricity, the snake's body stiffened, the head snapped up, and in my hands I felt the life throbbing back into the creature. For one split second everyone froze, as if turned to stone, myself included. Then, as the deadly head jerked round towards me, there came a spontaneous cry of "ooh sheet!" from the workers, as involuntarily I hurled the snake up into the air before joining the surge of bodies striving to create distance between themselves and the now obviously very much alive "mamba."

By the time the dust had settled, there was no sign of the tree snake, which had obviously only been stunned in the first place and was by now probably striving to achieve as much distance between itself and us as we were from it a few seconds earlier.

"Ho boy!" The old man spoke from his hiding place behind a log, his wrinkled, weather-beaten brow etched with concern. "Next time, the mamba spirit kill us all—sure thing!" And all the others, now slowly emerging from their hiding places, solemnly nodded their heads in awed consensus.

Bidding farewell to them all, I casually mentioned that I was heading back to the central forest area to pursue my quest for the elusive Gaboon viper. Expecting exclamations of shock or dismay that I would actively seek out these deadly creatures, I was surprised when the old man, who seemed to be the only one with a spattering of English, spoke up again.

"You want Gaboon?" It was more a statement than a question. "We have Gaboon. You come see." And taking me by the elbow, he guided me along a narrow pathway leading through the sugarcane field, the others following closely behind, chattering excitedly as we went. Soon we came upon a clearing where a half section of a two-hundred-liter steel barrel stood, topped off with a piece of hardboard being held down with two rocks.

"You look inside," the old man gestured, "You find Gaboon—fifty rand, please [approximately seven dollars in those days]?" He waved me forward.

I was beginning to understand now. Removing the rocks and then the board, I gazed into the depths of the hollow drum, my eyes taking a few seconds to properly adjust to the dark interior. And there it was—what I had been searching for all along—a beautiful specimen of a Gaboon viper. I shook my head in dismay. It appeared that anything resembling a "mamba" was taboo, the reputation of the snake being well ingrained in legend and folklore, but a Gaboon viper was no problem. And I knew why. These snakes were so scarce and elusive that only those people working in their region on a daily basis might come across one. Ever in demand amongst herpetologists and snake parks, monetary rewards were offered for their capture. Cane cutters coming across a specimen would keep it safely housed until their contact arrived to collect.

My own search for the elusive snake so far having proved fruitless, this was not an opportunity I was going to let slip by. It appeared that, irrespective of what agreement the cane cutters might have with any other party or parties, they were not overly concerned about who took possession of their captive, as long as cash changed hands. Without hesitation, I paid the price, transferred the huge snake to a secure bag, and headed back to my camp like a happy Father Christmas with his bundle of toys. Not only had I found my specimen to film, but I had also saved the snake from a life in captivity, as I would release it again into the forest once I had secured the footage I needed. All in all, this was an interesting and successful day in the life of a somewhat still in training documentary wildlife filmmaker.

ڏ ڏ ڏ

Finally, after some eight months spent in the field and seventy-two eleven-minute reels of 16 mm film exposed, I felt that my footage was sufficient and ready for editing. In South Africa I had all the reels transferred to professional Beta SP digital video. From these I had time-coded VHS copies made to work from rather than risk damaging the professional tapes.

This enabled me to do a rough-cut edit in which I would reduce my twelve hours of footage to just two hours. Thereafter, a final edit would eventually reduce it all to the desired fifty-two minutes of broadcast time allotted by NDR.

The rough cut was a major task that took me the better part of the next three months to complete, with the resulting film released in Germany as *Die Natur der schlange* (*The Nature of the Snake*). The film was received with great enthusiasm in Europe and nominated for an award at the Grenoble Film Festival in France. Needless to say, I was thrilled.

Following the completion of *The Nature of the Snake*, I became, to a lesser degree, partly involved in the making of numerous documentaries featuring lions, baboons, vultures, desert elephants, and wild dogs. On occasion I was recruited to shoot reptile footage needed in the production of other reptile documentaries that were being produced at the time. However, remembering the unusual behavior I had witnessed while filming the desert chameleon section of *The Nature of the Snake*, another idea was forming in my head. It was an idea that would later result in the production of my second full-length wildlife documentary, to be titled *Dragons of the Namib*.

Thus, some time later, I once more found myself back in the great sand dunes of the Namib Desert, this time with my eye looking through the viewfinder of a newly acquired video camera specifically purchased for the making of my proposed project, a project that I believed in so strongly that I was prepared to attempt it alone, with or without encouragement from outside financial sources. It had become obvious to me that this was me at my most content. Admittedly it is a risky business; however, for anyone who loves nothing more than to live in a vehicle or remote tent-camp locations while recording the secret behavioral patterns of some wild animal or reptile, the rewards are quite satisfying. It is a life of outdoor wonder filled with four-wheel-drive travel adventure, campfire nights under starlit skies, and the subdued sounds of the surrounding wilderness.

Dragons of the Namib was a project that took over seven months to complete, time that I spent mostly in the sand dunes of the Namib Desert, where I habituated and followed the daily life cycle of another extraordinary female desert chameleon I named Ependa ("the brave one," in the language of the local Namibian Herero people). The film was later released on the National Geographic Channel, where it proved to be extremely popular and is still being aired today, some thirteen years later.

It was soon after the completion of this documentary film that I was approached by Tigress Productions, a UK-based film production company, that enquired if I thought it might be possible to make a one-episode documentary about my work in the field—how I locate reptiles and photograph them. I said that I believed this to be possible and, after a meeting in Bristol, the project was confirmed, with work beginning almost immediately. Little did I suspect at the time that it would be the beginning of a new era in my life, an era that would take me to the far reaches of the planet in search of wilderness and reptiles that I could otherwise only have dreamt of or imagined. It was to be an experience of mind-boggling proportions.

Chapter 12

The Making of *Snakemaster*

As must be expected when venturing out into wilderness regions of the globe in search of wild animals to film in close proximity, there will be risks involved. Though every precaution was taken to ensure the safety of myself and my team, the whole idea of the film was to demonstrate how certain wild animals live and behave. This to some degree necessitated that we expose ourselves to certain scenarios and conditions that were oftentimes potentially dangerous.

In particular, as "action presenter," I was expected not only to get as close to my subjects as possible but also to deliver a running commentary as I did so, simultaneously dividing my attention between the necessary camera angles and exposing myself to the particular wild animal at that time in my presence. And anyone who knows anything about working with wild animals will tell you that losing concentration for even one second, while doing the latter could lead to the unthinkable.

Not one to waste time, right at the beginning of it all, I simply went straight in and did just that—lost concentration for one second and almost paid the price.

In retrospect, I should not be surprised. I was new to the business of "action" film presenting. Sure, I had a world of experience in the handling of venomous reptiles. Certainly I had plenty of experience giving lectures and entertaining the crowds. However, with each of those scenarios, I was in complete control of every element of the action. Now suddenly

I was attached to a radio microphone that recorded every breath I took, every sound I made. Overhead was a boom microphone, and two video cameras were pointed at me from different angles. I needed to deliver not only the action but also the angles and dialogue that make up the stuff of adventure documentary filmmaking. (Sound recording is a complicated business and easily distorted, thus two systems were employed wherever practically possible.)

As if this was not enough, it had to all be done with stylish enthusiasm, for cinematic effect. *Holy mackerel!* And that first mistake I made could so easily have ended it all before it had even begun.

In spite of a few unfortunate "mishaps," I still consider myself one of the luckier herpetologists in that I have had few dangerous bites, even though I have, for the purpose of manufacturing antivenom, extracted venom from hundreds of snakes, performed countless public shows and lectures and have spent years in the field catching and photographing venomous snakes. However, of these accidents, without question, the most embarrassing remains the snake-bite I endured from the snouted cobra encountered on my very first shoot as *Austin Stevens, Action Presenter.*

There I was, some eighty kilometers out in the field, about to show my daring skills with a huge snouted cobra that I had just enticed out from under a long, dead log in the Swakop Riverbed. As familiar with cobras as I am, having worked with so many over the years, I did not calculate for the potential capability of such an old and wizened specimen. As a slightly improvised old saying might go, *familiarity breeds complacency.*

As is usual for African cobras, the snake struck out at me deliberately as I hunched down close to it. Expertly I flipped my arm out of reach of the strike. I had done this so many times before that my reaction was second nature. With the action picking up now, the camera crew moved in for closer effect as the cobra struck out again . . . but this time in an unusually angled direction, resulting with one fang just catching my index finger as it was speedily being retracted.

Suddenly there was a rush of blood, and I was quick to realize that a vein had been penetrated. There is no more serious bite than a venous bite. By this route the venom can very quickly be transported throughout the body. The realization struck me that I might have only minutes to live!

My first rule of filming has always been, where possible, to *keep filming*, no matter what. I feel it is important to record every incident, planned or unplanned. Even in the case of a life-threatening occurrence, as this now turned out to be, I felt it important to keep one camera rolling, lest it all be for nothing. There were enough members in the team to lend assistance while still having one cameraman operating. I was very serious about this. Thus, under my explicit instruction, one cameraman somewhat reluctantly kept rolling while other crew members gathered around to do what they could to assist me.

Having antivenom with me, I began preparing for treatment should it be necessary. On closer examination of the wound, I concluded that the fang had sliced *through* the vein rather than injected *into* it. Hope flared as I considered the possibility that the initial rush of blood may have flushed away any venom. Hurriedly packing up our equipment into the two vehicles at our disposal, we steadily made our way back across the burning desert, heading for the Cottage Hospital in Swakopmund.

Covering the distance in record time, at the hospital I was placed under observation for two hours, after which time it was decided my life was most likely not in any danger, though further observation was advised. However, I felt certain that, had any venom entered my bloodstream, I should long ago have registered the effects. I now experienced an overriding need to get the job done. Against my better judgment, and that of the medical staff, I led the crew back out into the field in the unlikelihood that I could locate that cobra again and complete the shoot.

With my finger all bandaged up and fairly painful, I must admit I was feeling weak, somewhat disorientated, and nervous. I felt that I had to do this immediately, so as not to lose my nerve. *Can't afford to be a ninny!*

As luck would have it, and as I had dared to hope, the cobra had simply returned to the security of its log, probably quite pleased with itself for having nailed me on the finger earlier in the day. And, as could be expected, the snake was not thrilled to see me again. Immediately going into the offensive, it rushed towards me, hood raised menacingly. The snake struck out viciously, exerting as much effort as possible in a blatant attempt to kill this *man-thing* that would not go away. This, in conjunction with the bloody footage of the actual bite, and the treatment administered in the field and at the hospital, was in itself a winning combination to be cut into the sequence.

Finally I was able to deliver my piece to camera while simultaneously demonstrating the snake's behavior and defensive strategy. I knew it would hold any audience spellbound. Snapping up dozens of close-up shots as the cobra dramatically postured just inches from my Canon 35–105 mm lens, I secretly rejoiced in my returning confidence in the face of such a magnificent and potentially dangerous adversary. Finally, the action over, the shoot all wrapped up, we all breathed a sigh of relief. The snake, too, by this time aware that it was obviously not in any real danger from this antagonizing human, got bored and headed off to the closest tangle of bush.

I sat down, suddenly seized by a burst of uncontrollable shakes. This was not an action I wanted to repeat too often. Little did we suspect at the time that this film, which became known as *Seven Deadly Strikes*, would eventually lead to the making of the hugely popular *Austin Stevens: Snakemaster, Austin Stevens: Most Dangerous,* and, later on, *Austin Stevens Adventures,* which was a big-budget series of twenty-eight episodes that would be some eight years in the making.

My idea behind the scripting of the series was basic: I outlined it on just a few typed pages, noting down what reptiles and animals on the planet were of most interest to me. I then categorized these animals according to the countries they could most likely be located in, and set off to go find and expose them to the world of nature television. There was no script as such, just a rudimentary idea that could be built on and altered according to how matters progressed . . . or regressed, as might be the case.

The serious planning came with arranging flights to locations, places of accommodation, and the transport of everything that would be needed on each individual expedition. This was handled by a base team who worked tirelessly at their respective offices before, during, after, and between each shoot. The crews for the early episodes of the series, including myself, consisted of eight people. This number was later reduced to six as carefully calculated budget money was steadily eaten away by rising travel and production costs. Most of the crew was based in the UK, but others were from South Africa, Canada, USA, and Australia, with my calling Namibia home at the time. As much as possible, it was important to have the same members of the team recruited for each expedition so as to build up familiarity and work experience together. However, this was not always possible, as most members of the team were invariably freelance operators, often committed to other projects.

The transportation of film equipment was an eternal nightmare and cost throughout the making of the series, with sometimes as many as fifty heavy metal cases needing to be flown to airports around the world, from where they would then have to be further transported overland, often to some seriously inhospitable places over difficult terrain. Not all of the equipment was used all the time, of course, but it was essential that we not find ourselves missing something when the need arose. This was to be a big-budget series, compared with others in a similar class, with provision being made for the use of two high-definition video cameras, a 16 mm film camera, two lesser digital video cameras, twelve high-speed Nikon motor-driven still cameras for time-slice operation, and a nine-meter collapsible camera crane.

There were heavy battery packs, miles of cables, body-cam equipment (a complicated body-fit mechanism which allows supported free-roaming movement of a heavy video camera), reels of film, one hundred one-hour cassettes of video tape, mountain and tree climbing gear, tool boxes, lighting equipment and stands, tripods, monitors, sound-recording equipment with more battery packs and more digital tapes, diving equipment and underwater-camera housings . . . the list was seemingly endless. Vehicles and drivers were hired to transport all of this to and from airports, oftentimes in areas of difficult terrain. Local porters would be employed to physically carry the necessary equipment on their shoulders, sometimes with the aid of horses, camels, mules, and, on one location in India, even an elephant.

Some locations would necessitate as many as five flights with aircraft of varying sizes to reach the designated destination. Four-wheel-drive vehicles were used where roads or tracks were available, boats and canoes where water was encountered. Horses and mules most often played a part, while the rest of it was up to hard, physical manpower. Desert areas usually allowed for a minimum of transportation problems, while jungle travel usually consumed everything available at our disposal just to get through.

It is important to note that, from the onset, it was decided that the filming of this series was to be as thorough as a full feature-film production, with every effort being put into the artistic and wide-screen creative design at the time, incorporating only the top people and equipment available. This was not to be a happy-go-lucky, over-the-shoulder, one-camera production. It was to be a cinematic experience for the viewer, as much as it was planned to be an exciting adventure, taking place through twenty-five countries around the world.

Thinking back now, considering all that we had to contend with, it is a wonder that we managed the energy, stamina, and patience to finally capture the action sequences that we did.

CHAPTER 13

THE GIANT RETICULATED PYTHON OF BORNEO

Reptiles being my specialty, it was decided that the entire first series would revolve exclusively around these fascinating creatures. The bigger and deadlier, the better! This was to be Austin Stevens at his best . . . or worst, depending on who was to be the judge. Anybody in the business knows that being on television potentially affords one the opportunity to disappoint the entire watching population at one time. So at least there was no pressure.

Though the pilot episode, *Seven Deadly Strikes*, featured venomous snakes only, nonvenomous snakes can also be potentially dangerous. The largest and heaviest-bodied snakes found on the planet are nonvenomous. As mentioned earlier, these giant serpents have rows of long, needle-sharp teeth fixed in their jaws, and, though these snakes can have a terrible bite, they have no apparatus for delivering venom. A person unlucky enough to be seriously bitten by one of the so-called "giant snake" species will need stitches rather than antivenom. These snakes are constrictors, the recurved teeth designed only to secure the prey. With these teeth firmly imbedded, the snake then pulls the prey animal into its waiting coils. Once trapped within the coils, escape is impossible, and death by constriction a certainty.

Some of these snakes measure over seven meters in length, with unsubstantiated records claiming nine meters and more. Whatever the case, a six-meter-plus snake is a powerful creature, capable of constricting an adult human. Fortunately these large serpents do not usually consider humans as prey but will not hesitate to defend themselves if threatened . . .

especially if it is an Asian reticulated python, the longest recorded species in the world, and well documented for its irritable temper and eager inclination to bite. Was there any doubt then that I should end up on the wrong side of one of these?

I had of course on numerous occasions previously, while working with captive specimens, experienced the muscle power generated by giant snakes. Once when tackling a large green anaconda in the Amazon, I came close to being drowned by the sheer weight of the reptile. The anaconda is potentially the second-longest snake in the world, while at the same time being recognized as the heaviest bodied, capable of catching and constricting prey as large as a donkey.

However, though the anaconda I tackled naturally tried to bite me in self-defense and easily pulled me into the water in an attempt to break free of my grip, it made no attempt to constrict me, rather concentrating all of its efforts on escape. It is generally accepted amongst herpetologists that constrictors apply their constricting technique only to kill their prey, not as a self-defense strategy. So what went wrong in Borneo?

ൟ ൟ ൟ

Borneo is one of the largest islands on the planet, much of which is covered in dense jungle and undisturbed by human encroachment. It was here that I set out to find the reticulated python. I had worked with a four-meter specimen in captivity, a snake so powerful that I was unable to control it alone and needed at least two other keepers to assist me. So you can imagine my dismay when I came upon a specimen almost seven meters long, alive and well . . . and defiant!

Amazingly, after spending many hours tracking the snake through the undergrowth, I was disappointed when first I spotted it amongst the roots of a tree submerged in a slow-moving stream. The parts of the body that were visible suggested that it was a specimen of less than average size, I guessed around four meters. A formidable snake to be sure, but not the giant snake I was seeking to catch on film. The pieces of discarded skin that

I had collected along the way suggested that the snake was in the process of shedding. This would explain the reptile's submerging itself in the water, to help loosen the old skin.

The size of a snake's head usually gives a good indication of what lies behind it. However, though I could see parts of this reptile's body through the murky water, there was no sign of the head. A snake is capable of remaining submerged for long periods of time on only a single breath. This made me somewhat nervous, as I was well aware of the danger of a strike from those tooth-filled jaws. Nonetheless, having pointed out the submerged snake to my crew, and giving them time enough to prepare their cameras and sound apparatus, I approached cautiously.

"Keep some distance," I warned my first cameraman as he closed in behind and slightly to the side of me. "I am not sure exactly what we have here." Further back, encompassing a wider view, the second cameraman positioned himself. Above my head the sound technician's hand held a microphone suspended on an extendable boom pole, ready to take in every sound. On my belt was a battery clip feeding the tiny microphone fastened to the inside of my collar.

As I approached, the brightly patterned coils of muscled body just below the surface did not move, not even a ripple. The body was partly obscured by a tangle of roots growing down into the water. Bracing myself with legs spread wide and shoulders hunched, I carefully pushed my right arm through the closest coils, right up to the elbow, and pulled upward with all my might.

Expecting to heave the snake bodily out of the water with one powerful, fluid motion, I was somewhat taken aback when nothing happened . . . the coils did not budge. Grunting, I tried again, forcing my arm in deeper and encircling what I imagined to be a number of slippery coils at one time. Spreading myself now with one leg up to the knee in the water, I reinforced my grip to once more apply all my strength in an upward motion. Still nothing happened. I was baffled; it was like trying to lift a tree stump!

For the first time, I contemplated the possibility that this reptile, barely visible below the surface of the murky water, might be somewhat bigger than previously anticipated. Or possibly the snake might have attached itself to the underwater root system growing down from the overhead tree.

Fully aware that the cameras were all the while still rolling, I changed position. With both legs now in the water, I recklessly plunged both arms in amongst the reluctant coils of snake in a now-desperate attempt to bring them to the surface. I needed to get this snake out of the water and onto dry land, where I could better evaluate its size and deliver a piece to the waiting camera.

And it was at this very moment, bent over forward with both my arms encircling the coils of the resisting snake, that I saw the bubbles suddenly rise to the surface, not 50 centimeters from my face, followed closely through the murky gloom by an enormous head. And I knew, without any shadow of doubt that, if I did not drop everything and leap for safety, I was going to lose my face . . . *literally.* My experience with the African rock python in the stormswater drain all those years ago remained forever etched in my mind. I clearly recalled the frightening agony of it and did not even want to imagine what would be the outcome of a similar scenario now with a huge reticulated python . . . the meanest of all the python species.

"Get back!" I screamed to the team, as the water in front of my eyes seemed to boil to life. "Get back!"

And like an offshore volcano erupting through the surface of the sea, the giant snake's head exploded upward, jaws wide open, baring six rows of glistening teeth, curved like hooks. Upward it came, gushing water ahead of it as I desperately released my grip and hurled myself back and to the side for all I was worth. Like a gleaming lance, the head rose up towards me, and, though I was fast and agile, I had no hope of avoiding the inevitable. Missing my face by centimeters, the huge mouth shot passed my turned head to unerringly redirect towards the next most obvious movement . . . my flailing arm.

At first there was no pain, just a powerful sensation of tugging, with my arm being forced behind my back. Then came the seething mass of coils spewing forth from the water. A seemingly endless stream of body as thick as my thigh effortlessly flowing out of the water towards me, enveloping me whole. And I was suddenly rudely awakened to the fact that, unwittingly, I now found myself on the wrong end of the biggest and most powerful snake I had ever tackled. I had overlooked the signs, misjudged the scale of what I saw, and once more rendered myself into the arms of disaster.

I have heard it suggested that I am "accident prone." I strongly disagree with this rather fatalistic statement and offer instead the fact that I just simply do a lot of different things that are dangerous. However, I do not offer any excuse for myself when delivering myself into trouble by my own stupidity. I am well aware of the fact that large pythons are known to submerge themselves in shallow water in wait of potential prey approaching to drink. And though these snakes generally do not consider humans as prey, it is known that children and small adults have been taken, more by mistake than by plan. Any movement approaching the submerged snake would be considered prey. In this case, I was it. And having now hooked its rows of inch-long, needle-like teeth into my body and with its killer instinct fully aroused, the snake was bringing its powerful coils into play to constrict its prey to death.

My team was, of course, as shocked as I was by the sudden eruption of unpredicted action. From one second to the next the whole scene had metamorphosed from serene exploration to explosive action of potentially life-threatening proportions. Still somewhat stunned by this turn of events, I only fully began to realize my predicament when the first coils began to apply pressure; I was suddenly aware of the fact that I was powerless in the snake's hold. I had never in my life before felt such raw power.

This was not the four-meter snake I had imagined when first spotting it in the water. This was a much larger snake, possibly close to the seven-meter mark, a snake easily capable of constricting an adult human. It was too late now to explain to the snake that this was all a big mistake, that I was not in fact its preferred prey. Instinct ruled the action, and with its mouth firmly gripping my arm for leverage, the giant snake pursued the process of constriction.

Forced to the ground at the edge of the water on the bank of the stream now, with all my strength I attempted to remove myself from the grip of the coils, but to no avail, as more coils slowly worked their way around my body. Bright red blood flowed freely from the lacerations inflicted by the teeth embedded in my arm, steadily soaking into my shirt sleeve. Frantically struggling to grip the head of the snake with my free hand in the vain hope that I might dislodge it, the upper most coil around my shoulder suddenly slipped up and onto my neck. Sensing the gap, the giant snake quickly applied pressure to take up the slack. It was at that moment that I knew I was in serious trouble, and out of my depth. The giant coil, thick as my upper leg, was now applying pressure to my neck. Added to the pressure already being steadily increased around my chest, within seconds I could not breathe and, with my last exhaling breath, I screamed for help.

True to the professionalism on the part of my crew, and our original agreement, I had been left alone to handle what I was there to do: wrangle snakes and display them to the viewing public in all their forms, shapes, sizes . . . and temperaments. And though obviously aware that matters had taken a somewhat unexpected turn, the cameramen had continued to film regardless, even when aware of the seriousness of the initial attack and the blood flowing from my bitten arm. However, all this changed instantly on my call for help, and within seconds there were three people around me, desperately, nervously, grabbing at coils of snake.

"Grab the body!" I called out, the sound of my voice stifled by the pressure on my throat. "Grab the body and unwind it!"

By now I had a grip on the neck of the snake, just behind the head, ensuring that it would not suddenly strike out at anybody else. As it turned out, this was not an issue, as the snake doggedly continued to maintain its grip on my arm, as is its nature. Releasing its grip before the prey has stopped struggling might render the prey able to retaliate, often with sharp teeth or claws that might injure the snake. Instinctively, it held on and continued to apply pressure, while all around me my crew grabbed and pulled and strained to remove the powerful reptile from my body. This was no easy task, as the snake relentlessly fought back.

It is not easy to describe the muscle power that is present in the body of a seven-meter reticulated python, but eventually with three men pulling on the lower coils and another two assisting me with the upper section, I was freed enough to breathe again and eventually escape those deadly coils. I had worked with many giant snakes in the past, and so had some inclination of their strength, but never before had I experienced the true power of such a snake in feeding mode. This is when a constricting snake exerts *all* its power, knowing that its life depends on holding its prey securely. It is not unusual to find large pythons in the wild displaying old healed wounds received from badly caught prey animals that were able to retaliate.

Finding itself under "attack" from multiple enemies, thankfully the python finally released its grip on my arm to try and defend itself by attempting to bite those closest to it. A fortunate occurrence indeed, as it is not a simple matter to remove so many recurved teeth from your flesh if the snake in question does not cooperate.

Gripping the snake behind the head with both hands now, I was at least able to ensure that nobody else gets bitten. Blood flowed freely from my lacerated arm, but as is the case with sharp razor cuts, and thanks to the fact that the teeth had been voluntarily dislodged and not forcibly removed, the flow soon slowed and congealed. The wounds stung but were not unbearably painful, nor did I consider them terribly serious, as only a dozen or so teeth had actually penetrated. I had been lucky . . . *very lucky!* And I do not want to even think about what would have happened if that enormous mouth full of teeth had struck me in the face!

"Thanks guys," I said, breathing a sigh of relief as the giant coils were finally being disengaged from my body. "I'll take it from here. Get ready . . . once I let go of the head we're going to have one angry monster to contend with."

With great relief everybody scrambled for their equipment and positions, grateful to make distance between themselves and the seething mass of powerful coils and that giant head filled with teeth.

Out of the water now and spread out on the open ground alongside the little stream, this particular reticulated python now proved itself to be just as bad tempered in real life as was reputed in text—not surprising, as it had been subjected to such abuse and the loss of its "prey." While the film crew scrambled to recover their hastily dropped equipment—and I for my camera—the giant snake raised its head up high, over a meter into the air, and slithered after me with vengence in its eyes, lunging at me repeatedly as I attempted to photograph it. I had never before seen anything like this. Without question, this snake held a grudge and was determined to settle the score. Again and again it raised its head up high, chased after me wherever I positioned myself, and struck out viciously, its mouth extended at full stretch, showing rows of recurved teeth, a few still stained red from my blood.

I have seen countless snakes show aggression when called upon to defend themselves, but they quickly regain their composure and head for cover when the danger is passed. Never before had I seen a snake actually lose its temper and actively seek revenge! This is the only way I can think to describe its behavior. By this time the snake was well aware that I was not its usual prey, and was certainly not interested in eating me, but it was still dedicated to biting me some more, as though this might in some satisfactory way compensate for the 'abuse' it had endured in my presence.

This was also the first time I was not able to physically *release* a snake I had been working with back into the wild. Defiant to the end, the giant snake refused to depart, watching our every move, daring us to come closer. Keeping a wary eye on the ever-present serpent and with enough fascinating footage recorded, we finally packed up and headed back into the jungle, the crew nervously looking back over their shoulders as though fearful the irate snake might follow.

That evening back at our camp, discussions were solely dedicated to the day's unusual encounter, the director even suggesting that the giant snake might search us out in the dark of the night, seeking revenge. Everyone laughed out loud, as it was a somewhat humorous and unlikely scenario. But when the campfire was extinguished and we settled into our flimsy tents, with a myriad of mysterious and unidentifiable jungle sounds frequenting our ears . . . not a single man or woman amongst us that night slept with less than at least one eye open.

CHAPTER 14

THE KOMODO DRAGON ACCIDENT

Venomous snake-bites were naturally high on the list of potential accidents that might occur during our excursions, considering the nature of the series we were making, but there were other dangers as well. There were spiders, mosquitoes, leeches, stinging plants, ticks, and waterborne diseases to consider, not to mention extreme weather conditions, food poisoning, precarious plane flights and landings, crime and terrorism, viruses . . . with the list going on and on. Many of these we experienced in one form or another and at one time or another, but never anything serious enough to halt production of the film series. But it is often those things that one least expects that may sometimes bring about the worst scenarios. And so it was to be on the Komodo Islands, where we found ourselves in search of the largest and most ferocious lizard in the world: the Komodo dragon.

These giant lizards were first discovered in the early twentieth century on the Southern Indonesian Islands of Komodo, from where their name derives. Direct descendants of a fifteen-meter-long reptile that lived some fifty million years ago, there are today only a few thousand surviving, scattered amongst a handful of islands: Flores, Padar, Gili Motang, Rinca, and Komodo. As is usual where wildlife is concerned, these magnificent remnants from the age of dinosaurs have been forced out of other islands because of human pressures. These flesh-eating giants of the lizard world can weigh up to 160 kilograms and reach lengths of over three meters. Their mouths are rimmed with rows of bacteria-laden, serrated teeth, which are flat, serrated, and shark-like. Reliant on their powerful jaws and their formidable dentition to secure their prey, Komodo dragons, like most reptiles, replace broken or dislodged teeth continuously, so as to never be without. The serrated teeth, which are situated towards the front of their jaw, allow for tearing chunks of flesh from their prey, which they swallow down whole. These usually consist of wild pigs, deer, or even water buffalo. There have also been some recorded cases of humans being taken.

Armed with powerful claws, shark-like teeth, and a muscular tail, Komodo dragons are formidable creatures capable of actively hunting down and killing large prey. Though their preferred prey is the Sunda deer and wild pigs, Komodos will also feed on carrion (dead animals). By constantly flicking their forked tongues in and out of their mouths, they collect scent particles from the air (as do snakes), which are analyzed in the Jacobson's organ situated on the roof of their mouth. This powerful sense of smell enables the dragons to detect their prey—and carrion—from kilometers away.

The high-toxicity saliva bacteria present in the mouth of a Komodo dragon is acquired while eating carrion, the lizard's mouths affording the bacteria a prime habitat in which to thrive. If prey is not immediately killed and escapes, the highly dangerous bacteria from the dragon's saliva quickly bring about infection. The Komodo then tracks the scent of the prey as the wounded animal slowly weakens from the infected bite, a process that can take several days.

Komodo dragons are extremely territorial reptiles, and males will fight other males to gain mating right to females. This species is considered to be one of the most intelligent reptiles on the planet, and the people of the Komodo Islands revere them as a mystical ancestors, treating them with respect.

వ వ వ

Our first stop was to visit a cave on the island of Flores, midway between Australia and Indonesia, where scientists had recently discovered evidence of a hobbit-like species of humans that grew no taller than a meter. The species inhabited Flores as recently as thirteen thousand years ago, which means it would have lived at the same time as modern humans. Skeletons of these tiny humans were found in the same sediment deposits on Flores that have also been found to contain stone tools and bones of dwarf elephants, giant rodents, and Komodo dragons. This suggests that these little people lived side by side with Komodo dragons, possibly hunting them . . . or being hunted by them. It was unanimously decided that a visit to the caves on Flores was a must for opening our story, to introduce our adventure with Komodo dragons.

Once again it was to be an elaborate expedition to ensure a top-quality production incorporating a team of porters, guides, boats of various sizes, and even a helicopter. With the caves situated some distance into the jungle over rough terrain, boxes of equipment had to be laboriously transported by hand through the wet, steaming undergrowth. With the high humidity, sweat poured off our bodies. Once inside the complex of caverns, we were forced to climb up rickety pole ladders held together with strips of woven bark and through jagged limestone tunnels that scraped our knees and ripped our clothes. Here the air was cooler but even more humid. More sweat poured off our bodies.

The Flores caves are unusual in that many areas open up into the light of day, enabling vegetation to take root at various locations. This encourages wildlife species to seek refuge and shelter within the caves. Along the way I found a monitor lizard, which gave me a merry chase as I attempted to catch it for display on camera and for some personal pictures of my own. Shortly thereafter, on an overhead ledge hidden by cascading branches from an unknown tree taken root there, I came across a juvenile reticulated python of about three meters long.

Small in size—compared with the one I tackled in Borneo—but true to its well documented disposition, the snake immediately struck at me as I climbed up towards where it lay. Once in hand after a few near-miss strikes, the irate snake proceeded to show its further displeasure by defecating all over me and attempting, any which way, to strangle me as I struggled to display it for the camera. It was like trying to hold an octopus, and I made short work of the scene, releasing the snake back where I had found it as quickly as possible. Experience was teaching me that reticulated pythons, large or small, were not snakes to fool with.

Finally we came to the mouth of two huge intersecting caverns, where the director decided we would stage the opening introductory scene. It was to be a simple scene, with me walking casually along through the various caverns describing where we were and why—nothing dramatic from me, just an introduction to the episode with the spectacular dimly lit caverns as the backdrop.

Within minutes the area was littered with equipment as the team set up for the shoot. A cameraman controlling a body-cam was to follow at my side as I walked, while a fifty-meter cable system was being rigged to swing another cameraman overhead as I passed a particular area of the cave. Battery-operated studio lights were strategically employed to create diffused ambiance, and special sound arrangements were set up at various points along my route, as well as on my person, to clearly record my every word through the echo of the caverns. A forward camera incorporating a long lens would film my walk-and-talk head-on, from a distance. A full day's work for an estimated thirty seconds of film . . . but what a spectacular setting for an introduction. It would all be worth it.

There is a certain tense anticipation when the introduction to each new episode is about to be filmed. Much care is taken, every detail considered, as we know that this scene must procure the interest of any watching audience and immediately draw them in. In the case of a scripted scene, as this was to be, I would as best possible distance myself from everybody beforehand, to memorize what must be said and consider how I should deliver the piece. Most times it was certain that numerous takes would be necessary to finally get everything synchronized to the satisfaction of the director, the sound engineer, and, in this case, the three cameramen. No pressure here. . . ?

The short distance I was to cover while delivering my opening introduction would take me along a steep-sided ledge and through an archway that led to an outside opening. My simple introduction would be naturally dramatized by the wondrous surroundings of the actual cave itself as much as by the content of my words. Three times I practiced the walk, repeating my lines as I did so, pacing myself so as to make it all fit exactly to scale. With three cameras running—one of them passing overhead at a fair speed—timing was critical. All around me the bustle of organization and preparation of equipment echoed along the cave walls. Finally the director came over to where I was rehearsing.

"Ready when you are," he said, looking at me enquiringly. I was once again reminded that everything hinged around me. All the people here on location—my six-man crew, the porters, the guides, the helicopter and pilot on standby, the boats and crew waiting in the bay, not to mention all those working around the clock back in the edit studios in the UK—were all in one way or another relying on me to deliver.

I swallowed nervously. I am always nervous when preparing for a scripted piece, especially introductions and endings. Throw a cobra in my way and watch me go, with plenty to say and do without having to give it a second thought. But tell me I have to deliver a specific selection of words and phrases in a particular order and in a specific time, and I get butterflies in my stomach. This has been the case with me for as long as I can remember.

"All set," I replied, sounding more confident than I felt. But I knew I would get into the swing of things once we were running. No problem.

Okay, let's do this. And turning to face the crew, the director called out, "Places, please. First take. When you're ready." And looking around critically, he added, "Clear the floor please. Move those cases out of sight . . . and the ropes, please. All those not participating . . . out of sight now! Thank you."

There followed a few moments of shuffling and maneuvering until finally all movement and sound ceased.

Looking around critically, and now removing himself to a safe location from where to oversee it all, the director made final calls:

"Camera one . . . ?" And from the camera one operator . . . "Speed!"

"Camera two . . . ?" And from the second camera operator . . . "Speed!"

"Camera three, overhead . . . ?" And from the third operator, hoisted high above in a harness and pulley system ready to be released . . . "Speed!"

"Sound . . . ?" And from the soundman . . . "Rolling!"

And with one last critical look around . . . "Quiet please! . . . And . . . ACTION!"

Suddenly everything was in motion. Cameras and sound equipment were all around me as I walked along my designated route, rattling off my piece. Other than the delicate timing required for the scene, it should have been a fairly simple shoot. And indeed all was going well . . . right until a loose stone dislodged under my booted foot, twisting my ankle sharply and forcing me to stumble and fall to the left off the steep edge I had been negotiating, and gravity hurled me down towards the jagged rocks below—all in one split second of time!

A searing pain tore through my ankle and calf as I fell. In that moment, registering the rocks rushing up to meet me, I twisted my body in the air, offering my back rather than my face and chest to absorb the inevitable collision. With my full body weight now behind the fall, I hit the jagged rocks with terrible force, screaming as I did so. Pain exploded through my back, as though the very life were being crushed out of me. Terrible, terrible pain forced the air from my lungs and left me gasping for air that would not come. Desperately I screamed in agony, only to find myself rendered incapable of anything more than a hoarse, breathless howl, followed by suffocating blackness.

Consciousness returned within seconds, my mouth wide open and my chest burning like fire from the lack of oxygen. My head hurled backwards, and I desperately tried to catch my breath, but with no way to make it happen. As my diaphragm and surrounding muscles spasmed from the crushing blow they had received, the laryngeal muscles contracted to produce only an aspiratory strident sound.

And the pain of it was terrible!

Suddenly my team was at my side, worried faces looking down on me, frightened and unsure of what to do.

"He's struggling to breathe!" The director called in alarm. "Get him onto level ground, quickly!" The sound of his voice filtered through the roaring agony that suffused my body and brain. Hands reached for me as my vision once again grew dark, the agony multiplying as my constricted diaphragm stubbornly refused to relax. I knew I was suffocating, and I was rendered powerless to do anything about it.

Then suddenly, as I was bodily lifted to level ground, air miraculously flooded back into my lungs! Like a burst of fire, it came in, almost as painful as when it had been so dramatically forced out. Then another breath . . . and another . . . each one less painful than the last. The dimness in my brain cleared, as did my vision. I was alive and could breathe again. *Oh, thank you! Thank you! Thank you!* Never before had good old everyday taken-for-granted air felt so good in my lungs.

My euphoria was short-lived, however, as with the return of my breath I was now able to focus on the advancing pain in my ankle, already swelling at an alarming rate. My back, too, pained terribly with each breath I took, and I knew with some certainty that some of my ribs were broken. Stubbornly, I tried to stand up, feeling the need to be vertical.

"Don't move!" ordered the director, as he stared down into my face, his hands feeling through my hair, presumably for signs of a head injury. "Stay still until we can assess your condition." He turned to the others gathered around. "Get the medical kit, and bring me the sat [satellite] phone. This shoot is over."

His words struck me like a blow to the stomach. This could not be happening! Surely this was just a little setback; I would be fine again in a day or so! Again I attempted to raise myself, this time using my foot to push with . . . and the pain of it seared up my leg like fire. Screaming in agony I looked down, and for the first time began to comprehend the true dimensions of my injury.

My entire foot had swollen to twice its normal size, with a purplish, yellowish tinge already beginning to show. If not broken, then at the very least my tendons were torn. This was to be a long-term recovery. I shifted my position slightly, a move that rendered a spasm of pain through my back, a reminder that there was *that* little matter to consider as well!

Remaining at my side where I lay on the floor of the cave, the director continued to issue a string of orders. It was imperative that I be moved back to base camp as quickly as possible. A difficult route lay ahead, as we had to head back out through the cave system, followed by some miles of dense jungle with rough terrain. We had walked in carrying all our kit and equipment. I would be lucky to get myself up and out in one piece.

My whole body now seemed wracked in agony. Having rested on the hard floor for some twenty minutes, I once again, with the aid of several crew members, attempted to get myself vertical. My breath came in short, fast, painful gasps, with the agony in my foot doubling in size as the blood flowed down towards the stricken limb.

Psychologically, at least, standing erect made me feel better. There is no more demoralizing a feeling than being laid out on the ground in pain, especially in front of my crew. But I was up now and determined to remain so. One of the local guides appeared with a crudely fashioned, forked branch cut from a nearby root system, which he presented to me for a crutch. Crude though it may have been, it did the job admirably, and I thanked him. I could now hobble along under my own steam, mostly unsupported.

All around me the crew was hurrying to pack up the set in preparation for leaving the area, while two local porters were dispatched ahead to report our situation to base camp. From there an attempt would be made to drive a vehicle as close to us as possible so that I might be transferred to the closest town in search of a doctor. Meanwhile the first priority was to get me out of the cave system itself and back out into the jungle. This was the more difficult of the many hurdles that lay ahead, as we had to negotiate the steep climbs up and down the same rickety pole ladders we had scaled on the way in. This took two hours to achieve, with every step of the way offering a new experience in agony.

Finally emerging from the mouth of the great exterior cavern, our bodies drenched in sweat, we were greeted by the smiling faces of the two local porters sent ahead to report our situation and organize a vehicle. This they now proudly displayed to us in the form of a dilapidated 100 cc Yamaha motorcycle that had definitely seen better days. And while incongruous at first, it made sense. Where the bulk of a four-wheeled vehicle could not possibly pass through the dense undergrowth to get close to our position, a motorbike certainly could, as they had themselves now proved. Consideration of how exactly I was, in my condition, supposed to be transported back through the jungle on this vehicle seemed not to have been calculated.

The director, meanwhile, via satellite phone, had finally made contact with our "fixer," Charlie, who was based in Bali, the person overall in charge of our arrangements concerning the expedition. On hearing of our predicament, Charlie immediately set the wheels in motion for my extraction from the island. There was apparently no adequate medical facility on the island itself, other than a lone doctor who dispensed simple medicines from his home.

"I will contact the SOS doctors' team immediately," Charlie's voice emerged through static over the satellite phone. "They'll be on the next flight out. If you can get Austin comfortable in a room somewhere in the town, I'll arrange that the local doctor at least take a look at him."

"How long before the SOS team arrives?" The director asked, sweat running down his face and onto the satellite phone. He peered anxiously in my direction.

"Two days," came the reply. "The only flight to the island is in two days time. You just have to sit tight. Let me know when you get back to the town and where you are. I'll get things organized from here." He rang off.

Two days? Holy mackerel! The director looked over in my direction, where I practiced clumsily to stay upright on my primitive crutch. Suddenly aware of his attention, I looked up. "What?"

"There is no proper hospital on the island. We have to get you to town and then on a flight to Bali. The next flight is in two days. How do you feel?"

Wincing with the effort just to breathe, not to mention to stand upright, I lied. "Not too bad," as I almost fell off my crutch. More frustrating than anything was the thought that the whole expedition would now be delayed for who knows how long. I could just imagine the paperwork involved in the insurance claim. One episode delayed meant the whole series would be delayed—time schedules disrupted, editing and delivery schedules extended, crew and equipment rebooked, flights and accommodation rearranged, to mention just the basics. And all this on the first day's shoot. *I had not even seen a Komodo dragon yet!* I tried not to dwell on the logistics of it, because right now I had to get myself out of this jungle in one piece. The rest would take place all in its own good time. I looked at the battered little Yamaha and grimaced. This was going to be the hard part.

"Help me onto the back of the bike and let's get going," I said, sounding more confident than I felt.

With the driver of the motorbike settled into the seat, I was carefully lifted up behind him, from where I could encircle my arms around his waist for support. Using camera tape, my crutch was somehow attached along the side of the bike, upon which I could rest my swollen leg. And with another two local porters running alongside the motorbike, we began a journey of some four kilometers through the dense jungle over terrain that no vehicle was ever meant to cross.

It was a journey of horrific proportions that I will never forget, as pain seared through my body with every bump and jolt, twice sending me into the air and off the bike as I screamed my agony to the indifferent surrounding vegetation. By the time we finally emerged from the jungle to a waiting, expectant gathering of locals and four-wheel-drive vehicles, I was reduced to a jabbering, incoherent bundle of pain. Kilometers behind, the rest of the porters and crew trudged along with full packs of equipment, not expected to arrive back till sometime after dark.

For me the worst was over, as I was carefully stretched out on the back seat of a vehicle and driven to a local lodge. There I was assisted to a room with a double bed and adjoining bathroom. Here I was to remain for the next two days and nights, during which time the local doctor came by to offer assistance and advice. I was doused with painkillers that seemed to have little effect, and finally with sleeping pills, which, thankfully, knocked me out.

The story of my accident had spread like wildfire throughout the little town, and indeed the whole of the island. Many locals visited the lodge, asking about my condition and wishing me a speedy recovery. Some even apologized for the wrath their "cave spirit" had chosen to render upon my person, assuring me that this would surely have been avoided if I had made a sacrificial offering before entering the sacred cave. A few special herbs scattered into a fire . . . some secret chantings and a chicken slaughtered by the hand of an island Shaman . . . was all it would take, seemed to be the general consensus. How come I did not know this?

Everybody on the island knows this!

The pain in my chest and back continued undiminished throughout the two days waiting for the plane to arrive from Bali. Getting to the bathroom involved carefully rolling my body off the bed to settle on hands and knees, affording me mobility enough to crawl painfully along to the bathroom toilet. The local doctor agreed with my belief that ribs were indeed broken and strapped my chest with stretch bandages, affording some slight feeling of security against my fragility rather than any actual relief of pain.

When shifting into certain positions, I could feel jagged ends of broken bones gritting against each other in my back. It was not a pleasant feeling. My ankle meanwhile remained enormously swollen and extremely tender to the touch, making it impossible to stand on. Depression set in. It was once again in my life a time to endure.

As scheduled, the Bali flight finally arrived two days later with the SOS team on board to assist and accompany me back across the ocean. Deciding to at least make use of the time and effort already expended in getting to Flores, some of the film crew remained behind to shoot as much footage as possible of scenic views and any other aspects of the island that might be usable when we finally returned to complete the shoot. The director and the production coordinator traveled with me to Bali.

The turbo-prop, twenty-seat plane was cramped and uncomfortable, but we made good time. Within two hours I was in hospital and being X-rayed. The result proved my assumption correct, with no less than four ribs completely snapped off close to the spine. My ankle, on the other hand, showed no break, but tendons and muscle had been badly torn, a serious condition that could leave permanent weakness if not carefully treated.

Two weeks later I was on crutches getting onto a Cathay Pacific flight back to South Africa, and on to my home in Namibia. A further two months passed before I was able to begin lightly walking on the damaged foot. Another month and I began to do some light training, which at first produced a fair amount of pain in both my back and my foot. However, the exercise relieved the frustration of just waiting and promoted the feeling of building up again. Another month and I informed my team that I was ready to work.

The adventure that followed, as we probed with our cameras into the mysterious life of the Komodo dragon, was one of the most thrilling I have ever experienced. This included an unusual occurrence when a subadult dragon was found scavenging amongst our kit in the boat, where the lizard presumably had picked up the scent of our food packs. This animal was almost two meters in length, large and powerful enough to resist all our attempts to encourage it to leave the boat. A chunk of raw meat attached to the end of a pole eventually lured the giant reptile onto the gunwale of the boat, allowing me access to the tail and a final shove over the side. One does not want to share a little boat with a ravenous, meat-eating, prehistoric reptile.

Once in the water, the lizard took off at a healthy pace towards the shore, some hundred meters away, moving as effortlessly as a shark. On impulse, I dove in after it, the excitement and thrill overriding any thoughts of a logical outcome. Stretching out in my fastest stroke, I was finally rewarded when I caught up to the lizard, my outstretched fingers fleetingly touching its tail as it swam. Startled, the dragon swung around in the water, eyed me with some distaste, then dramatically increased its pace, leaving me floundering behind.

Thinking back now, I realize how foolish I was to allow my enthusiasm to overwhelm me. Nobody ever went swimming with a Komodo dragon before, and with good reason! There was no telling how it might react. Exhausted from the fast-paced swim and in deep water as I was, if the dragon had turned on me, there was no telling what would have happened. Having considered this, however, I will never forget the thrill of it, the look in the dragon's eyes as it turned and reacted to my touch. This was, after all, a top predator, powerful enough and armed with claws and dentition enough to dismember and eat a human being, and I was swimming with it, out in the ocean surrounding the wild islands of Komodo! I cannot help but think I would do it again anytime, should the unlikely opportunity ever arise.

Oh, and yes . . . this time we *did* pay our respects to the cave spirit before beginning the return shoot . . . with Shaman, herbs, fire, slaughtered chicken, and all. Little wonder everything went smoothly.

Don't knock what you don't understand!

A fiery sunset enhances the stormy sky while on location in Tanzania.

An aloe tree in grassy plains after good rains in the Namibian Desert; an area I regularly frequented for scenic and reptile photography.

Here I am caught on camera displaying a variety of nimble ballet techniques unconsciously acquired over a lifetime of dodging striking snakes; in this instance an aggressive juvenile African rock python.

This black spitting cobra species found in Namibia, typically has scattered bars across the length of its body, though not always.

Catching a large Zambian black spitting cobra by the tail for relocation away from the track where it had been defiantly posturing.

The Welwitschia plant, found only in Namibia and southern Angola, is the oldest living plant, some specimens being over 2,000 years old.

Photographing the awesome scenic beauty of the Augrabies Canyons in South Africa. A paradise for numerous desert mammal and reptiles species.

A species known to cause most snake bite deaths in Central and South America, this giant lance-
viper located in Costa Rica, provided a frighteningly exciting sequence on camera.

The mysterious beauty of the Cyprus Swamps of North Florida is home to many species of venomous reptiles, including cottonmouths and copperheads.

Known for its abundance of wetland wildlife populations, the Everglades of South Florida are now also home to many invasive species.

The infamous and poisonous cane toad of South America, introduced into Australia, continues to spread and decimate native species which attempt to feed on it.

Locating alligators in the Everglades is not difficult; attempting to pose with one for a film piece on camera proved to be more difficult.

The largest reptile in North America, an adult alligator is a top predator, reaching almost 6 meters (20 feet) in length.

An airboat, a canoe, and a reputable local guide are essential when exploring the vast waterways that make up the Florida Everglades.

Catching a large cottonmouth in the Everglades. This species is highly venomous and known for its bad temperament.

Precariously balancing an HD camera and tripod in my canoe in preparation for a fill-in scenic sequence incorporating the gloomy surroundings of the Everglades.

An introduced species, the Burmese python, is now well established and breeding in the Florida Everglades, posing potentially catastrophic consequences for native fauna.

Ayers Rock—or Uluru, as it is now known—stands majestically alone under a stormy sky in the vast desert landscape of central Australia.

So named for their habitual north/south construction, the "magnetic" termite mounds of Northern Australia are unique to the territory and make for scenic pictures.

Underwater filming and catching of a sub-adult Australian freshwater crocodile in the Northern Territory.

A powerful predator, the beautifully marked perentie monitor lizard is Australia's largest lizard, reaching over 2 meters in length.

Catching and removing a spectacled cobra from a public area.

Demonstrating the cobra's defensive hooded posture for the camera.

The Asian cobras display a much shorter and more rounded hood than their African cousins.

While attracting a cobra's attention with one hand, I am able to touch the back of its neck with the other, without fear of being bitten.

A rare sighting of a foraging white-coated black bear or "spirit bear" as it is known amongst the First Nations people of British Columbia, Canada.

A mother and sub-adult cub keep a watchful eye as the camera crew position themselves for some close-up filming.

When it is all said and done, after a long day of sweat and toil, any available free space is acceptable for a nap.

CHAPTER 15

SNAKE VENOMS AND THE FER-DE-LANCE

To produce a polyvalent antivenom (a single serum that is effective against the venoms of a group of snake species), a cocktail mix of snake venoms is introduced into the blood stream of a horse, in dilute, nonlethal proportions. These proportions are then gradually increased as antibodies form to combat the venoms. Eventually the horse's system is capable of accepting a normally lethal dose of this snake-venom mixture without experiencing any ill effects whatsoever, the antibodies having increased sufficiently to overwhelm and neutralize the venoms. The animal is now immunized. Though any variety of animals may qualify to be used for this process, the domesticated horse holds the advantage of size, which allows for the draining of many liters of blood from it, making it the perfect animal for this process. The same horse may be used for many years, continuously supplying large quantities of its valuable immunized blood. The blood plasma contains the antibody and is separated and purified into crystal-clear, liquid serum. Some serums are produced in powder form, ready to be mixed with a saline solution before use. Some snake species require specific antivenom, and for these a monovalent serum is prepared.

Many antivenoms produced in the world today are polyvalent, covering a number of venomous species occurring in the same country or in close proximity to one another. This is a saving grace, as the need to positively identify the snake (though still an advantage) is no longer of primary importance—one serum may cover all the venomous species found in any one particular region. In most developed countries, snake-bite is a rare occurrence, with more people being killed by lightning than by snake-bite. However in some developing countries, where much of the population is rural, the incidence of snake-bite is far greater, sometimes numbering in the thousands each year.

Snake venoms are made up of an extremely complex mixture of enzymes and proteins, which scientists and biologists have not yet been able to duplicate. Thus, to continue the manufacture of antivenom, laboratories are forced to rely on suppliers who extract venom from living snakes. As discussed earlier, this is done by "milking" the venom from the snake, usually by allowing the reptile to bite through a thin plastic membrane stretched tightly over a conical flask, or in some cases, by massaging the venom glands while the fangs are supported over the edge of a collection container. Some snake species are capable of delivering large amounts of venom at each "milking," while others, especially smaller species, may yield only minute quantities at a time. It would take roughly ten days for a "milked" snake to replenish the lost yield. Once extracted, the venom is freeze-dried, in which state it remains concentrated and toxic for any length of time. Considering the specific nature of the venom extraction business—the number of snakes required and the obvious difficulties, costs, and potential dangers present in collecting the venom—it is not surprising that snake venom has become a valuable product that is often in short supply.

Snake venom may be thought of as a modified digestive juice, and in fact venom does play a part in aiding the digestion of prey consumed by snakes. In the more highly developed species of snakes, however, the primary purpose of the venom is to kill the prey as quickly as possible. In the case of a dangerous amount of snake venom being injected into a human victim, an adequate amount of antivenom should be administered as soon as possible.

Antivenom is the most important element in the treatment of snake-bite. Depending on how much venom has been injected by the snake will ultimately determine how much serum will be needed. This naturally varies greatly according to the species and size of the snake, how long the snake was attached to the victim, and the size of the victim. A small child will more quickly succumb to the effects of snake envenomation than an adult, for example. Considering that most highly venomous snakes need to inject no more than a drop of venom to potentially kill an adult human, it must be appreciated that most often *many* ampoules of serum will be needed to neutralize the symptoms arising from a serious bite. While this number may greatly vary from two to twenty—or more—in some cases as many as a hundred 10 ml ampoules have been required to save a life. Thus one can understand and appreciate the need to keep up a constant supply of snake venoms for the continued manufacturing of antivenom. And considering that there are roughly three hundred highly venomous snake species spread around the globe, one can only imagine how many snake 'milkings' would be required to keep up with demand.

In a somewhat different direction of exploration, still further demand for snake venoms has arisen as scientists probe deeper into the possibilities of using these venoms for medicinal purposes. Research has revealed that some snake venoms may hold the key to some of the worst human diseases. From research projects that are underway, there is evidence to suggest that snake venoms—or fractions thereof—can be used with surprisingly effective results. Cancer tumors in animals, for example, shrink when injected with certain venom extractions. Hemophilia, a bleeding disease, has been controlled in laboratory tests with clotting factors taken from the venom of the Russell's viper of Asia. Drugs based on the venom of the Malayan pit-viper can be used to relieve phlebitis. Cobra venom can be made into a nonaddictive painkiller with the strength of morphine. Scientists have discovered that snake venoms are composed of as many as forty or more different proteins, so complex in nature that scientists are unable to duplicate them.

Considering all of this and the fact I was known to be travelling around the world on a quest to photograph venomous snakes, I was not surprised to be contacted by a venom research laboratory asking me to collect venom from certain species for analyses, should the opportunity arise. Though I had not practiced snake 'milking' for some years, I was of course well familiar with the technique from my days working at a snake and animal park, so I agreed. The research in question involved closely scrutinizing samples of venoms taken from wild specimens of the same species from different regions, which would afford the opportunity to study any variations in composition. It was thought that what the same species of snake was feeding on in different regions might affect the toxicity and/or composition of the venom.

I had, over the years of my employment at snake parks, extracted venom from a wide variety of venomous snakes, depending on what species was available and what venom was required at the time. Unused serum, depending on how it is contained and housed, will expire after a certain number of years on the shelf, so generally speaking there is always a demand for fresh venom. Usually, under ideal conditions, extracting venom from snakes is a fairly simple task for the practiced herpetologist. "Milking" freshly caught venomous snakes on location in the field can prove to be a bit more uncoordinated and nerve wracking. Here conditions may be far from ideal, with very basic apparatus being employed in uncomfortable locations and most often involves handling angry, rebellious snakes, keen to retaliate to their handling with a deadly bite.

In Queensland, Australia, I came across a huge king brown snake curled up under the rotten floor boards of an old, disused wooden barn. Seeing that this enormous snake displayed few outward signs of distress or anger at my catching and handling of it, I considered it to be a perfect specimen for venom extraction, suspecting that it would deliver a good yield. And indeed it did, biting down firmly into the plastic membrane over the flask and injecting a huge amount of the deadly venom. When attempting to remove the fangs from the plastic membrane however, the snake refused to let go, biting down harder. Even after releasing my grip on the flask the snake held on tenaciously, leaving it dangling precariously from his jaws. Obviously excited that it was able at last to vent its frustrations it had so cleverly suppressed when first caught, the snake now pursued its path of revenge with a passion. Eventually I was forced to cut the elastic band securing the plastic membrane stretched over the top of the flask, allowing the membrane to collapse into the snake's jaws while I removed the flask to safety. Still not dissuaded, the snake proceeded to stubbornly chew at the plastic and would surely have swallowed it had I not quickly extracted the membrane with a pair of forceps. It was a frightening reminder of just how dangerous these snakes could be if provoked. Had it gripped onto my arm and held on to it as it did to the flask, the amount of venom injected into my system would have secured my death that much quicker.

Spitting cobras are able to eject their venom more forcibly than other snakes. The venom of spitting snakes is also more fluid than that of other snakes, allowing it to be forced more freely through the fang openings. Thus, true spitting cobras have no need to throw their venom at an attacker (as is the case with the rinkhals) but instead are able to direct the venom spray in any desired direction by simply turning their head while contracting the muscles surrounding the venom glands. Considering that this venom spray may reach a distance of three meters, gives some indication of the force with which it is being ejected.

While filming an earlier episode of my reptile series one morning, I was astonished to find very obvious snake slither-marks in the sand surrounding my vehicle, in which I had bedded down the previous night. Knowing full well that a snake may be attracted to the warmth of a vehicle engine on a cold desert night, I was careful to check out all openings in the chassis for fear that the snake may still be present. As matters turned out, it was a wise thing to do, as I soon located the snake comfortably curled up on the engine block. Startled by the sudden movement and the sudden exposure to daylight as I lifted the hood, the snake quickly advertised its surprise, and its species, by raising its head and jetting a spray of venom in my direction. A Namibian spitting cobra! These snakes can grow to almost two meters long and are known to be quick to defend themselves, spraying copious amounts of venom in the hope of dissuading an attacker.

Fortunately, because of the ever-present desert glare reflected off the sandy floor, I had already donned my sunglasses, which prevented venom spray from entering my eyes, the only place it could cause me damage. Knowing there was a project underway to make a specific anti-venom for this species, I carefully untangled the snake from the wiring of the Nissan's engine compartment and made preparations for a "milking." The angered snake, meanwhile, continued to spray venom at my every movement until my sunglasses and the rest of my face and head were sticky with the stuff.

Finally securing the snake behind the head, I introduced the customary flask with covered plastic membrane. Not expecting much, considering that the snake appeared to be expelling most of its venom at me, I was surprised to see two clear jetstreams of venom *zing* down into the flask with such force and duration as to make the flask vibrate in my hand. This continued for no less than four or five seconds, leaving the little flask almost a quarter filled with venom. I was astonished, but a further surprise lay in store.

It is a fact that venomous snakes control the amount of venom they deliver. A (more or less) lethal dose of venom is injected into a prey animal to kill it; usually a few drops is all it takes. A startled snake, on the other hand, instinctively striking out in a defensive mode, often delivers no venom at all. This situation is referred to as a "dry bite." An angered snake, however, when offered the opportunity to vent itself by way of a premeditated, revengeful strike, will often deliver a much larger quantity of venom. The Namibian spitting cobra, angered by my handling, clearly demonstrated its dissatisfaction by first repeatedly spraying venom at me and then by ejecting a huge amount of venom through the plastic membrane into the flask, a technique *designed* to stimulate the snake into delivering venom through the false sensation of an actual bite. The cobra's venom glands should, to all intents and purposes, by this time have been largely depleted, but when I released it a few minutes later, I was shocked to find myself once again under attack as the snake further vented its anger by once again showering me with streams of accurately directed venom. I was astonished! The snake seemed to possess an endless supply of stored venom, much of which it obviously had held back in spite of the 'milking.' I was aware, of course, that spitting snakes held a considerable amount of venom, but nothing had prepared me for this. Another lesson learned, as finally, with a disgusted last disdainful look in my direction, the cobra slithered away into the dry desert bushes.

Then came the day of my confrontation with the most vicious snake I have ever encountered in my entire career as a herpetologist—the giant fer-de-lance viper of Central America. I say "giant" because this particular snake, which would usually average about a meter to a meter and a half in length, measured over two meters in length, closer to two and a half meters, in fact. A formidable reptile in any herpetologist's book, but also a species that I had been specifically asked to extract venom from, should I be so *lucky* as to encounter it.

The fer-de-lance, or lancehead viper, as it is commonly known because of its distinct, sharply triangular head and its frequent pattern of a dark arrow or lancehead marking, is a wide-ranging and prolific snake occurring from Mexico through Central America and into South America. These snakes have a virulent venom that destroys tissue and blood and are known to have caused many human fatalities. Like most snakes, this species will most often take flight when disturbed; if threatened, however, the fer-de-lance will defend itself vigorously. It is a species well known for its aggressive temperament and generally given a wide berth when encountered in the wild.

I had in fact come across two lance head vipers, both of which were of average size, during my several trips to film reptiles in South America. Of these, one clearly displayed its readiness to defend itself by striking out repeatedly on being approached, while the other slithered off at a hurried pace, apparently preferring escape to confrontation, as is more usual with most species of snakes. Being less than a meter in length, the first, more aggressive specimen posed little danger to me, as its striking distance was limited, which allowed me to comfortably get within range for some close-up photography. The Costa Rica episode, however, presented a different scenario—one that could have easily cost me my life.

There are basically three ways to find snakes in the wild, the first and most obvious being to physically search them out with methods applied according to the species you are after. Ground-dwelling snakes might be located under rocks or fallen tree stumps, etc., while arboreal species can be camouflaged amongst dense vegetation and hollow tree, and snakes known to eat frogs are usually found close to streams or dams. Therefore, depending on what species is being searched for, one can limit the search according to these basic principles.

The second method of reptile location can be employed if one is spending a fair amount of time in any one particular area of search. In this case it can prove productive to inform the locals of your quest, especially those laboring in the outdoors, as people spread out across a wider area naturally have more chance of encountering a snake while simply going about their everyday business. This can be especially beneficial in rural areas, where laborers may be planting, harvesting, or bush clearing. Word spreads fast, and generally workers will be only too pleased to have someone on call when a snake has been encountered.

To a lesser degree—but proven to produce effective results—is simply being alert to the cacophony of sounds reverberating from the surrounding wilderness in which you find yourself, especially where vegetation is dense and filled with a variety of insect, mammal, and bird calls. A sudden lull in the otherwise persistent screech of cicadas, for example, may indicate that something has disturbed them, while just the opposite is usual when birds are alerted to a foreign presence. I have on numerous occasions been made aware of the presence of a snake by the excited chattering of birds grouped together high up in a tree top, where I would otherwise never have spotted the reptile. In Costa Rica, however, it was a troop of capuchin monkeys that alerted me to the presence of the lancehead viper, which, in spite of its camouflage, had been detected by the monkeys' excellent eyesight as the snake moved stealthily through the undergrowth.

My crew and I had become aware of capuchins in the area, as the monkeys made their curiosity concerning our movements evident by their brief appearances above us while foraging for fruit in the tree tops. We were filming general fill-in sequences while following my search pattern through the dense undergrowth close to a clear stream. The astonishing thing was that, when the snake had first been spotted by the capuchins and their initial, excited alarm calls reverberated throughout the immediate surrounding jungle, some members of the troop actually came across to where we were filming, as if to alert us as well. In fact, one capuchin was so adamant that we take notice that it maneuvered itself to within just a few meters above us, where it appeared to all the world as though it was excitedly beckoning for us to follow. I will never know with certainty if this was indeed the case or not, but it certainly was enough to get our attention.

"There's definitely something going on up ahead," I commented to the crew as we all stared up to where the capuchin bounced frantically up and down on a flimsy branch above our heads. "For the monkeys to be this excited, there has to be a reason. Let's take a look." I indicated to the lead cameramen that he better be ready for anything. Not needing to be reminded, the lead cameraman was already preparing himself, hoisting the camera high up on his shoulder while the second camera operator and sound technician positioned themselves from a different angle. This had the potential of being one of those rare occasions where everybody was ready to catch the action right from the start. Following the chattering capuchins, we cautiously maneuvered our way through the undergrowth, our eyes and ears alert for the slightest glimpse or sound that might give some indication of what was going on.

In spite of this, the first strike—when it came—was completely unexpected. Another step, and I would have been on top of the snake, which obviously had long been aware of my approach, preparing itself for the worst. Its camouflaged pattern so perfectly blended the creature into the surrounding foliage that my eyes had missed it completely, until I almost stepped on it. Glimpsing just the beginning of the movement—almost too late—instinct and fast reflexes were all that saved me, as I hurled myself sideways off my path of direction to plunge unceremoniously flat on my side in a tangle of bushes. For a stunned moment, I was unable to fully comprehend what I had just witnessed. As if in slow motion, my brain had registered the wide-open mouth reaching towards me at an impossible height—above my waist line—enormous hinged fangs pushed forward to their maximum. A seemingly impossible feat! Instantly the massive head retracted, disappearing once again into the foliage. Above me the capuchins were going ballistic, having apparently viewed the entire scene from an aerial point of view.

Scrambling frantically on hands and knees, I worked my way back a few meters, suspecting the strike action was about to be repeated. "Stay where you are, guys," I called out to the crew, who were spread out around me at a safe distance. "It's a huge lancehead viper . . . and it's mad as hell!" Our established routine when filming dangerous reptiles was for me to lead into the first action sequence, thereafter directing the cameramen as to when and how safe it was to move in closer for the more dramatic sequences. However, my creating distance seemed to satisfy the snake that the danger had retreated, and the giant head remained hidden. By the size of that head—and its reach—I estimated the snake to be well over two meters in length, and, having just witnessed its defensive disposition, I knew I would have to proceed with extreme caution in approaching this specimen. My excitement aroused, I knew this was a snake I had to see and photograph in its entirety.

Knowing now where the viper was positioned, I decided to approach with my meter-long snake tongs extended out ahead of me, so as to hopefully divert any further strikes. "Get ready, guys," I called to the team. "Whatever happens from now on . . . keep the cameras rolling."

The hope that my snake tongs would suffice in protecting me from another strike proved to be an underestimation of the snake's capabilities, as the very next lunge reached way over and beyond the tongs, forcing me to once again jump backwards, dropping the tongs as I did so. Never before had I witnessed a viper with such a reach. Around me the cameras rolled nonstop from a safe distance, while above us the cacophony of capuchin calls reached a crescendo. The viper was more exposed now, its most recent lunge having been delivered with such force as to have drawn it further out of the foliage onto a cleared, pebbly area close to the stream.

Butterflies in my stomach, my nerves a-jangle, and sweat breaking out on my forehead, I slowly picked up my snake tongs off the ground. There was no way I was going near this snake bare-handed. Most often, in the case of a slender, slow-striking snake (like a cobra), I would be able to maneuver myself into a position where I could reach for the tail and raise the snake off the ground for safe handling. This is not possible with the short, stubby, fast-striking vipers, and totally impossible with this extreme example of a two-meter-plus monster that confronted me now. This snake's estimated speed of strike I knew to be somewhere in the region of seven meters per second. From within reach, no amount of agility could save me from a direct line of strike. In its present state of mind, that of active self-defense, I dared not even approach this snake with my still camera without risking a bite; and a bite from this snake, as far from civilization and medical attention as we were, would mean certain death—*a slow, horrible, excruciatingly painful death.* My mind reeled at the thought of the amount of blood and tissue-destroying venom this giant snake could deliver. Getting good close-up pictures was one thing, but getting killed for it was another consideration entirely.

At the same time, I knew it was important to get a sample of its venom for the snake-venom research laboratory. I considered my options and made a decision, calling the crew together. It was not often we could prepare ahead for the action about to take place. We huddled together, all the while keeping an eye on the lancehead viper, which remained where it was, folded into a number of tight "S"-shaped coils that were as taut as a spring, defiantly ready to defend itself. Partly exposed as it was now in the dappled light filtering through the canopy, I could appreciate the beauty of the creature, as its yellow tongue flickered in and out, continuously testing the air for smells. It was a magnificent specimen for sure, but knowing that I had to somehow secure it with my bare hands sent shivers down my spine. Seemingly satisfied that the snake was being taken care of, the capuchins now began to move off, their curiosity outweighed by their relentless need for food. This provided welcome relief from their chattering, which had begun to unnerve me, as I felt the need to concentrate fully on my handling of the deadly viper.

Taking a deep breath, I divulged my proposed strategy to the crew: "My best bet is to get the most difficult part taken care of first. That is to say, secure the snake, head and body." This of course would be easier said than done, but seemed the most logical way to get the shoot running. The crew concentrated intently. There was no room for misinterpretation.

"Once I have the snake firmly behind the head, I will take us through the venom extraction process step by step—all on camera. By doing this, we will not only have attained some unique footage, but I will have drained the snake of much of its venom supply, thereby reducing the severity of any later accidental bite to my person . . . should we be so unfortunate."

I of course knew well that a snake never yields all its venom supply, even when being "milked," and that only a few drops were needed to kill an adult human, but I figured it sounded more positive for the crew. Certainly, the less venom injected, the better chance of survival. However, considering that it only took a drop or two . . . I could not at that moment in time take into consideration *all* the many facets, factors, and potential hazards of what I was about to do . . . or I would never do it. I knew the dangers; I would take it all as far as I trusted my abilities and experience.

"However it goes," I continued, "we will have some great footage in the bag, and I can then release the snake for us to collect some close-up photography as it moves off." I could see doubts etched in the faces around me, but none were voiced. Everybody knew I had simplified the proceedings. This snake was an unknown quantity, larger and potentially more dangerous than any other viper we had encountered. In some weird herpetological or cinematic way, it made sense. Basically, if I was to get bitten before, during, after—or not at all—the cameras will roll and, one way or another, we will have some unique footage. "Let's do it," I said.

The meter-long Pillstrom snake tongs, manufactured in America, that I incorporate into the action (on occasion) are very well designed. Their actual grabbing action is very sensitive and accurate, enabling gentle manipulation of any snake too dangerous to approach bare-handed. In this instance, considering the potential reach of the viper, I would have to carefully secure the giant head with the tongs before allowing myself to reach out with a bare hand. This would be the most critical moment, as, without a doubt, any snake will jerk and twist in an attempt to pull out of the tongs. My timing would have to be accurately gauged between the gentle closing of the tongs on the snake's neck, the snake's reaction to twist and pull out, and the placing of my hand behind the head. Once my hand began moving in to take the head, there was no turning back. It will be done right . . . or I will be bitten. There are no two ways about it. And knowing that a viper with a head this size could be expected to have fangs over three centimeters long, my grip had to be accurate and firm. Otherwise the snake will twist in my hand and stab me with at least one fang, which is more than enough to cause trouble. Thinking back, I shiver at the thought of everything that could have gone wrong, way out there in the jungles of Costa Rica, endless kilometers from civilization and medical treatment.

Finally, with everybody in position and ready, I cautiously approached the snake, still warily keeping its defensive pose at the edge of the foliage. This was a rare example of a reptile prepared to stand its ground. Being left alone, it would have eventually moved off to go about its business. Attracted by our presence, however, and having already been forced to defended itself once, this snake was primed and ready, secure in its ability to do lethal damage. Snake tongs outstretched, I closed in to within two meters of the deadly head, which now angled towards me, tongue rapidly flashing in and out as beady eyes gauged my approach. The first strike came lightning fast and high, forcing me to lunge back out of reach. I changed angle and approached again. Though I had been ready for it, I was still astounded by the strike's incredible height and reach. Another strike . . . which, if anything, reached even further and higher than before. This was one determined snake. A few more strikes and the snake began to hover, as though undecided whether to continue this path of defense, or run. This was what I had been hoping for, and, very slowly, to avoid further alarming the snake, I maneuvered the tongs so as to circle the snake's neck, and gently closed them.

With a powerful and violent thrust, the snake twisted its head and bit at the tongs, squirting a jet of thick, yellow venom across the lower lever action. Releasing the grip immediately, I stood back nervously to regroup. My heart was pounding. That bite could have been my hand. The snake has to be relaxed in the tongs grip, for just a split second, in which time I must gauge it and grab with my hand. Under ideal laboratory conditions, I had secured large puff adders for venom extraction countless times, but this snake was twice as long and far more agile. The snake stared at me defiantly but did not strike out as I approached again. Secretly I hoped that it was beginning to realize that I was not intending it any harm; I was just being a nuisance.

It was on the third try that I finally decided to take the plunge. I have no explanation as to how I might have recognized the moment, other than my many years experience working with venomous reptiles. There comes that fatalistic moment when, in some mystic way, my thoughts correspond with those of the snake, as though reaching a consensus and knowing that the time is right. Bending forward and grabbing for the snake's neck as close behind the head as possible, I immediately released the tongs to free my left hand to grab the body. I knew if the body was not immediately secured the snake would shake itself free of my grip with little effort and certainly puncture my hand with a fang in the process.

Finally having the head in my grasp, I wrapped the powerfully wriggling two-plus meters of body around my arm so as to restrict its movement—a slight miscalculation in this case, as the snake's powerful pull almost jerked its head free of my fingers. Quickly I unwound the body again and tried a less constricting grip, leaving the body partly suspended between my two hands and partly resting on the ground. On the biting end, meanwhile, the snake's jaws worked ceaselessly, both left and right hinged fangs clearly visible below the bottom lips, where they were attempting to reach my hand. Thick yellow venom dripped down onto my fingers. This snake was so agitated now that it was already releasing venom. I had to get those fangs into a flask quickly!

Already prepared with a plastic membrane covering the top, I quickly fished out the venom flask from my rucksack, using two free fingers from my left hand, a hazardous maneuver that I wish never again in my life to repeat while clutching such a potentially lethal, writhing body in my grip. Watching those venom-loaded fangs probing determinedly just millimeters from my fingers was nerve-wracking, sending my heart rate through the roof. All this was happening while I positioned myself strategically for the cameras and kept up a running commentary. The snake now secured in my hands, and with flask at the ready, I indicated the "all clear" for the lead camera to move in for close-ups, so as to best exploit the anticipated "milking" action. All in place, I brought the enormous head towards the flask and gently pressed the lips over the edge.

The force of the bite registered instantaneously, so powerful as to almost wrench the flask from my hands. Delighted to finally be biting into something—*anything*—the giant head pushed forward, the opposing hinged fangs, each at least three centimeters in length, chewing at the plastic. Not designed to withstand such an onslaught, the membrane gave way, leaving the fangs barred and still grinding away over the far side of the flask opening, dispatching copious amounts of the sticky yellow venom over my hand. I was truly shocked; it took all my wits to keep my composure on camera while at the same time feeling the wet flask slipping from my grip. For safety reasons, I knew I had to release this snake as quickly as possible. Snake venom is not generally harmful on the skin—unless there is a cut or graze allowing for absorption—but I was not comfortable being exposed to so much of it. Aside from the venom running down my hand, there was a significant amount settled in the bottom of the flask from the first initial bites. As I had surmised, the amount of venom contained in the glands of this snake was remarkable. It was time to call it quits . . . while I was still ahead.

Carefully pulling the snake's fangs back from the flask, the powerful body immediately attempted to twist in my grip, using leverage from the coils still partly wrapped around my arm. The snake was exerting great force, but with my left hand now free of the flask, which I had placed on the ground, I was able to loosen the grip. Once again the fangs were exposed and gnawing away in an attempt to reach my fingers. This was now one *very* angry snake, and I didn't blame it. I was doing everything one should not do to enrage a venomous viper. A quick close-up of the snake's head into the camera lens completed the scene, and I got ready to move away.

The method of release is simple—but dangerous—especially with a muscular viper of this size. With the rear end of the snake's body still gripped in my left hand, as close to the tail as possible, I hurled the squirming head away from me, swinging the snake in a long arch safely clear of the ground. Dangling free now, the snake immediately lunged at me, its fangs just grazing my shirt at chest height. Normally I am very careful to place a snake I have been working with gently back down onto the ground, but after witnessing what this reptile was capable of and anticipating another lunge that I knew was likely to reach me this time, I spun round and flung the reptile into the nearby stream. There it floated, in defiance, head raised, gazing directly at me, as though daring me to try that again. I was shaking all over. This was not something I needed to do too often.

Gathering ourselves together, the crew and I all breathed a sigh of relief, the crew assuring me the whole episode had been captured in its entirety (and from multiple angles). There remained now only the matter of my personal still photography. Being semisubmerged in the cool stream for a while appeared to have calmed down the viper. Probably fed up with the whole business of our presence, the snake swiveled its body around to slide gracefully across the water towards a protruding log, affording myself and the camera crew artistic photographic opportunities. As unperturbed by our movements as the snake now appeared to be, we remained careful not to approach too closely, a common miscalculation when one's eye is fully concentrated through the viewfinder of a camera. Considering that this snake not long ago was being angered to the extreme, here again was clear evidence that, if left alone, even a highly venomous snake will choose flight over fight.

Our filming with the snake completed, I rounded off the shoot by delivering a final piece to the camera, as was the norm, before packing up to move on. Of the snake there was no sign, having silently slithered back into the undergrowth as we worked. I estimated a snake that size to be anywhere from ten to fifteen years old. I could not help but wonder what all it had experienced throughout its life, and what, if anything, it thought about what had just happened. Would it ever be seen by human eyes again? Or was I the only person ever to have that privilege? Retrieving my backpack, I joined the crew as they headed out in search of more natural wonders. It was a day I will never forget.

ട ട ട

There are many factors to be considered in the event of snake-bite, and no two cases will be the same, whether or not the species of reptile involved

167

is the same. While the use of a tourniquet has proved to be of value for delaying systemic envenomation with elapids (fixed front-fanged, neurotoxic species, e.g., cobras), it is not generally recommended for viper bites. Experimental evidence has shown that the systemic spread of venom is via the lymphatics, thus the application of a crepe—or stretch bandage—covering the bite and entire effected limb is promoted today as the most helpful first-aid measure to be applied to *any* snake-bite. With this procedure, as opposed to a regular tourniquet, neither venous nor arterial flow is affected, thus reducing the chance of later gangrenous effects. Though the treatment of snake-bite cases will vary around the world according to the species involved, there are a few basic first-aid rules:

- Keep the victim calm.
- Immobilize the victim, or at least the bitten limb.
- Transport the victim as quickly as possible to a hospital where antivenom is available.

For those who venture into the wilds (safari, rock climbing, caving, etc.), it is essential to study the subject of snakebite further, as hospitalization and treatment may be days away. An antivenom kit should always be included in any field trip that which ventures far from civilization and, more importantly, each person should be familiar with its contents and application. Snake venom poisoning is a *serious* matter and one would be wise to consider *prevention*, rather than having to cure.

CHAPTER 16

DCI PROMOTIONS

Outside of the actual physical process of making a television series, there is also the promotional side to be considered, something I knew little or nothing about. All that was about to change, however, when one evening I was contacted by Animal Planet USA, informing me that I was expected to attend and perform at the annual *Discovery Channel International Up-Front Promotional Tour*. The tour would take place over a period of two weeks, including live performances, promotional photo shoots, and television interviews with the likes of Regis and Kelly, Tony Danza, and David Letterman, amongst others. These would take place in New York, Chicago, Detroit, and across the USA to Los Angeles. This was the big promotional tour to which all potential buyers of advertising time and space were invited from around the globe to view the next year's program line-ups. My series, having now proved itself through its ratings, was considered *the* wildlife adventure program to watch; thus, as action presenter of the series, I was expected to attend, perform, and promote.

And so it came to pass that my appointed publicist, Amelia Naido, was waiting for me when I arrived at the Ritz-Carlton Hotel in New York. She was a young American woman of Asian-Indian ancestry, dressed in a red business suite with a white blouse and high-heeled shoes. She brandished an air of overconfidence that immediately suggested someone accustomed to doing things her way, and unaccustomed to criticism. I took an instant dislike to her.

Entering my suite in the Ritz-Carlton on that first day, I was not prepared for what awaited me. The rooms were huge, with a separate bedroom, lounge, and study areas, tastefully decorated and fitted out with heavy, polished, oak-wood furniture. The bathroom was even more stunning in pale marble with black and gold trim, an enormous spar bath, a double wash-basin fitted onto oak cabinets, and a marble-and-tile enclosed shower cubicle the size of a small room, bathed in subdued lighting filtering through numerous frosted glass shades. Decorated and engraved floor-to-ceiling mirrors added to the luxurious effect of size and grandeur. Soaps, conditioners, perfumes, baskets of fruits, sweets, and reading materials were strategically placed, with a 'bath menu' that offered any imaginable delight of your choosing. The liquor cabinet was the size of a wardrobe, and pamphlets brought to my attention that I had free access to the gymnasium on the fourth floor, including free massage anytime I felt the need. *I could get used to this!*

On the huge double bed I found a wrapped and decorated box addressed to me, a welcoming present from Discovery. This turned out to be a very expensive B&O sound-dampening headset, something I had always wanted. Next to the bed, at the window overlooking Central Park, stood a huge chocolate cake, at least a meter tall, designed in the shape of a snake entwined around a branch. The card read, *The Ritz-Carlton Hotel Welcomes the Snakemaster.*

I was stunned! *All this for me?* I was being treated like a movie star, whereas in fact I was little more than a herpetologist turned wildlife filmmaker with little more to offer than my knowledge and experience in the field.

The days and nights that followed merged from one activity into the next, starting with Amelia's insisting we go shopping for new clothes suitable for me to wear on the upcoming TV shows. I am particular about what I wear, and it was inevitable that Amelia and I would clash (especially on this). Not accustomed to being challenged, she stood her ground. "This is the latest fashion," she insisted, frowning and holding up a baggy combination of designer pants and shirt that I would have preferred not to be seen dead in. We were in a ridiculously expensive and as unlikely a named store, Banana Republic.

"You will be performing in front of a live audience of top executives, television personnel, and celebrities, not to mention appearances on national TV . . . with the likes of David Letterman, no less," she said as she stamped her foot and glared at me.

Amelia always brought up David Letterman when attempting to emphasize the importance of the role I was to be playing during this promotional period. It seemed that, above all others, it was considered a great honor to appear on the *Late Show*. Though I knew little about the politics behind the world of American television, I had learned enough to realize that Letterman was placed right up there next to God (as far as TV hosts are concerned). From what I personally had seen of his show, I couldn't fathom it, as my only comparison was to the UK's Graham Norton, who, to me, had a completely different style and approach. Admittedly, however, Letterman did interview some of the world's biggest celebrities, and promotion was after all what this whole business was about. It made sense not to be critical until I had gained more experience in this field.

Until this promotional tour, my part in the television *business* had been mostly running wild through the undergrowth with a film team on my heels as I pursued wild animals. To now find myself involved at the other end of the spectrum was an eye-opener. This was the *business* side of the product I was supplying, that which made all the expense viable. The gamble, it seemed, was to spend money to make money. And for someone of my meager means, who valued every cent and just got by supporting myself with wildlife photography, it came as quite a shock. My first-class airplane ticket to New York alone could have supported my simple lifestyle for two years. I could not begin to imagine what my luxurious Ritz-Carlton suite was costing per night. It was all quite bewildering.

The first days consisted of exhausting interviews with a variety of TV and celebrity magazines, with each night inevitably ending in an ostentatious dinner at one or another of New York's well-known socialite restaurants. Then came the day of media training, a new experience for me, where I was subjected to a lecture, and then rehearsed—on camera—to answer a series of questions that I might be confronted with during live television broadcasts.

I was astonished to learn that, depending on whose program I was being featured, there were questions that were to be avoided, while others were to be encouraged. I was also astonished to realize that I was under such scrutiny as not to be free to voice my own opinions if they were not considered in line with American television's "political correctness" at the time.

Finally the big day of the Discovery Networks Presentation arrived, with my series, *Austin Stevens: Snakemaster*, being advertised and presented to all attendees beforehand in a boxed collection consisting of photographs and a video cassette of my Borneo adventure episode. The supporting blurb read as follows:

There are only two kinds of snakemen—the quick, and the dead! Now, meet the quickest.

Dear TCA Attendee:

As you are preparing for July's Television Critics Association, we wanted to prepare you for our new presentation.

Meet Austin Stevens. A herpetologist, award-winning photographer, filmmaker, author, Kung Fu artist, and extreme adventurer, Stevens is as fascinating as the deadly creatures he scours the world to find, study, and photograph.

Stevens wrestled with the feared and revered Giant Anaconda in the Amazon and calmly photographed extreme close-ups of the King Cobra in the remote forests of India. But he is the first to admit he isn't completely fearless. A typical American spider, a high-rise elevator, big cities, and small closed places can raise beads of nervous sweat on his forehead.

Animal Planet's new series, Austin Stevens: Snakemaster, *premiering Tuesday, October 5, at 8 p.m., follows Stevens as he travels around the world, from deserts of the American West to the dense jungles of Costa Rica, the outback of*

Australia, and the forbidden forests of Borneo, to explore and photograph some of the world's rarest and deadliest snakes and animals.

Enclosed is a tape of Austin's incredible journey across Borneo, in search of the Reticulated Python—a snake known to grow to 30 feet and capable of swallowing a man whole!

Animal Planet's presentation is part of the Discovery Networks TCA time slot on Thursday, July 22, 10 a.m.–12 p.m. Panel to include: Austin Stevens: Snakemaster, herpetologist, award-winning wildlife photographer; Graham Booth: executive producer, Tigress Productions.

The show was presented in grand style, with hundreds of potential advertisers and connected television executives, celebrities, and personnel comfortably seated in a huge theatre bristling with television camera crews, sound technicians, and affiliated paraphernalia. At the head of the sloped seating arrangement was a raised stage area where the presenters could introduce attending artists, backed by a huge screen where film segments pertaining to each category were to be televised. Further screens were strategically placed around the theatre, affording a perfect view of the proceedings from any part of the theatre. It was, in essence, a Hollywood-style presentation, with top television executives hosting the show, featuring numerous "talents" being called up to stage to present their new shows for the year to come.

The executive producer of my series, Graham Booth, flew out from Bristol especially to attend the shows and offer support, something which I was most grateful for. I was, after all, just a simple wildlife photographer from a little-known desert country suddenly hurled into the frenetic world that is American television promotion. This was all new to me, and it felt good to have somebody from my personal team at my side. Far more familiar with this type of business, Graham confessed to me that he had never before experienced anything on the elaborate scale of what we were now being presented with. DCI was pulling out all the stops, as could be expected, with all potential advertising sales in the immediate future depending on the success of the these shows, whose sole purpose was to advertise the content of DCI's programs for the year ahead. The more potentially successful and popular the advertised programs were judged to be, the more lucrative the advertising slots. *Austin Stevens: Snakemaster*, I was assured, was high up on that potential list. The pressure was on, and I was expected to perform.

Performing in front of cameras in the presence of a live audience is of course very different from performing in the field. Here there is no chance for a retake or an edit. And though I became accustomed to performing public demonstrations and lectures during my years as a professional herpetologist at reptile parks, that was a long time ago, and it certainly was not usually in the presence of such an elite audience. Strangely enough, I was not *that* nervous about it all, possibly because the full extent of what I was involved in had not yet fully registered. My first on-stage live performance would soon remedy that.

Up to that point I had been watching the show from the sidelines, out of sight and behind the curtains. I had been afforded only limited rehearsal time, enough only to know my positions required on stage during my performance, with the rest being left up to me. A radio microphone was attached to my collar, and the cable fed under my shirt to a receiver attached to my belt in the small of my back. A brush-over from a makeup artist, and I was all ready to go on cue.

Numerous shows from a multitude of categories were being advertised, with the likes of *Queer Eye for the Straight Guy* and *American Chopper* being amongst the last leading up to mine. In the wildlife documentary adventure series, my show had been promoted as *the* one to watch for and was held back till the last minute possible, with the audience having been treated to on-screen snippets at various intervals throughout the presenting of all the other shows.

Finally the moment arrived, as with much fanfare and enthusiastic introduction, the master of ceremonies, the chief executive of DCI himself, announced my show to the eager audience while on the giant screen behind him a dramatic video segment of my encounter with a king cobra, as I laid my hand down upon the snake's enormous head, was shown for all to see. My last words from that segment, "I have always wanted to do that," were my cue to appear on stage. This I did to tumultuous applause, desperately trying to overcome the untimely nervous sensation that seemed to suddenly envelop me. Putting my best foot forward, I strode across the stage to shake hands with the esteemed head of DCI, at the same time acknowledging the crowd with what I hoped passed for an enthusiastic wave and a smile.

"Austin, we are so pleased to have you on the show. But tell us, *why* do you do the things you do? And what everybody wants to know: *Why* is it that you felt you had to place your hand on the head of that king cobra? Surely this is playing with your life?"

This was my cue to rattle off my basic history, how I felt about photographing wildlife, and how I was pleased to bring my adventures into the homes of the world in the hopes of dispelling some of the myths and fears generally associated with snakes and other reptiles.

"Austin, you seem to be fearless in the face of such potentially dangerous animals. Is there *anything* that you *are* afraid of?"

This was now my cue to explain that, while I had studied and understood wild animal behavior, my fears evolved from the more mundane everyday things, like being claustrophobic and unable to travel in elevators, while at the same time the thought of being in a swaying high-rise building terrified me. It just seemed so unnatural. I also pointed out that I was rather nervous around spiders. This the audience lapped up with astonished delight. They had just seen footage of me reaching out to touch a wild king cobra on the head . . . and now I confess to being afraid of spiders. *Hilarious!*

"Well Austin, from the footage we have seen so far, it looks like your series will be an exciting treat for all our viewers. Now I believe you have brought something to show us, am I right?" This was my next cue, all prepared and ready to go. Stepping over to a mysterious suitcase that had been unobtrusively present on stage throughout my appearance, I bent down and began to unfasten the catches.

"Yes, I have. As you've all seen on screen, I have just returned from filming in India." Steadily my hands worked on the suitcase latches, as though having some difficulty undoing them. I continued chatting: "On my arrival here in New York I was astonished to find I had acquired some extra baggage, a stowaway no less. And so I thought to bring him along for you to meet." And with one fluid motion from the now-open case, I plucked out a four-foot-long Asian cobra and swung it precariously by the tail over the edge of the stage, where the first rows of seated audience sat, eagerly leaning forward for a better look.

Startled by the sudden handling and exposure to the bright lights illuminating the stage, the snake emitted an audible hiss, flattening its neck into a defensive hood, poised to strike. For one split second, in mid-air, I released the snake, to regrab it more securely just over the edge of the stage, where it threatened to drop into the now-not-so-enthralled audience. This must have given the appearance that I was throwing it at the audience, and there was an immediate scramble for distant places as the first few rows of seats were hastily evacuated. *Oh Lordy!* Though I do like to entertain my audience, this was not the time or place for something like that, and I just knew I was going to be seriously reprimanded later.

With the cobra now safely back on stage, I hastily broke into dialog concerning the reptile, demonstrating how it makes a defensive hood, as though to attack, though all the while attempting to escape rather than fight. Somewhat settled down again, the audience remained skeptical, with the front rows of seats closest to me remaining unoccupied for the duration.

Soon my segment was concluded with loud, if somewhat nervous, applause from the audience, and I was free to leave the stage with my cobra safely tucked away back in the suitcase. The snake had of course not traveled from India with me but was borrowed from a private collector for the occasion. There were three more such shows to attend over the next few days—in three different cities—and I noted that on each occasion the first three front rows closest to the stage were left vacant. I think it had been decided that this particular "talent" was a *loose cannon*, somewhat unpredictable . . . and precautions were taken.

The meet-and-greet gatherings taking place after each show were another eye opener for me, the first being held at the New York Museum of Natural History, surrounded by displays and a full-sized blue whale suspended overhead. In the dining area, it was obvious that no expense had been spared. Dining tables and chairs were scattered around the hall amongst elaborate displays of palm trees and water features. A buffet offering just about anything and everything imaginable spread out as far as the eye could see under the subdued wall lighting, while the bar, constructed completely of ice, with the Discovery logo engraved in its front, seductively offered to satisfy any thirst.

Crowds of people were milling around, many of whom approached me to introduce themselves, congratulating me on my performance at the show and my TV series in general. The mood was festive, with Amelia introducing me to people in the business as well as to numerous well-known TV and film stars. During the two weeks of the promotional tour, I would meet Donald Trump, Daryl Hannah, Kevin Costner, Cindy Crawford, Tony Danza, Carmen Electra, and Alyssa Milano, to name but a few. It was indeed a dazzling time for a simple, desert-dwelling wildlife photographer like myself.

In between these DCI promotions and parties, I was expected to do live television appearances with popular hosts such as Tony Danza, Regis and Kelly, and David Letterman, to which I was always requested to bring snakes with me. I was, after all, the *Snakemaster*. People wanted to see snakes—the bigger and more dangerous, the better. I was not keen on the idea. Time slots allotted for each of these shows were precise, allowing just so many minutes on stage, with no margin for error. I voiced my concerns to Amelia, pointing out that, without venomous snakes to contend with, I would have much more time to explain who I really was and what my series was all about, to discuss it all in greater depth . . . but she would not hear of it.

"Your series is titled *Austin Stevens: Snakemaster!*" She announced dramatically, as if I didn't know. "That's what gets the public excited. The title alone indicates that you will be handling highly venomous snakes. The audience will expect it. And that's why you are the *Snakemaster*, because nobody does it better than you."

This clever and strategic mix of rebuke and praise was a typical publicist ploy to keep the talent in line. She took a breath. "Just make sure that as many times throughout your performance as possible, you state clearly that your show can be viewed on Animal Planet, and give the time slot." She stared at me, a frown all over her dark features. "And don't go frightening the hosts by bringing the snakes too close to them, especially Letterman. He really wants you on his show, but he is terrified of snakes. So behave! I know how you like to spice up your performances, but, if you kill Letterman, my life is over!" And, as if a second thought, "yours, too!"

Having little idea about the wrangling of venomous reptiles live in a public arena, Amelia suggested that I display five snakes on each show, I disagreed immediately. The time slots allocated would not accommodate for so many, allowing time for little but wrangling. How was I supposed to communicate with the audience and host? These were to be highly venomous snakes and, as such, needed my full attention so as not to get myself or anybody else bitten.

"But we want lots of snakes," Amelia argued, stamping her Prada high-heeled shoes. "It has to be *dramatic*! The shows will be viewed by millions of people around the world."

I sighed. Here we go again! "Dramatic will be more evident in quality rather than quantity," I said. "I'm suggesting just three snakes, three very *dramatic* snakes." I paused for effect. "Number one, a full grown eastern diamondback rattler, the biggest rattler found in America, sometimes reaching over two meters in length and thick as a man's arm. A local species that the viewing audience can immediately identify with. One of the most dangerous snakes in the world." Amelia leaned closer, her interest aroused.

"Number two, an exotic species that performs well when handled, like a cobra spreading a hood. Something very different from the rattler, from another world." Amelia's eyes gleamed now as she imagined the impact of it on camera in front of a live audience and being broadcast into millions of homes.

"Then, as a grand finale, a *giant* snake. And not just any giant snake, but a beautiful albino giant snake, something around four meters long.

A heavy-bodied snake that, except for its size, is otherwise docile and harmless, and can be touched or handled even by the host . . . if he or she so desired."

Amelia stared at me, her eyes wide and shining with the image of it all. I knew there were plenty of private snake keepers all over the USA, some making their snakes available for film shoots. I did not think it would be a problem to get what I wanted. Having just three snakes to work with allowed for more communication time with the hosts of each show, as well as with the audience, and more time to get the message across. And by introducing one harmless specimen, usually an Asian python that could be handled safely, was always a show grabber.

To give credit where credit is due, Amelia jumped on the phone and within a matter of hours had arranged for the snakes I had requested—with keeper—to arrive at the studios where and when the shows were scheduled. These specimens would be made available for all the New York, Chicago, Detroit, and LA shows. Now things were really moving along.

CHAPTER 17

SNAKES ON THE *LATE SHOW*

Arriving at the NBC studios in my chauffer-driven, sleek, black Town Car, I was greeted by the astonishing site of crowds of fans surrounding the entrance to the building, all waving sheets of paper and pens, screaming for autographs.

Holy Mackerel!

The first episodes of my TV series had just recently been aired; surely this could not all be for me? How could they possibly know I would be here? The Town Car pulled off to the side, and I watched nervously as the chauffer came round and opened my door. Tentatively I stepped out and was immediately enveloped by a surge of people, surrounding me, still waving papers and pens, and calling for my autograph. I was astonished! *Was I indeed a celebrity in New York City?*

It was only later that I discovered that this was a 'usual' occurrence, where fans gathered on a regular basis in expectation of seeing someone famous entering the NBC studios, where they knew various TV and film stars—amongst other famous people—were being interviewed on the *Late Show* on a regular basis. Probably most of the crowd calling for my autograph didn't even know who I was, but were just content in getting an autograph from *anybody* entering the NBC studios, with the assumption that they must be famous in some capacity or another.

Furiously I signed autographs, reveling in the exhilarating emotion of it. Every dog has his day, and I was going to lap it up. There is no greater feeling than "adoring" fans pushing, shoving, and calling for your personal attention, for your personal signature, something that they would display in a special place amongst other memorabilia to cherish forever. (Or, more likely, as I was later also to learn, sell on eBay when the price was right.) Once again I came to realize that there was still a lot to learn in this business.

Finally escaping the "fans," I was ushered into the building where Amelia and everyone else were waiting for my arrival. I had a quick touch-up in the makeup room, a few minutes with the sound engineer as he fitted me with an on-stage microphone, followed by a lecture from Amelia and the stage manager as to what to expect and how to act . . . nothing was left to chance. I was to enter at this exact point, at that exact moment, from this particular angle, and face in that specific direction. And Letterman was at *no* time to be approached with *any* snake.

I then went to meet with the snake keeper, who held the reptiles in closed containers awaiting my attention. It was decided that the only practical way to manage the snakes was to have the containers already stashed out of sight behind a closed-front table on stage, well away from Letterman's usual place of operation. Letterman would then approach me from a particular angle, all the while keeping a safe distance once any reptile was exposed.

If I was not nervous before, the feeling was now steadily growing in me. How was I supposed to remember every little move and detail that was being described and dictated to me? How was I supposed to handle and control venomous snakes safely, while at the same time having a discussion with one of the world's most famous talk show hosts, trying not to get him—or me for that matter—killed in the process, and all the while still offer interesting entertainment, not to mention correct camera angles. Whatever happened to good old fashioned spontaneity—going with the flow?

Finally, with all possible details discussed, I was set free to watch the first part of the show from behind a curtain, as it was being recorded in front of a live studio audience. On his own instructions, for reasons I was never to discover, Letterman's studio temperature was air-conditioned to a freezing 16°C (60°F). I immediately pulled on my jacket, which would have to come off again before I went on stage. My arrangements with the positioning of the snakes would come into play during the break, after which time I would be out of sight, on standby for my cue. I began to shiver; whether from nervousness or cold, I don't know, but I just decided there and then to push all the added hullabaloo out of my head and simply do what I do best, the only way I know how. The world would be watching . . . I just had to be myself.

My immediate job description was to entertain and enthrall an audience, supply good visual material for the cameras, make a good impression as a representative for Animal Planet, get my conservation message and broadcast time slots across, while at the same time attempting some intelligent Q&A with Letterman. Piece of cake.

Part of my character, however, is that I like to include people in what I am passionate about. What is the purpose of trying to describe to someone how amazing and smooth the glossy scales of a snake feel to the touch when you can just hand them the snake to feel for themselves? At the same time, I do understand that some people have an indoctrinated fear of snakes, most often acquired through false information, mythology, or both. But that is why I am present, the expert, controlling and handling the snake in such a manner as to make it completely safe for anybody else to touch. I am not asking or expecting that person to suddenly be converted into a "snake lover," but only to experience a little of what I am physically demonstrating.

In my experience, most people are thrilled by an opportunity to safely come into close proximity with a reptile. There is a fascination that draws them in. A chance to safely be close to—or even touch—one of these feared creatures so enveloped in mysticism and adverse publicity. And one would imagine that this opportunity offered on your very own TV talk show, before millions of viewers, would be a dramatic and unusual inclusion. Indeed, on all the other TV shows I did across America, there was much excitement concerning this very opportunity, with some presenters even helping me handle the harmless species, game to dare and thrilled by the opportunity.

Not so with Mr. Letterman. The fact that the man allowed me on his stage at all was a credit to his professionalism. Letterman has a real fear of snakes, venomous or otherwise. But I respected his fear, and after the showing of a short clip from one of my series episodes, he introduced me to the audience and the world at large. Then, with some further stern, though good-natured-warnings not to pull any stunts in his direction, he cautiously leaned over towards me and read aloud, for the benefit of the audience, the signs printed on my reptile containers: "Danger. Venomous snakes. Do not open."

Looking up he pointed a warning finger in my direction: "No heroics! No cowboy stuff! Just show us what you've got."

He backed away, a meter or two off my left shoulder. His discomfort was obvious, and the audience loved it. Probably nobody had ever seen Letterman really nervous before. Even Paul Schaefer, the leader of the Letterman show-band, who usually continuously offered comment while Letterman was doing interviews, was now completely quiet as I introduced the first snake, an enormous eastern diamondback rattler.

The snake immediately showed its displeasure by rattling its tail, filling the studio with the sound, while I actively controlled it with a combination of my bare hands and a hook stick. The snake was big and active . . . and potentially deadly. The audience lapped it up and "oohed" and "aahed" and strained their necks for a closer look, while three cameras rolled, displaying in close-up my every action on various screens and monitors around the studio.

Letterman, now some *three* meters behind me, strategically maneuvered his distance between the snake and himself, making it very difficult for me to coordinate my angles for the cameras while at the same time attempting to converse with him, answer his questions, and entertain the audience facing me . . . a frustrating task when handling two meters of fast-striking, highly venomous reptile.

This is the main reason I dislike handling venomous reptiles during live TV talk-show interviews. My attention, by necessity, must be wholly focused on the potential danger the reptile represents, allowing me little freedom to otherwise communicate articulately with my host and the audience, with scarcely time for meaningful conversation and Q&A. With all attention drawn to the activity of the reptile in question and my handling of it, little else is achieved.

The fact that Letterman was so nervous about the activity of it all led to him asking numerous questions in quick succession, all rolled up on top of one another, often without allowing me time enough to answer comprehensively. Being suddenly exposed to the bright lights of the studio, the snake was alert and lively. In terms of action, the show was going great. In terms of education, the audience was not getting much, especially with some questions posed by Letterman in a nervous attempt at humor.

"Do rattlesnakes drink coffee?" And my quick automatic response, in similar vein, while grabbing at two meters of fast escaping snake, was, "Oh, they love coffee."

Any herpetologists watching were going to have a field day with that one. I was joking of course . . . going with the flow! Why on earth would a rattlesnake get to be fond of coffee?

"Why is he rattling?" Letterman asked at one point.

"Because he's getting rattled," I answered automatically again, without malice, but with full concentration on the snake's head trying to get at me.

The audience clapped and laughed and seemed to love it all, apparently blissfully content to be visually entertained without the accompaniment of any educational value being dispensed in their direction. The rattlesnake continued to rattle.

"Put it away," Letterman said, motioning from his rear view of the proceedings. "Show us what else you've got."

Dispensing with the rattler, which continued to rattle furiously in its container, I quickly pulled out the next snake: an Asian cobra. The snake was fast and agile—much more so than the rattler—and immediately tried to escape my clutches. This necessitated a lot of skillful maneuvering on my part just to keep the cobra on the table surface I was working on, as it continuously slipped over the edge as though to escape, then would as quickly pull back and slip across to the other side. Letterman was not impressed, and further increased his distance between us.

I was finding it increasingly difficult to communicate with Letterman standing behind me while still facing the audience, till finally I swung round, with dangling cobra in hand, in an attempt to include him more closely with the action. This did not sit well with Letterman, whose discomfort was becoming all the more apparent, and he pointedly reprimanded me, emphasizing that I should please refrain from throwing the snakes in his direction.

In all honesty, and in my frustration with not being able to have close participation with the host, I was just attempting to include him in the action, never intending to exacerbate his nervous disposition. (No one would believe me.)

"You can put him away now, too," Letterman suggested, continuing to keep his distance. "Show us what else you've brought."

Gratefully I maneuvered the cobra back into its container. I felt relieved. The worst was over, and Letterman was still alive and kicking. I had just one more snake to show, and it was a harmless species: an albino Asian python, a beautiful, placid specimen some four meters in length. I turned to face Letterman.

"This next snake is completely harmless, but I could use a helping hand in getting it out of the container," I suggested, peering at Letterman hopefully. What an accomplishment if I could get Letterman to actually hold a snake on his show. The ratings would skyrocket. Cautiously he moved nearer, to peer into the container at my feet, which housed the snake. My hopes rose significantly. He was actually coming closer, and the look in his face told me that he was experiencing serious internal conflict with his fears. Then suddenly he looked up.

"You brought the snake . . . you take it out." And he stepped back, apparently content for me to struggle on my own. I sighed. It was worth a shot . . . but no gold star for me.

Bending down to collect the huge snake, I made a big show of struggling to bring it up and drape it around my body. The audience, always predictable, "oohed" and "aahed" and voiced their amazement as more and more of the huge body was exposed. I was obviously struggling to hold the weight of the animal, and turning to Letterman, who once again had retreated to his safe position behind me, I gave it one more shot.

"I could really use a hand here. If you could just take the tail end . . . ?" I swung the tail end in his direction. But Letterman was having none of it.

Backing off further, he waved his hands in dismissal. His mind was made up, no matter what I had to say, he was not going to touch any snake . . . today or ever.

Disappointed but resigned, I supported the heavy snake wrapped around my body on my own, while Letterman and I for the first time were able to exchange some meaningful Q&A, simply because I could be more relaxed with a nonvenomous species that was of no threat to either of us.

As we wrapped up with closing statements and reminders of where and when my show would be aired, and with loud applause from the enthusiastic audience and music from the band, the show drew to a close. Thankfully, I unwrapped the python from around my body and placed it back into its container. It was all over. And after so much fuss and preparation, the whole episode seemed to have passed so quickly.

With the show concluded, through all the chaos involved with the packing up of equipment, stage props, and other paraphernalia, I attempted to make my way over to Letterman, in the hope of shaking his hand and expressing my appreciation for being on his show, but within seconds he was out of the studio, without so much as a wave or a goodbye. I turned away with mixed emotions and headed out of the studio, somewhat confused, not sure if I had done a good job or not.

The very next day, by coincidence, I was spending some free time sightseeing through Times Square, when I ran into the show's production coordinator. We recognized each other at the same moment in the crowd. Stepping aside for a few minutes chat, I expressed my concerns to her about having achieved the right impression on the show. All I had gotten from Amelia was that it was a great show and everything went well. This was standard response for whatever I did.

I knew I had done well with the handling of the snakes and providing entertainment for the audience, but were my actions towards Letterman inappropriate, in the grand scheme of New York television etiquette? Had I offended or broken some secret rule by being myself?

She looked me straight in the eyes and said: "It was a good show, the difference being that you were not intimidated by Letterman." And with that simple sentence, over which I would ponder for days to come, she wished me all the best with the series and waved a cheery goodbye.

All further TV appearances went really well, with nobody getting killed or maimed, and only one slightly uncomfortable moment when Kelly (of Regis and Kelly) got her head stuck under the weight of the four-meter python and I had to pry her free. Considering her nervous disposition around snakes, she took it light-heartedly, clearly demonstrating her professionalism to audience and cameras alike.

On another show, to the delight of the in-house audience and television viewers around the country, Carmen Electra daringly took it upon herself to assist with the handling of the large Burmese python, setting a precedent for all future shows. For my New York media trip grand finale, I went on the *Tony Danza Show*, where I met Alyssa Milano. There we stretched the python out for display on stage amongst four New York firemen. Everybody loved the friendly, beautifully marked albino Burmese python, though still keeping their distance and remaining nervously cautious around the venomous species.

In Los Angeles I posed for a photo shoot that required me to be laid out on the floor covered with about forty snakes. Another presented me face to face with a king cobra. Yet another required that I spend time in soaking-wet clothes while holding a python suspended at arm's length above my head, like a modern-day Tarzan having just saved Jane from the coils of death. I came away from that one suspecting that I had developed pneumonia.

Much medication and warm clothes later, however, I was well enough to be treated to some glorious open-air lunches in the sunshine on Venice Beach, and some wonderful dinners at well-known LA restaurants, including Ago, part owned at the time by Robert DeNiro, and known to be frequented by stars, socialites, and paparazzi alike. Here our table was personally visited by the head chef, who announced to all present that Austin Stevens, *Snakemaster*, and the Discovery team was in attendance. This invited raucous applause and a flurry of autograph signings.

I attended the launch of the Bruce Willis film, *The Whole Ten Yards*, and saw Bruce, one of my most favorite actors, from a distance. I walked the star-studded "Walk of Fame," spending some time to study many of the names and handprints displayed. I saw Dustin Hoffman walking and talking on a cell phone and met Daryl Hannah, Cindy Crawford, and Donald Trump at a publicity shoot. It was an exhilarating time of new experiences in a different world, and I could not help being caught up in the Hollywood-style fever of it all.

But, of course, all good things must come to an end, and in what seemed to be no time at all, the promotional tour was over. There was some sadness as I said my goodbyes to people I would in all likelihood never see again, and within a very short space of time, I once again found myself spread out in a first class seat of a jumbo jet on route back to Africa, my thoughts roaming back over the weeks just passed. It was a time I will never forget . . . my fifteen minutes of fame, living the life of a TV celebrity, in the good old U.S. of A.

CHAPTER 18

FOREIGN TOADS AND PYTHONS

Foreign animal species introduced into environments where they do not belong have in recent years been a topic of much conversation and debate. For centuries animal invaders have bridged oceanic gaps, sometimes by natural means, more often by aid of human activity, sometimes knowingly, often unknowingly. Many foreign species were innocently or ignorantly introduced by early settlers, while in more recent times, more often for profitable gain, aesthetic pleasure, or in an attempt to solve a preexisting problem. The South American marine toad's introduction into Australia, where it is better known as the cane toad, is a perfect example of how a poorly researched, seemingly benign introduction of a species can lead to an environmental tragedy. Australia has a huge range of introduced species, but it was the problem of the cane toad that caught my attention while photographing reptiles in the far northern regions, where I was based in the small town of Kununurra.

Cane toads first made their appearance on Australian soil in the mid-1930s, when a hundred specimens were imported, bred, and released in Northern Queensland in an attempt to control the infestation of cane beetles that were destroying sugar-cane crops. It soon became evident that the experiment was not successful. Being a robust, ground-dwelling species, the toads were not able to reach high enough to devour the beetles, which settled on the upper stalks of the cane.

Left to their own devices, the toads flourished, breeding rapidly, with each female laying thousands upon thousands of eggs, which quickly hatched tadpoles. These tadpoles in turn quickly metamorphosed into fast-growing toadlets. Up until this time, Australia had no toad species of its own, so there were no natural predators to assist in the control of the invasion. The cane, or marine, toad is considered to be the most toxic toad in the world, being toxic throughout all the stages of their life cycle. The poison, which is secreted from glands along the neck and shoulders, consists of a concoction of chemicals causing rapid heartbeat, excessive salivation, convulsions, and paralyses. It soon became evident that introduction of the toad now threatened native species that might attempt to feed on them. Not only that, but the toads themselves proved to be indiscriminate feeders, eating other frogs and their eggs, as well as insects, lizards, rodents, and even juvenile snakes. The more food available, the bigger they grew, with some specimens measuring over 25cm in length.

Cane toads have proven themselves to be one of Australia's worst environmental disasters, having now spread across most of Queensland, into New South Wales, through much of the Northern Territory, including the world-renowned wetlands of Kakadu National Park, and heading steadily towards the borders of Western Australia. Recognized now to be responsible for the reduction of many species of Australian wildlife, urgent studies are underway in an attempt to remedy the problem. There is currently no effective control method that can be applied to cover the vast area the cane toads already occupy. Some scientists are working with gene technology in the hope of discovering a biological control method, while others are attempting to find a sex pheromone that may be used to disrupt their breeding cycle.

Meanwhile, in some of the more remote areas of the country, community involvement in the form of physically apprehending the offending toads is being applied by those more personally concerned and energetic citizens. And it was with just such a group with which I made contact one night while traveling a deserted stretch of road in search of reptiles, not far from Kununurra. Astonished to see a number of people hopping and bopping across the road in my headlights, I pulled my vehicle over to the side. My first impression was that it might be a police roadblock, but I soon discarded this thought, as no uniforms or patrol cars were evident. As I exited my Land Cruiser, a member of the group gathered randomly across the road waved a torch in my direction. Accustomed to the dangers of encountering strangers on the roads of Southern Africa, I was at first wary, but a friendly voice from the person approaching soon set my thoughts to rest.

"Hello, mate," he said. "Hope we didn't startle you. We're the Toad Busters." He flicked his torch around. "The buggers are everywhere." And, as if on cue, two huge toads hopped out of the undergrowth onto the road. Momentarily ignoring my presence, my new acquaintance lunged after the toads, bending to grab one in each hand. This sent his torch clattering onto the road, where I quickly recovered it for him, as his hands were otherwise occupied with squirming toads. "Thanks mate; my name is Ned," he said. Care to join us? We're the last line of defense preventing the toads from crossing into Western Australia." I looked at him in astonishment. Suddenly all became clear to me. These were the guys I had been told about in Kununurra; the group of concerned citizens who were *physically* attempting to arrest the spread of the cane toads across Australia's Northern Territory. "We ride the roads at night and flush out the surrounding areas, catch as many toads as we come across and bag them. Then we take them back to Kununurra where we euthanize them quickly and painlessly with CO_2 (carbon dioxide).

Introducing myself as we headed towards his accomplices down the road, I explained my mission to film specific reptiles in the area for my series. And the realization suddenly came to me that it would be interesting to include a segment concerning these dedicated people and their endeavors against the onslaught of the cane toads. But I was curious: Was there any practical hope that this hands-on approach might work, considering the vastness that is the continent of Australia and the already widespread distribution of the toads? I put the question to Ned. "Not a hope in hell, mate; but at least if feels like we are doing something until a better alternative is found."

Through the rest of that night till just before dawn, my time was spent flushing out toads with my new-found friends. And as the night progressed, I became steadily more aware of the immensity of the problem, as bag after bag was filled to capacity with toads. Hundreds of toads, flushed out from the surrounding area of just one single roadway! A roadway that seemed to stretch out endlessly in our headlights as we followed it through the night. I could not even begin to imagine how many toads remained out there, across the vastness that is the Northern Territory. If ever there was a mission impossible—*this was it!*

Late the next day, after introducing my film crew to the Toad Busters, we asked to join them on their next night out; to take an on-camera look at the project and the people behind it. The Toad Busters embraced the idea with enthusiasm, pleased to advertise their efforts wherever possible in the hope that the project would catch on and spread to more communities. So it came to pass that, two nights later, with everyone refreshed and eager to go, we set out once more to flush out the invading toads. It all fitted in well with our film schedule, as we were at the time in search of a particular species of Australian black snake that was known to frequent this region. One of the best methods of locating snakes is by slowly cruising tarred roads at night with headlights on full. Retaining the heat long after the sun has set, these roads are an invitingly warm area where snakes will often linger. This appeared to be the case with the toads as well, as many were encountered sitting in the road, presumably lulled by the warmth as they crossed.

By midnight, with the aid of battery-operated camera lighting, we had collected sufficient film footage around which to design our segment. This included personal interviews with members of the Toad Busters, providing a forum to explain the toad problem and their method of physically addressing it. Also caught on film was a series of rather comical snippets displaying adult men and women hoppity-skipping like playful children across the roads on their haunches and knees in pursuit of the agile toads. As "presenter," I was naturally expected to demonstrate the same, almost tripping flat on my face a few times as I did so. Catching a large specimen, which I brought up close to the camera, I was able to squeeze some droplets of the white poison from the toad's glands, clear visual demonstration of its presence. All in all, it was an interesting segment to include in my series.

Throughout that night searching the roads, we had not encountered any evidence of snakes. Ned assured me that this was due to the presence of so many cane toads: "Cane toads have no known predator in Australia, with the possible exception of keel-back snakes, a harmless species that has been seen to attack and eat small cane toads." He paused, shining his torch around so as not to miss any toad that might be sneaking passed. "Many Australian mammal and reptile species will take native frogs, so it is not surprising that the toads might be confused with these. Freshwater crocodiles, goannas, tiger snakes, western quolls, and even dingoes are known to eat cane toads, usually dying shortly afterwards from the effects of the poison." Ned sighed heavily, as though it all lay on his shoulders alone. "It's a sad state of affairs, mate. If something is not done to prevent the spread of the toads, much of our native wildlife will succumb to the onslaught—in a very short space of time."

I digested this information for a minute. Could this really be true? Could a whole range of species eventually be eliminated from the continent by this introduced infestation of toads? For the first time I began to fully comprehend the enormity of it all and sincerely hoped that the segment we were putting together might help promote awareness, not only locally in Australia, but worldwide—a warning against further indiscriminate experiments with our natural environment.

As my crew and I were scheduled for an early-morning start to shoot aerials from a helicopter, we wrapped up and prepared to call it a night. Before leaving, Ned approached me. "We will be staying out till dawn," he said. "Would you mind taking a few bags of toads back to town with you? We have so many piled up; it would relieve the pressure a bit, give us more space in our vehicle. You can just dump them in your cottage overnight. I'll take care of them when we get back."

"No problem," I said. "Just cram them in the back of the car. I'll leave them just inside my cottage door for you to collect tomorrow. I'll be out with the crew for the day." Thanking me, Ned brought over four huge bags writhing with toads. Each bag a heavy armful, was probably loaded with fifty toads or more each.

Back at the ranch where we were renting cottages during our stay in Kununurra, I dumped the bags of toads on the floor just inside of my doorway, as promised to Ned. Exhausted from the night's activities, I unceremoniously ripped off my clothes, hurled myself naked onto the low bunk-bed, where I instantly fell asleep, flat on my back.

What felt like just minutes—but was in fact some hours later, at the onset of the first light of dawn—I was slowly brought to wakefulness through a haze of sleep as something tickled my forehead. Unconsciously I brushed my hand at the irritation, but it persisted, with a further irritation now affecting my chin. Slowly my eyes opened, sticky with sleep, and I peered down over my nose. At first I could not properly distinguish what I was seeing through the gloom. Then two large golden eyes came into focus, staring at me from my chest. Suddenly the eyes hurled themselves forward, a gaping mouth leading the way, and a fly was smartly plucked from my chin. *Holy mackerel!*

Pulling myself upright, something dropped past my face. A huge stomach with four stubby legs fell to my chest, where it collided with the "staring eyes," and together they hopped off down the bed. Urgently, I looked around, beginning to suspect the problem. *Toads! Hundreds of them! Everywhere!*

Lunging from the bed, my bare feet connected with more toads, frantically squishing their way out from under my soles. And there followed a ludicrous display of complicated ballet pirouettes and leaps that till then I was not aware I was capable of, as I took to tippy-toeing on air in a vain attempt to dodge more toads. Still drugged with sleep and performing thus in the gloom of dawn, I lost my balance and crashed to the floor, where I was immediately set upon by a horde of toads, happily leaping over my naked body. Seemingly attracted to my writhing presence on the floor, or possibly contemplating revenge for being stuffed into the bags the night before, the toads gathered round, their bulging eyes focused on me with that inscrutable stare.

In my dazed state, I tried to recall any case of a human ever being eaten by toads. I knew that crabs ate dead bodies . . . ! Illogically alarmed, I quickly stood up. Instantly there came a chorus of guttural croaks—just a few to start with . . . then a few more, quickly followed by a crescendo of croaking voices, as all the toads stared up at me unblinkingly, their throats vibrating with the sounds of their calls. I blinked my eyes and shook my fuzzy head. It was all surreal. The scene might have resembled that of some naked mythical underworld Toad-God being uproariously paid homage to by his loyal minions. *Holy mackerel!*

By now I was fully awake. A quick glance over to where I had dumped the toads earlier revealed two of the four bags lying flat, ripped at the sides, their original contents now spread out excitedly exploring my cabin. The rips must have occurred while squeezing the bags in or out of the Land Cruiser. I had probably spilled toads as far as I had carried the bags, until once deposited in the cabin, the toads were free to emerge in their own time throughout the night. Glancing around the steadily brightening room, my eyes detected mayhem everywhere. Having said their piece, the toads were now scattering far and wide, keen to continue exploring the mysteries of this fascinating place they now found themselves in.

Hurriedly I searched for my clothes, only to find my shirt occupied by two toads, while another three appeared to have gotten themselves entangled in my pants! Wrestling them free, much to the apparent disgust of the toads present who clung on till the last shake, I managed to get dressed. Emptying a rucksack full of camping equipment, I began the arduous task of recovering all the escaped toads. A daunting task, as I soon came to realize, it would take some time to locate them all. There were toads in the open clothing cupboard, under the bunk-bed, on the bed, even under the covers. Some were stuck up behind the gas stove, while others explored the wonders of the bathroom shower and toilet; more were in the linen basket, buried snugly out of site. For rather cumbersome ground-dwelling amphibians, the toads were proving themselves extremely dexterous in going places no toad should ever be encouraged to go. I could imagine that, for weeks to come, cleaners might still encounter the odd toad or two, while future occupants may be awakened to some unusual in-house activity.

Having collected as many toads as were immediately accessible, I laced up the rucksack, which fortunately was designed with air holes in place, in similar fashion to those of the toad bags. Leaving a note for Ned, I explained the situation, suggesting that he take a further look around the place for any more elusive toads. Accustomed to checking my boots for scorpions and other potentially dangerous critters when in the bush, I was not surprised to find a squiggling toad in one boot as I tried to put it on. What did surprise me, however, was the chorus of guttural toad calls emanating from my Land Cruiser when I opened the door. As suspected, toads had already been escaping from their bags long before I had reached the cabin. *Déjà vu!* My thoughts flitted back to the baby puff adders born in my Land Rover, as for the rest of that day toads appeared miraculously out of nowhere, nearly resulting in an accident when one croaked its distress on finding itself pinned under the accelerator peddle.

As a herpetologist, naturally I am keen on frogs and toads, and it is with some sadness and regret that I found myself faced with the need to destroy these members of the latter group, however necessary it might be. It is a stark reminder of how humankind can so easily disrupt the balance of natural things, resulting in not only an environmental tragedy, but also the need to euthanize so many animals, innocent of any intentional crime.

ک ک ک

Of the numerous species of so-called "giant snakes" that are kept as pets by amateur and professional herpetologists alike, the Burmese python of Southeast Asia is one of the most popular. Known for their pleasant disposition, these snakes have been imported into numerous countries, where they have been bred and sold into the pet trade. And while it is true that these snakes are of a pleasant nature and feed well in captivity, they are capable of attaining great size, some being measured at over six meters in length and weighing close to a hundred kilograms. Over the years, some of these snakes have either escaped or been released by pet owners who are no longer able to care for animals that grow beyond a manageable size, in some instances resulting in breeding populations establishing themselves where conditions are favorable. Nowhere is this more evident than in the subtropical wetlands comprising the Florida Everglades where the first Burmese python was spotted as far back as 1979.

Between 1996 and 2006, an estimated ninety thousand Burmese pythons were imported into the USA for the exotic pet trade. Between 2001 and 2005, more than two hundred Burmese pythons were observed by rangers and water-management workers within the boundaries of the Everglades National Park, with more sightings being reported north of the park's borders. The discovery of a nest of eggs finally convinced conservationists that the pythons had begun breeding in the wild.

Known to eat reptiles, birds, and mammals up to the size of deer, authorities became alarmed when an impact study published in 2011 concluded that populations of mid-sized native mammals appeared to have declined as the number of Burmese python sightings increased. Considering the potential size attained by these snakes and the fact that they are known to be long-lived (able to reach twenty-five years of age in the wild), it is not difficult to imagine the carnage that might ensue by their introduction into the Everglades. Despite the infestation being relatively recent, because of native species already threatened by human activity and habitat encroachment, python predation is of particular ecological concern.

Florida enacted laws to prohibit the release of exotic animals into the wild. In 2012, in an attempt to control the number of exotic snakes imported into the USA and specifically South Florida, the Burmese python, African rock python, and yellow anaconda were declared illegal. In May of 2013, a Burmese python measuring 5.7 meters (18.7 feet) in length was killed by a Florida man. It is, to date, the longest Burmese python encountered in the Everglades.

My interest in the Everglades' python infestation was aroused some years earlier, when my team and I proposed to include an episode concerning the pythons in my series. At that time I was not fully aware of just how critical the situation was becoming, until one day I came across a four-meter Burmese python killed on the road, presumably by a vehicle passing in the night. I was astonished. I had been led to believe that a number of juvenile specimens had over the years escaped captivity and were considered a *potential* threat that *might* manifest itself in the future. To find a four-meter specimen killed on the road was a wake-up call that clearly demonstrated just how serious this problem had become. That there were enough of these sizeable snakes already sufficiently established that they were being killed on the roads astounded me. While filming in Asia, I had searched every nook and cranny for a sizeable specimen, finding only one large female after weeks of searching. The Burmese python is in fact endangered in its home territory, yet in the Everglades, half a world away, they were becoming that abundant as to be killed by passing traffic!

Making contact with conservationists and herpetologists working in the Everglades region, I was informed that any Burmese pythons located were destroyed, except for a few specimens being fitted with tracking transmitters for research monitoring. Once again I found myself confronted with the dilemma of wanting to preserve these beautiful creatures while at the same time aware that, by the ignorant hand of humans, these snakes, through no fault of their own, had to be declared vermin because of their potential impact on the native wildlife in a country far away from their own. Having already found a large specimen killed on the road, I could only imagine what surprises lurked out there in the vast wetlands of the Everglades. I decided to have a look.

The Everglades is a region of subtropical wetlands comprising the lower third of the Florida peninsula, fed by a slow-moving river that eventually empties from Lake Okeechobee into Florida Bay. While it is easy to imagine *thousands* of Burmese pythons of various sizes slithering through the dense swampy foliage in relentless search of native prey, I soon discovered it to be another matter completely to locate one. If ever there was place to hide, this was it. Pythons are expert swimmers, completely at home in swampy areas. My team and I, on the other hand, laden down with equipment and restricted to the shallows, found ourselves at a great disadvantage. Eventually incorporating the use of airboats, we were at least able to cross speedily from one vegetated area to another, but considering the raucous vibrating noise emitted by these machines, I imagine any wildlife was forewarned kilometers before our arrival.

Some animals being slower to react than others, however, during the days that followed we were fortunate enough to come across and film a large snapping turtle, which conveniently surfaced close to the airboat; a bad-tempered venomous water moccasin, which I caught and displayed for the camera; an agitated opossum that snarled at me threateningly from an overhead branch; and a number of alligators of varying sizes.

I have a particular fondness for alligators, having raised three specimens from hatchling to adult size while curator at the reptile park in South Africa. My first encounter with one in the wilds of the Everglades, however, took me somewhat by surprise, as it suddenly appeared from the gloomy depths of the waist-deep waters I was wading through, camera in hand. It was just meters from where I stood, and I am not sure who was more startled, me or the alligator, but both of us reacted at the same instant. A medium-sized specimen, no more than one and a half meters long, the gator swirled around to make its escape, while I in turn instinctively lunged for it, throwing all caution to the wind . . . and as it turned out in the excitement, my camera as well, hurled unceremoniously into the water in an attempt to free my hands to grab at the tail of the fast disappearing alligator!

"Roll camera!" I screamed to my team as I splashed and lunged forward through the resisting swirl of water. "Keep rolling—I'm going to catch it!" From behind me I was barely aware of the flurry of activity as the crew followed up. My discarded camera furthest from my mind, my only thought was to catch this alligator so I could film it. What a great scene that would make: allowing me to point out specific features of interest on the reptile's body while actually holding it in my arms. *I just had to do this!*

Lunging headlong now, my arms outstretched ahead of me, I grabbed desperately for the mottled body in the murky water at my feet. I had done this successfully before with a similar-sized freshwater crocodile while filming in Australia; no reason it shouldn't work with an alligator. As it turned out this was not to be the case, as the alligator in question, unlike the freshwater crocodile, appeared to take particular exception to my hands closing around its neck, coming to the surface in a powerful eruption of muscular, twisting, water-thrashing body! And for just one second it seemed that I might achieve my goal as I raised the reptile clear of the water, until with a final powerful, twisting thrust of its tail, the alligator ripped free of my grip and lunged back into the murky darkness of the water, where it disappeared from view.

"Did you get that?" I called urgently back to the crew. "Did you get the action?" I was all excited, adrenaline pumping through my veins. Even though the alligator had gotten away, I felt sure the animal's thrashing action as it fought itself free from my grip must have looked impressive in the late-evening sun, now setting low over the wide flat-water area of the Everglades where it had all taken place. "I got it," the lead cameraman announced, "but only the last bit of the action. Not enough to make up a sequence, I'm afraid. All happened too suddenly. Sorry. Should make a nice introductory snippet for the film, though."

Dripping wet, covered in swamp grass, my camera sacrificed in the effort, I was disappointed by this news . . . but not discouraged. I felt that at the rate we were going, by the end of this shoot we would have collected enough interesting footage to make up for this loss. A few minutes of underwater searching with my feet eventually located my camera in the silt, both body and lens totally ruined, of course. Fortunately the digital memory card was retrievable and, after blowing it out with a can of pressurized air, proved to be little the worse for wear. Inserting it into my spare camera body, my team and I proceeded with our search for the elusive Burmese python.

With all the emotional hullabaloo already evoked concerning the *huge* numbers of pythons speculated to be running unchecked in the Everglades, it was rather disappointing to not have encountered even one after eight days of searching. Though not unduly surprised, considering the vastness of the Everglades, I had nonetheless imagined by this time to have at least found some trace. Fortunately, the time spent searching was not wasted, as we were able to film numerous interesting examples of native flora and fauna offering itself to us as we explored the waterways from our air boat and canoe, and while on foot. One can never have too much general fill-in footage when compiling a documentary film.

Camping out in the Everglades, however, proved to be a nightmare, as swarms of mosquitoes, seemingly impervious to repellents, competed with each other for the privilege of draining the last drops of blood from our bodies. Meanwhile, raccoons lived up to their reputation as masterly exponents of night-time thievery by stealthily raiding our supplies whenever our backs were turned. Simultaneously, numerous pairs of glowing-red, unblinking alligator eyes reflected in the beams of our torches reminded us that we were ever under constant scrutiny, not only from the land, but from the water as well. All that was missing was a Burmese python.

Unexpectedly, it was the high-pitched distress calls of a juvenile alligator entangled in a piece of discarded nylon fishing net that brought me into contact with my first live, wild Florida Burmese python. No more than forty centimeters in length, the little gator called repeatedly, presumably in an attempt to attract the attention of its mother, who might be in the vicinity. As with crocodiles, alligators are protective of their young, the mother staying close to her brood for one to three years. Aware of this potential danger, I instructed the crew to keep a watchful eye while I quickly untangled the little reptile from the netting. We were in a marshy, heavily treed area right at the edge the deeper dark water, where a stealthily approaching adult alligator would be all but impossible to spot. With a camera recording my actions as the little alligator squirmed and twisted in my hands, unaware that I was trying to help, I managed to deliver a piece to camera concerning the thoughtless discarding of potentially hazardous materials into the Everglades, the entangled alligator serving as a perfect example. A short while later, still clicking away agitatedly, I released the alligator back into the surrounding swamp, hopefully to find the safety of its mother.

And it was at just that second, while keeping a tight vigil on the surrounding marsh for any sign of an approaching adult alligator, that I spotted the hint of shiny mottled scales slipping away in the dim, marshy undergrowth. I had found my python!

All thoughts concerning potentially dangerous alligators were quickly discarded as every nerve of my being turned to focus on where I was convinced I had fleetingly spotted the python. Following the sudden concentrated direction of my gaze, as though reading my mind, my crew came sloshing through the muddy water to my side, fully aware how important it was that we locate this snake that would represent the very basis of our documentary story. Plunging into the undergrowth, my eyes searched frantically for any sign of what I had seen. After two weeks of searching, time allocated in the budget was running out. If I did not find a python, the whole film was in jeopardy. Certainly we had collected enough footage to present an interesting story, but the key element that would tie it all together was still missing.

Then I saw it, silently slipping away through the gloom: the unmistakable skin pattern of a Burmese python. Not as big as I had hoped to find, but at around a guesstimated three meters plus, a good size none the less. "I've found it!" I called excitedly to the crew. "I've found a python!" Within seconds the film team was setting up for an on-the-spot shoot, as with one more cry of exuberance I plunged in for the catch.

As discussed earlier in this book, pythons have six rows of recurved teeth in their mouths, capable of inflicting a terrible bite. Though no venom apparatus is present, depending on the size of the snake and the locality of the bite, stitches are often required after such an encounter. The teeth are needle sharp, and when the gums are pushed back, may each be over a centimeter in length where bigger specimens are concerned. At a fairly modest size of three meters or so, it was to prove fortunate that my python was not yet that well endowed, as on my approach to grab it by the tail, the snake immediately retaliated by swinging its head around to lunge at me with wide-open-mouthed hostility. My peripheral vision detecting the motion of the strike in direct line with my face, I instinctively snapped back my head and outstretched arm, unavoidably leaving my torso vulnerable . . . and the angry snake clamped its jaws down firmly on the only remaining closest part offered to it: *my groin!*

Being razor sharp and recurved, the teeth not only cleanly penetrated through my pants and underpants and into the delicate flesh that is my manhood, but also hooked on, as these teeth are designed to do when biting into furry prey (no pun intended). Jumping back, the snake's head and body firmly attached to my groin. All unassociated thoughts instantly dissipated as it became suddenly critically important only to disengage that savage head from that most personal of regions, while at the same time preventing any unnecessary movement, especially the chewing motion that I knew was likely to follow. There were delicate matters to consider here! And all the while the cameras rolled. Though somewhat comical when viewed later on playback screen, I daresay it was not my finest hour on film.

Fortunately, in its eager, angry desire to kill me some more, the snake managed to dislodge itself just as my hand was about to encircle its neck. Pulling back quickly, the python delivered another strike, and another, forcing me unsteadily backwards to topple unceremoniously off balance, arms akimbo, flat on my back into the surrounding swampy marsh. This was not how I imagined my first encounter with a Florida Burmese python should be! Moderate in size it may have been, but this snake was otherwise proving itself to be proficient in its instinctive ability to defend itself. Lying on my back, half submerged in the mushy vegetation, the vicious snake coiled at my feet, ready to lash out again. I could not help but be grateful it was not a bigger specimen. Meanwhile, a slight sensation of pain and wetness was spreading through my loins. I sighed; I had experienced enough python attacks to last me a lifetime. And all the while, the cameras rolled, the crew making the best of my somewhat comical discomfort. *Would I ever live it down?* Consoling myself with the knowledge that only a very select portion of the footage would eventually find itself into the final product, I raised my weary, muddied body out of the swamp to prepare for the finale. The python glared its defiance at me, daring me to come close.

Taking great care not to further antagonize the snake, I eventually coaxed it into the lower branches of a tree with the aid of my snake tongs, where it quickly transferred its thoughts of fight into flight. This done, I had basically achieved my goal of locating a foreign Burmese python in the wetlands of the Florida Everglades. All that remained was that I display the snake on camera, present some interesting facts and figures, and photograph it. Most often the final sequences to any of my film episodes are delivered with an upbeat edge to it, something positive for the future. This time, however, as I ploughed on with my piece to camera describing the beauty and wonder of this snake while at the same time shooting a selection of close-up photographs as it climbed effortlessly up into the overhead branches, I was overwhelmed with the saddening thought that because of its locality, it was to be destroyed. I had spent weeks in the Everglades excitedly seeking out this Burmese python, the object of my adventure; but having achieved this goal now left me deflated and faced with the consequences of my actions. I had located the snake, displayed its beauty for the world to see, and unwittingly, in so doing, condemned it to death. To release the snake back into the Everglades presented a threat to native wildlife. Declaring the presence of the snake to the conservation authorities, automatically, by Florida law, demanded it be euthanized. A catch-22 situation. I had to do something.

Bagging the python, I transported it back to the airboat, where I placed it into a storage compartment for the return journey out of the Everglades. Contacting a friend who owned a reptile park in Tampa, I was fortunate enough to be directed to a private herpetologist in need of a Burmese python, and arrangements were made for the snake to be collected. I breathed a sigh of relief, a great weight lifted from my conscience. I considered a well-fed, contented life in captivity for this snake preferable to euthanasia any day. Although staunchly conservation-minded, I am not entirely immune to bending the rules when necessary. I was well aware that, in the broad spectrum of things, it was just *one* snake; but it was *my* snake . . . the only Burmese python I had personally uncovered in the Everglades, and I did not want the making of this episode of my documentary series to be the factor responsible for bringing about the demise of this beautiful reptile. With a lighter feeling in my heart, I packed up my belongings in preparation for the long flight home.

As conservationists continue to devise strategies and organize python roundups in the wetlands of South Florida, it remains at this time still uncertain what the final outcome will be. The Everglades and surrounding wetlands are vast, providing endless refuge for introduced invasive creatures of numerous descriptions. As is always the case anywhere in the world, once interfered with, the balance of nature is not easily restored.

CHAPTER 19

GRIZZLY BEARS IN BRITISH COLUMBIA

It might be safe to say that I have some sort of affiliation with reptiles, especially snakes. The advantage of filming with reptiles is that, for the most part, I have a reasonable amount of control around the animal. I am able to approach a reptile, photograph it closeup, and, if necessary, pick it up and relocate it. This was of great advantage in making my first series, which revolved almost solely around reptiles.

With my knowledge of reptile behavior, I was able to prepare my team for what to expect from any particular species we might encounter, plan ahead for possible eventualities, and position ourselves accordingly. My natural ability and experience with reptiles made it just a bit easier to collect the footage we needed for the series, and I was basically given free run for the design of each episode. The shows being aired on television were proving to be very popular with the viewing audience, so the suggestion was that we may be on the right track for more.

However, film-series production is an expensive business and impossible to achieve without the necessary financial budget firmly in place. And it stands to reason that those investing the funds would want a major say in the design and making of the series. This is unfortunate, because most often those making demands do not possess the necessary knowledge concerning what conditions in the field might advocate. For example, it is one thing to suggest that we get a cobra to strike into the lens, but quite another to ask for a black rhino to charge at the lens. Whereas I have some semblance of control instigating a cobra strike, I have little or no jurisdiction over tempting a two-ton black rhino to charge into the lens. (At least not without killing myself and most of the crew all in one go.)

And while I can appreciate the sponsor's desire for their man in the field to produce as much dramatic action as possible, it soon became evident that the more I achieved, the more was expected of me. Thus, when the decision was made that the new series be inclined more strongly towards mammals than reptiles, there seemed to be a general consensus that it would be business as usual.

By this time, everybody—from the directors to the editors—were accustomed to seeing Austin Stevens step up to a highly venomous snake of one species or another, bare handed and unafraid, and manipulate and control the scene through to a satisfying end. Why should it be any different with mammals? Throw in a lion or two here . . . an elephant there . . . and why not a grizzly bear for good measure? The possibilities were endless. What about the feared and revered spotted hyena, the most powerful pack predator in Africa? A pod or two of hippos . . . those two-ton amphibious creatures known to kill more humans in Africa than any other animal? And naturally, no such series would be complete without the appearance of the most elusive and cunning of all the African cats, the leopard . . . a stealth-killer without equal.

And should there be a call for an episode or two where snakes *are* encountered, make them *big* snakes of the variety that might be capable of at least strangling a human, if not actually capable of swallowing one whole.

Though to all of those mentioned above, I conceded with a certain stoic resignation, believing also that a certain amount of diversification was called for. However, I recoiled when glacial trekking in subzero conditions in search of the Canadian walrus, free-swimming with tiger sharks off the coast of South Africa, and deep-water night diving off the Baja Peninsular in search of the giant sea squid known to frequent those shores at certain times of the year was suggested. Here finally I put my foot down. I might sometimes appear to do stupid things, but I was not a fool!

My expertise lay in dangerous reptiles. While, to a lesser degree, I was familiar with most African mammal species, as well as having some knowledge of many exotic species from around the world, there were areas I felt I should not expose myself to. Aside from claustrophobia and spiders, some of my greatest fears revolve around extreme cold, man-eating sharks . . . and now that it had been brought to my attention, a giant squid at night . . . underwater . . . with its tentacles wrapped around my drowning body!

When all the kinks had finally been worked out and a program of exciting episodes had been designed and conclusively decided upon to the satisfaction of all parties concerned, I was confronted by Graham.

"The first episode will be shot in British Columbia, Canada, home of the grizzly bear." Graham informed me, rubbing his hands together with some obvious delight. "You will be flown out to a remote 'First Nations' location, a place called Klemtu, where grizzlies are known to congregate a few hours upriver. We've timed the trip to coincide with the yearly salmon run, so we know you'll find bears."

Great, I thought. *Nothing like throwing me in at the deep end.* September was technically fall, the first of the progressing BC winter months, which I happened to know included freezing windchill conditions and rain. Add to this the potential of being face to face with the largest, most unpredictable predator occurring in the northern hemisphere, and one of my worst nightmares was quickly taking shape.

Grizzly bears are the second largest of the bear species after the polar bear, with large specimens recorded at 680 kilograms, and measuring nose-to-tail lengths of up to 2.7 meters. This is a seriously large and potentially dangerous animal, and I knew that, to make good TV, I would be expected to get as close as possible to one of these unpredictable monsters.

I had some experience working with young hand-reared brown bears in the park at Hartebeespoort, but this would have little comparison to approaching a full-grown wild grizzly—no way to manipulate such an animal to pose correctly for a photograph. Unlike with reptile photography, I would not be able to maneuver myself around the subject with my usual casual ease. Wild grizzly bears were not likely to take kindly to my prancing around with my camera trying to get a good angle for a picture, especially my favorite kind: the close-up.

"No problem," I said, sounding more confident than I felt. "Can't wait to get a grizzly in my lens."

And the preparations began.

The region chosen for the shoot was on Prince Royal Island, located amongst the isolated inlets and islands of Canada's 'forgotten' coast, in the heart of the Great Bear Rainforest. This is an extremely remote area of British Columbia, some 520 kilometers north of Vancouver. There are no roads or tracks enabling access to the interior, making the area accessible only by boat or by air. Trees here can tower up to three hundred feet and reach the age of fifteen hundred years or more. These coastal forests have evolved to their biological splendor because natural disturbances, such as fires, happen infrequently and are usually small in scale.

The Great Bear Rainforest consists of some two million hectares of impenetrable ravines, rivers, and forest. Back home in Namibia, I lived next to one of the driest and hottest deserts on Earth, rendering me somewhat inexperienced for the challenge that lay ahead.

ଔ ଔ ଔ

Newly spawned salmon head downriver to the sea, where they spend between three to five years before returning to lay eggs in the same place they were spawned. There are many theories as to how they achieve this, but none are conclusive. It was a logical step to arrange my landing with that of the salmon migration, as this was a big yearly event on the bear's feeding calendar. Bears would arrive and congregate from many miles around to take advantage of the plentiful salmon swimming up the rivers. By following the salmon migration to their spawning grounds, I would almost certainly be led straight to the bear activity I was seeking and, hopefully, to an opportunity for some nice photography.

To reach the destination base location in BC, my flights were scheduled from Walvis Bay Airport in Namibia to Johannesburg, South Africa, then on to London, and on to Vancouver, the trip to be completed by charter of a seaplane flight, which in two trips finally delivered myself and my team to the tiny outpost of Klemtu, situated on the edge of the Great Bear Rainforest. From here it would be a four-hour boat ride to the area where we intended to begin the operation. A helicopter was organized for two days in the event we were able to do some aerial filming.

Flying in over the BC wilderness, the aerial view was breath-taking, displaying a seemingly endless expanse of rainforest with dotted rocky islands of green scattered across the deep-blue ocean along the edge of the mainland. From my tiny window, cramped into the old twin-engine sea plane piled high with containers of supplies and camera equipment, I watched as the scenery passed below and marveled that anybody could ever survive down there. Living in a desert land, I was familiar with the dangers of being lost or stranded in vast wilderness, but the impenetrable tangle of ancient forest passing below seemed a lot more daunting. Through the scratched and weathered porthole, I took some pictures.

As could be expected, the weather was wet and cold, with a windchill factor adding to the misery. While awaiting the arrival of the next sea plane flight in with another load of supplies and equipment, a satellite phone call from Vancouver informed me that my personal baggage had not arrived. The matter was being investigated, and temporary replacement clothes would be bought and sent out to me. As it turned out, my main suitcase containing all my painstakingly selected clothing and apparatus necessary for an extended stay in freezing rainforest conditions did not arrive until two days before the shoot was completed!

For four weeks I was flaunted in front of the cameras wearing badly fitting clothes selected randomly by someone in Vancouver with no idea of my preferred style, color, or need. Everything was in black, the favorite color of every known species of mosquito. The pants were too baggy and long in the crotch, causing raw patches where it hurts most. The shirts were of a light, warm-weather design, with the jackets made of a scratchy waterproof material that irritated my neck. My usual soft leather boots were now replaced by an extremely heavy-duty make of cold-weather, low-cut boots that allowed no natural movement of the foot and were fitted with hard rubber soles that sent me crashing painfully onto my back every time I negotiated rocky terrain. It was not the most comfortable shoot of the series.

Soon after arrival at Klemtu, I was introduced to Burt, my personal guide, who immediately set about educating me in the do's and don'ts of wild-bear encounters. Burt was of First Nations origin, slight of body, with a smooth face sporting a thin moustache. His face was serious as he gave me the break down to survival in bear country.

"You cannot run from a bear. A bear can run faster than you." He stared at me intently, allowing time for this statement to sink in, then continued. "You cannot swim across a river to get away from a bear. Bears can swim faster than you." Another pause, his dark eyes stern in their warning. "You cannot climb a tree to escape a bear. Bears can climb trees better than you." Continuous serious staring, as I waited for more. After about a minute I realized there *was* no more. That was it! My mind turned over what I had just learned. Basically you meet a bear in the wilds of BC . . . you die. End of story.

Holy mackerel!

Seeing as there appeared to be no more to the lesson, I felt compelled to ask, "So what, in your experience, is the best thing to do if you come across a grizzly bear in the wild?"

Burt's answer was matter of fact. "If the bear is very close and you cannot move away slowly, lie down on the ground, roll yourself into a tight ball, and cover your head. Chances are the bear will examine you, possibly nibble and claw on you a bit, and then lose interest."

I shifted uncomfortably. "And if the bear does not lose interest . . . if the bear is aggressive . . . ?" my words trailed off despondently. I was not sure I wanted to know.

For the first time a hint of a smile appeared on Burt's face, lighting up his eyes. "Bears kill about thirty-five people each year. Better not get too close to any bear." He turned to rummage in his back pack, allowing me a few seconds to contemplate my now seemingly dubious immediate future. Finally locating what he was searching for, Burt displayed the object to me. It looked like a can of mosquito spray with an unusually large handle arrangement. "We do not carry guns here. This is your only last-resort weapon against a bear attack. I carry it with me at all times."

Proudly he handed the can over to me to examine. I read the label.

BEAR REPELLENT (The ingredients being a powerful concoction of chili and pepper, loaded under pressure into a spray can.)
Do not use indoors.
Do not get on hands or skin.
Do not get near eyes.
Do not inhale.
In case of accident seek medical attention immediately!

I turned the can around to read a second label printed in large red letters.

OPERATING INSTRUCTIONS
Remove safety pin from trigger mechanism.
Hold can at arms length downwind towards bear and pull trigger.
Expel contents into bear's open mouth and eyes from close proximity.
Maximum range three meters.

So let me get this straight. One has to make sure the attacking bear is downwind from you, that its mouth and eyes are wide open to receive the spray effectively, and it is not more than three meters away. Sounds like a suicide mission to me. But then as Burt pointed out, bears can outrun you; outswim you; and outclimb you . . . so what have you got to lose? Line the monster up and blast away!

Oh Lordy, I thought to myself. This could be dicey to say the least. In Africa when you render yourself into close proximity with a lion, leopard, buffalo, rhino, elephant, or any potentially dangerous wild animal—even from a vehicle—you are always covered by a guide with a rifle . . . not a can of *repellent spray!* What makes a bear any different from the above mentioned? Especially the grizzly, with its huge size, powerful jaws, claws, and indeterminate disposition. *If ever there was reason to have a gun on hand, this was surely it!*

Don't get me wrong. I have never shot a healthy wild animal in my life, and hopefully will never have to. But when passing through a wilderness region where predatory animals are prevalent, without the potential protection of a gun, you could find yourself sadly lacking in defense. And one only has to see the film *Grizzly Man* to appreciate how easily things can go terribly wrong.

Voicing my misgivings, Burt assured me that, in the instance of the few human deaths recorded from bear attacks in the area, it all happened too fast for the person to realize the situation and fire upon the bear. He stared at me stone-faced, totally oblivious to the irony of this statement. I sighed deeply. This was my lot; I would have to take my chances and hopefully survive to tell the tale.

During the weeks spent exploring the Great Bear Rain forest by canoe and on foot, we came across not only grizzly bears but black bears as well. Within the densely wooded forest itself, most times the rough terrain, with its slippery, moss-covered rocks and long-fallen dead trees, made it impossible or too dangerous to attempt a closer approach. On open grassland areas, the black bears would usually spot us approaching and systematically maneuver to keep the distance between us and them. Just once we spotted a rare "Spirit Bear," an animal held in great esteem by the native people of the area. The Spirit Bear is in fact a black bear, but sporting a white coat. The female we came across had two cubs with her, one white and one black. The mother, instinctively protective of her cubs, quickly scurried them away into the forest, she herself disappearing right after them, giving me barely a chance to even raise a camera.

There were many minor adventures along the way. Canoeing the fjords, a humpback whale one day appeared from out of nowhere. Surfacing from the tranquil black depths close to my canoe in an explosion of froth and vaporized water from around the blow hole, it emptied its lungs, simultaneously nearly giving me a heart attack, as I floated in my flimsy canoe. On another occasion, a pack of six wolves briefly exited the forest to stare at my passing, and then disappeared back into the dark of the woods as quickly as they'd appeared. A raccoon raided my camp one night while I was sleeping, digging around presumably in search of scraps. Another near heart-attack, as naturally my initial waking thoughts screamed . . . *bear!*

Crossing a strongly flowing stream one day, its bottom a cauldron of smooth, rounded rocks, I slipped and tumbled headlong into the freezing water, my full back pack taking me straight to the bottom. By the time I had regained my footing, my carrying weight had doubled as the water saturated every bit of my clothing and equipment. The cold took my breath away, and I suspect that, for the third time in this particular expedition, I came close to a heart attack—this time for real—as the cold knocked the breath out of my body and seemed to freeze my very soul. With the weather threatening rain, and cold mist smoldering at ground level, it took many hours of fireside maneuvering to finally get everything more or less dry again, but it was the beginning of a bout of bronchitis that hampered me for the rest of the shoot and all the way back to Namibia. *Never a dull moment.*

Though numerous grizzly bears appeared randomly along the edge of the forest, it was not until I reached a particular spot along a river I had been negotiating that I finally got my chance for a closer encounter. Had I known just *how* close, I might not have been so keen.

ষ ষ ষ

The place was picture perfect, with the river splitting around a wide, grassy plateau surrounded by steep cliffs of granite that reached high into the misty sky. My first glimpse of the place from my canoe revealed two grizzlies splashing around in the water some distance away. By their active behavior and splashing back and forth, it was obvious they were hunting salmon. By the time I had secured my canoe to a washed-up log and prepared myself for a trek across land, two more bears had appeared, joined minutes later by two more. I had found the mother load. This was bear heaven!

Contacting my team by radio, I gave them my GPS coordinates, suggesting they drop everything and head out my way ASAP. There were bears to be filmed. Close by, Burt had also beached his canoe. Quickly he made his way over to where I was preparing my kit and cameras. Burt was a keen photographer himself, sporting some impressive long-lens equipment. He carried these with him wherever we went, ever ready to make use of any photo opportunity. The team consented to this, as long as it did not divert from Burt's duties as guide, for which he was hired.

As well as being my guide, Burt was also responsible for carrying the bear spray and watching my back whenever I might be close to bears. Moving in for some close-up photography, my attention would be fully absorbed in the moment, leaving me vulnerable should another bear approach. Every move I made would be filmed by the camera crew, who would take up position some distance away so as not to place themselves in harm's way (and so they'd have a clear, long-lens view of all the action). The bears in this case, half a dozen by now, were mostly preoccupied with chasing after the elusive salmon to pay much attention to me. It was perfect opportunity to get in close.

I have always been fascinated with close-up wildlife photography, and this has served me well where reptiles are concerned. With reptiles, I was always able to get really close, often incorporating a macro lens for detail. Later, when including mammals into my photography, I was faced with a new challenge. Still feeling the need for the effects derived from close-up work, but not able to coordinate the larger animals as I might a small reptile, I was faced with the daunting task of getting as close to my subject as the situation might allow, incorporating as wide a lens as possible to create the effect I preferred.

This is by no means always possible, and certainly can lead to trouble, as many of these animal subjects are potentially dangerous. And here now again, far out in the extreme wilderness of British Columbia, surrounded by feeding grizzly bears, my plan was to get as close as possible for that ultimate shot. The trick always, as I had learned through experience, was to know how far one could push the envelope. As I have heard said; *Only those who risk going too far, will ever know how far they can go.'*

The real danger comes with those factors that lie outside of your control. No matter how cautious or knowledgeable you might be, there is always room for the unexpected.

With the arrival of the rest of the team, we set about planning our strategy. All around us, as though summoned by a dinner bell, grizzlies were arriving for the feast. Our strategy was not complicated. With Burt as guide and knowledgeable bear-behavior person, one cameraman, and one sound engineer following at a respectable distance behind me, I would set out to creep up to the feeding bears to get some close-up pictures. The second camera team would remain close to the canoes and film from a distance with the long lens. We would be in contact by short-range, hand-held radios. Nothing to it. All angles and sides covered. What could go wrong?

Hunched over, dragging our equipment with us and keeping as low a profile in the long grass as possible, we set out. Burt, carrying his own camera and a can of bear spray, moved out some distance on my right, the far side from the bears I was heading for, giving both the close- and long-range camera crews plenty of clearance, so as not to be caught in the shot.

"Don't worry about my positioning," Burt called softly as he moved off through the grass. "You concentrate on the bears. I'll keep my distance but be close enough if you need me."

Good to know, I thought to myself. As any wildlife photographer will tell you, once you have your eye in the viewfinder, lining up your subject matter, all concentration is in that direction and the rest of the world disappears. It was imperative under these particular circumstances, with bears appearing randomly out of the tall grass, to have someone watch your back.

The grass was green, tall as a man in places, and soaking wet from the perpetual rain and mist. The mud underfoot sucked at my boots, making progress slow and awkward, with every second step landing me in a muddy hole. There were at least eight bears in the area that we had spotted, with no way to tell how many were emerging from the distant forest. In the tall grass, most bears were only visible when they stood up. The only bears constantly visible to me were those few already engrossed in fishing along the edge of the river. I headed for these, every nerve on edge as my eyes swept the surrounding area. I hoped Burt was doing the same. Any warning message from him would be transmitted to my camera team, who would relay to me vocally, as I did not carry a radio. This was a very different scenario to my earlier film series dealing with reptiles, where there was no threat of ambush and the whole team could work together in close proximity.

Not far behind, my camera team kept pace with me, a reminder that any risks I might take spilled over to them. I needed to get close to the bears, and the crew needed to be close to me when I did so. Such is the nature of the business we were involved in: the making of "good telly" as one British cameraman often remarked. Of Burt, there was no sign. He had melted away into the grass some distance off to one side of us, presumably checking the perimeter for any approaching bears.

It took some twenty minutes of navigation, but finally I exited the tall grass where it thinned towards the edge of the river. The two grizzly bears I had spotted earlier were now chest deep into the fast-flowing river, running this way and that, snatching at the fast-fleeing salmon heading upstream. The bears' antics were somewhat playful, and it dawned on me that, although fairly large in size already, these were young bears, subadults, not yet proficient in the art of catching their slippery prey. Stealthily, I headed towards them, hoping that their concentration on what they were doing would preoccupy them enough to ignore me. Close behind me, the camera team exited the tall grass and prepared to roll camera. We were now all exposed on the rocky slope along the edge of the river.

Visible on my left some distance away along the exposed stretch of riverbank, the first camera team had the advantage of height and ran long-lens surveillance on the proceedings. Behind me a radio crackled into life.

"Grizzly approaching from behind, moving at a steady pace towards you guys. Watch your distance."

Though I carried no radio with me, not wanting any extra distractions, I could clearly hear the message broadcast on the film crew radio some twenty meters behind me. Looking around, I could not see anything over the tall grass back from the riverbank and wondered where Burt was. Had he not spotted the bear? Burt was supposed to be our backdoor warning system. Quickly, I backed up closer towards where the camera crew was stationed at the edge of the grass. With numerous bears in the area, mostly invisible to us from our location, I was not about to take any chances.

"Give Burt a call on the radio," I suggested. "Find out if he can see the bear." A few calls later rendered no response from Burt.

The two young grizzlies meanwhile had curtailed their activity in the water and started in our direction. It was obvious they had been alerted to our presence. One made a tentative move in our direction, then stopped, then made another. The second bear followed suit. Their curiosity was aroused and they wanted a closer look.

"Grizzly still moving in your direction," a voice from the first crew sounded over the radio, more urgent now. "About sixty meters behind you and moving steadily. Better back away along the riverbank."

Good advice! However, at that very moment, the two bears from the water were slowly heading towards us, leaving little room in which to maneuver. Where the hell was Burt? Why was he not answering his radio?

Then suddenly I saw a movement further up the bank, just at the edge of the grass. I recognized the long, white Canon camera lens immediately. It was Burt, and he was taking pictures of the bears in the water. He was taking bloody pictures of the bears frolicking in the water when he was supposed to be watching our backs! Aaaarrrgh! I was furious!

Suddenly, from behind me, I heard a commotion and turned just in time to see the camera crew scuttling for distance as a huge grizzly appeared out of the grass, not ten meters from where I crouched on the riverbank. At the same time, exiting the water, the two young bears picked up their pace, now loping towards me . . . and the realization hit me like a ton of bricks. I had just done the unthinkable! It was not coincidence that these three bears were heading steadily in our direction. This was the mother of the two subadults in the water. And the *very first rule* of safety while in the company of bears, or any other animal for that matter, is *never get between a mother and her offspring!*

Holy mackerel! Finally my life was over. There was no escape.

Then I remembered Burt, and with no further reason for stealth, I turned and screamed for his attention.

"Burt! Over here!"

But Burt was already running towards me, his camera forgotten, his hands grabbing for the bear spray attached to his waist. In a second he had it out and was struggling with the removing of the cap and the safety pin. With panic in my heart, I watched Burt's frantic approach, and I saw, as though in slow motion, his hands pulling desperately at the trigger mechanism of the can, until with a sound of snapping metal, the whole apparatus came loose and flew through the air. The operating mechanism was unserviced and rusted, traveling now uselessly through the air to clatter onto the rocks, and in so doing, rendering my last hope of salvation inoperable.

Excitedly, the two young bears loped up the bank towards where their mother and I stood facing each other. Burt, now without the means to assist me, wisely backed off, crouching so as to attract as little attention as possible. The mother bear had now stopped dead in her tracks, eyeing me maliciously through small, unreadable eyes. Then, with a grunt, she threw herself up on her hind legs to tower over me, her jaw open wide . . . and I all but had a heart attack. Vaguely in my head, as though in a dream, I recalled the basic facts that had been drummed into me.

Bears can outrun you.

Bears can outswim you.

Bears can outclimb you.

Right now my legs were in desperate conflict with the first rule: *never run from a bear!* Oh dear Lord . . . I now so desperately wanted to run from this bear. Somehow I fought the urge. There was nothing to be done but stand dead still and embrace my fate.

I have heard it said that, if a man has nothing to hope for, then at least give him something to do. So slowly, very slowly, I raised my camera and took a picture.

Then the impossible happened. The two young bears stopped where they were half way up the riverbank, swaying their heads, as though uncertain of my presence between them and their mother. And just when I thought my time had finally come, the great bulk of the mother twisted slightly away from me, dropped back down onto all fours, and slowly sidled past me, her eyes never leaving me as she did so. Another few steps and she was past, allowing my heart to regain some of its former rhythm. Gathering together, the three bears greeted each other enthusiastically, confirming my belief that they were indeed a family group. Their greetings concluded, they entered the water to once again pursue their feeding on the salmon.

With deliberately slow movements, both Burt and I moved away back towards where the film crew was positioned. I glared at Burt. I was *not* impressed. His job was to watch out for us, not take pictures for his personal collection. We were relying on his knowledge and experience working in bear country, and the fact that the bear spray was unserviced and not operable made my blood boil. It was bad enough to have to rely on someone else to watch your back, but worse if that person is unprepared and incompetent. I was really angry and voiced my feelings to the director. Lives were on the line here, and I wanted Burt out of the picture.

In reality, of course, being in as isolated a region as we were, hundreds of kilometers from anywhere, there was no chance to arrange a replacement guide, leaving me weary and deciding finally to carry my own personal can of bear spray. Admittedly, though, having experienced the awesome size of a grizzly closeup, I seriously doubted it would be of much use.

Fortunately, as it turned out, the incident had a positive side to it. Enough footage had been recorded during the event to enable the scene to play a dramatic part in our story. Another week of continuous filming followed, during which one night I came within touching distance of a black bear and on another occasion managed once more to fall into a freezing stream. The latter resulted in my beginning to show all the signs of acute bronchitis by the time we were finally heading back to civilization. My missing baggage had been located and returned to me as we were wrapping up our shoot. What can I say? At least it had not all been permanently lost and was able to tackle the half-dozen flights back to Namibia in properly fitting attire.

Thus, the first episode of my new series was filmed and heading for the edit studios in Bristol, where afterwards it would be judged and no doubt cut to shreds and reassembled by the powers that be. It remained to be seen what my fans and public at large might have to say about the new direction my shows were taking. It was an established fact that the reptile series was hugely popular. Would my adventures with mammals have the same appeal? Only time would tell.

CONCLUSION

Once the dominant form of life on the planet, the reptiles and amphibians of today are largely reduced in numbers and variety. Some are relatively unchanged from the age when dinosaurs dominated the land and offer fascinating hints as to what life was like at that time.

Reptiles, especially snakes, are a hard resource to sell to the public at large as worth conserving. Not only are these not of cute and cuddly genera, but the fact that some snakes are venomous has unwittingly condemned all the species. In fact, few snakes are dangerous to humans; rather, most are generally shy and elusive. Should a human encounter a snake in the wild, there is a greater chance than not of the snake being harmless, and it is certain that the encounter is by accident, with no evil intent on the part of the snake. Should one encounter a snake, it is certainly best to either keep still or step back and away. Snakes do not actively seek out humans (as humans are generally too large to be considered prey), and so are experiencing as much fright as the human and will usually take flight in the direction of the closest cover. As stated before, a venomous snake is generally only a threat if it has been stepped on or cornered, in which case it may possibly strike out in self-defense.

ട ട ട

The style of my adventure television series developed as it did because I was allowed, to a large extent, the freedom to respond according to what each situation called for. Armed with a basic script, my team and I visited wilderness areas in a variety of regions of the world in search of particular species of interest, to photograph and film them as best possible in their natural surroundings. Naturally, we experienced numerous encounters with a variety of wildlife species along the way, and these would gradually dictate the shape of the story behind the expedition.

Wildlife documentary programs are designed not only for their entertainment value but with the idea in mind to encourage viewers to become more aware of the natural world and of the wild animals that exist in it, their behavior, and their position in the intricate chain that connects all natural things. I have heard it argued that if not for zoos, people would have no opportunity to view and learn about wild animals from various locations of the planet. With modern-day technology, however, the media of television not only brings wildlife programs directly into the living rooms of every home but does so in such a way as would never be seen in a zoo. And it does this without the need to confine any wild animal to a life of incarceration. There is no greater media of education than television. Thus it is the obvious way to introduce wilderness and wildlife of the world, that people should have a better understanding of it, fear it less, and hopefully be more encouraged to protect it.

It has been said that "a picture is worth a thousand words." I find this to be true, and especially relevant where wildlife is concerned. Never can one describe the wondrous colors to be found in the shiny, textured scales of an exotic snake or the wings of a particular hummingbird. But in one close-up picture, all is revealed. Most people in their lifetime will not see many exotic animal species in their natural habitat, especially not close up. It is important to bring these animals into their homes in the form of pictures and film, so that they become aware of the wonderful beauty that we still have on this planet. Hopefully, this will in some small way arouse awareness and help promote the conservation of all living species.

I am seldom without a camera close at hand, even if it is simply my little pocket Sony Digital Cybershot. You just simply never know when something of interest will pop up. I photograph anything that might interest me, with special attention of course given to all wildlife subjects. I do personal wildlife trips whenever possible. In doing so, I am free to take my time and concentrate on what I want. It does not matter how long it takes. I usually travel in a campervan (for example, when in Australia) or a four-by-four double-cab vehicle when in Africa. This enables me to carry all supplies and equipment I might need with me and leaves me free to remain in any place as long as is necessary to get a particular photograph. When it comes to big-game photography, one can only wait and watch, but when attempting to photograph reptiles, I am forced to seek them out actively, as these creatures, especially snakes, are shy and elusive, and therefore not often seen in the wild.

Wildlife photography is largely a luck-of-the-draw situation, especially when the behavior of any species is factored in. The trick is to be patient and ready when the action hits. And at this time, should the action be fast and furious, it would be important to have camera and lens equipment that is fast enough to capture the moment.

Unfortunately, I myself am not a particularly patient person by nature and struggle with this part of the deal. I actually prefer something that I can help create, like a snake or a frog in a beautiful setting, where I can maneuver around the animal and specifically plan my shots. This of course can also sometimes call for fast-action shooting, like when a snake is striking out or takes off at a fast slither, but at least I have some control and can shoot off as many pictures as I like from a variety of different angles. I cannot do this with a charging rhino or elephant, for example, because I have to consider my own vulnerability in getting the shot. So, while one does what one can to create a wild-animal photograph of some artistic value, it is not always possible and might depend entirely on where the animal is positioned or what it is doing at the time.

While filming my adventure series, I was faced with a mixture of these two scenarios. I would sometimes have a cobra standing for long periods of time with its hood expanded while I easily moved around the reptile, shooting off one lovely picture after another. Other times, I would be fearing for my life as a wild animal, such as an enraged black rhino, charged down on me, forcing me to run for the nearest tree. Needless to say, the latter produced very little in the way of beautiful photography.

I believe that each wildlife photographer will settle into his or her own style of photography. Some, like myself, will be content to get what is possible within the bounds of practicality. I have never expected to make a living from wildlife photography alone, but rather from what surrounds it, such as writing, or making documentaries. More important has been my appreciation and experience of being in wild places and doing a documentary, rather than delivering the finished product. My preferred style of photography is to get as close to the subject as possible with as wide a lens as possible, so as to encompass as much of the surrounding background. This style of photography in the face of wild animals can prove to be dangerous and should not be attempted by anyone unfamiliar with the behavior of wild animals.

At the same time, however, when working with smaller animals, like snakes, lizards, or scorpions, for example, there is little to beat a good 105 mm macro lens for up-close clarity—shooting at F22 (which increases the depth of focus) with a hand-held flash—for great pictures in the field. Ultimately, to each his own. There are some great wildlife photographers out there who put a tremendous amount of time and effort into bringing these wildlife images into our homes through books, magazines, and television, and I hope only that I have played some small part in this.

I myself do not have a large collection of cameras and lenses, preferring to keep my kit compact and light. To the contrary, when filming on location, my personal camera kit is dwarfed by the loads of equipment needed for the production of the film series. The latter is a different matter all together, sometimes amounting to as many as fifty-heavy packed metal cases.

ʓ ʓ ʓ

While it is true that I do sometimes find myself in potentially dangerous situations, this is only by definition of who is judging. Having lived a large portion of my life somewhat isolated in the Namib Desert and other wilderness regions, I now find myself more terrified when faced with big-city traffic than when confronted by any wild animal. Put me in front of a venomous snake any day rather than on a congested city road. A venomous snake I understand, and have experience with, and know the rules, and consider myself in control. Not so in the rush-hour madness that kills hundreds of people around the world every day. It is simply a matter of knowledge and how you use it. Working with potentially dangerous animals might look more dangerous to those who don't have the knowledge or experience and understanding.

Having said all this, it remains a fact that I might place myself within the potential realm of danger on some occasions, but this is not out of ignorance, but rather out of calculated necessity, usually to get a photograph. And again, it is possible that something on occasion might go wrong or I may make a miscalculation and find myself in trouble. But what is life if nothing is ventured and we miss the true purpose of the expedition? The odds still remain more against that everyday pedestrian crossing the street in a traffic filled city.

I am often asked if the scenes in my films are real. When I am seen confronting a highly venomous snake or being charged by a desert elephant or struggling with a twenty foot python, what you are seeing is real. The introductory buildup or ending to the scene may sometimes be dramatized, as we do not always know what is going to happen, and the cameras cannot be rolling continuously throughout the expedition. So, should I, for example, suddenly come across a snake and run forward and manage to catch it, I then demonstrate the snake on camera. Should the cameraman not have caught the initial approach to my actual catching of the snake, once I have finished my segment, I can release the snake in question and reenact the scenario with the camera now focused and running. In so doing, we provide the introduction to the scene that the audience would otherwise have missed. Of course, music and well-placed close-up cuts would later be employed strategically to make it all as exciting as possible.

The length of time it takes to film a one-hour episode of my series often depends on how difficult the working terrain might be, how elusive or available the animals we are searching for might be, or both. But generally speaking, in terms of camera hours, we would shoot between sixty and eighty hours of tape to complete a one-hour episode, with one particular episode shot in Asia reaching the 140-tape mark. Once shot, this footage then takes about eight to ten weeks to edit and again as many weeks to prepare for final production. It is a lengthy, time- and budget-consuming business, of which the general public is not usually aware.

ৰ ৰ ৰ

Concerning the question of the conservation of the planet as a whole, I find myself unable to respond with moderation, or as it were, political correctness. One of the awesome enigmas of today is how to slow the destruction of the last remaining ecosystems on Earth. I could bring up the usual assortment of ideas about saving what is left, but you will have heard it all before. My views on conservation of the planet and all its natural resources and wilderness cuts right down to the heart of the problem, the "white elephant in the room," which is seldom brought to the forefront. I am referring to human overpopulation. Each and every problem facing the world today is either directly or indirectly connected to human overpopulation of the planet.

At this time our lagging space-program technology does not enable us to migrate to other habitable planets (should they eventually be located), so when the last tree is cut down and the last slab of concrete poured, where do we go? Already, most of our rivers are polluted, the ground poisoned, our seas raped and now used as dumping grounds, while our air becomes less breathable by the day, and the ozone layer has been destroyed to the point it is dangerous to go outside unprotected. Where wilderness and wild animals are concerned, barely a species can be mentioned without the word "endangered" being present. *We are exploiting this planet as if we already have another to relocate to!*

In simple terms, human overpopulation occurs if the number of people exceeds a region's environmental carrying capacity. The human population globally has ballooned from 2.5 billion to more than 7 billion people since

World War II. This has led to protracted confrontations between nations over ecological resources, with overpopulation now becoming a leading cause of conflict. Human overpopulation of the planet persists at a fearsome, unchecked rate, bringing with it habitat destruction, pollution, global warming, extinction, human poverty, and overall misery. Even apart from the deterioration of the quality of human and animal life, the planet simply cannot cope with the consumption and waste produced by more than seven billion people. Without drastic legislation and immediate implementation of strict measures, humanity as we know it has set itself on a downward spiraling course of self-destruction . . . a suicide mission of unimaginable proportions. A harsh reality . . . but a reality nonetheless. I believe no conservation philosophy is complete without the recognition that there can be no sustainability in the long term if the human population of our planet continues to increase.

Every few seconds of every minute of every hour of every day, somewhere in the world, a woman is giving birth. As my mother used to comment, *"Somebody please find that woman and stop her!"*

ය ය ය

Through my Facebook communications (facebook.com/AustinStevensAdventurer), I am constantly approached with questions about my life that cannot be wholly answered in so short a space as is usually provided. It is my hope that, by reading this book, those interested will experience some greater insight into the man behind the scenes. It has been suggested that I have experienced an interesting life, and though this may to some extent be true, I am very conscious of time wasted and the many mistakes I have made. For it not to have all been in vain, I have, in my later years at least, attempted to correct these mistakes by learning from them and never repeating them (in essence: attempting to become a better person).

No amount of money can buy back time. This becomes increasingly evident as one gets older. I am constantly in a semistate of panic because

I am acutely aware that every minute passed can never be recaptured and so am driven to try and make the most of the time made available to me. I have always felt that it is important, as far as is humanly possible, to spend as much of your life indulging in that which interests you. If you can achieve this, then the term "work" disappears from your vocabulary, rendering you free to experience the time you have been afforded on Earth to a fuller and more prosperous extent.

In my writings, photography, and wildlife-adventure documentary filmmaking, I wish only that I have in some small way contributed to the greater aim, that of promoting the beauty and overall magnificence of the wilderness and wildlife that has been afforded us, and generating a greater worldwide awareness for the need to protect it.

ACKNOWLEDGMENTS

Remembering back across the years of my life spent in reptile parks, in South Africa and in Germany, I wish to offer special thanks to Jack Seale (Hartebeespoort Dam Snake and Animal Park) and Jurgen Hergert (Nordharzer Schlangenfarm) for inviting me to share in their dreams. Without those times, much of this book would not have come about.

Concerning the later advent of my adventures on film, I wish to thank Tigress Productions (UK), Cineflix Productions (Canada), and Animal Planet (USA) for offering me the opportunity to experience a new world of adventures beyond my wildest dreams.

I wish to extend my warmest thanks to the many teams, film crews, editing staffs, researchers, and the multitude of other behind the scenes operators involved in the production of my TV series, all who helped make each episode into a spectacular cinematic experience.

My thanks to Amy, my beautiful wife, for her patience and advice offered during the writing of this book.

Also a great thanks to all my die-hard fans and Facebook followers (facebook.com/AustinStevensAdventurer) for their continuous encouragement and support. I really appreciate it.

And finally, my thanks to Jason Katzman, my editor at Skyhorse Publishing, for tolerating my persistence in having it my way, and in spite of this still making my work presentable for publishing.

Photo Credits

The author would like to thank the following people, whose assistance was helpful in putting together the photograph insert for this book:

Tigress Productions
Scubazoo Films
Romulus Whitaker
Chitral Jayatilake
Amy Stevens
Brendan McGinty
Warwick Sloss

All other scenic photographs that do not personally include Austin Stevens were taken from the author's private collection.